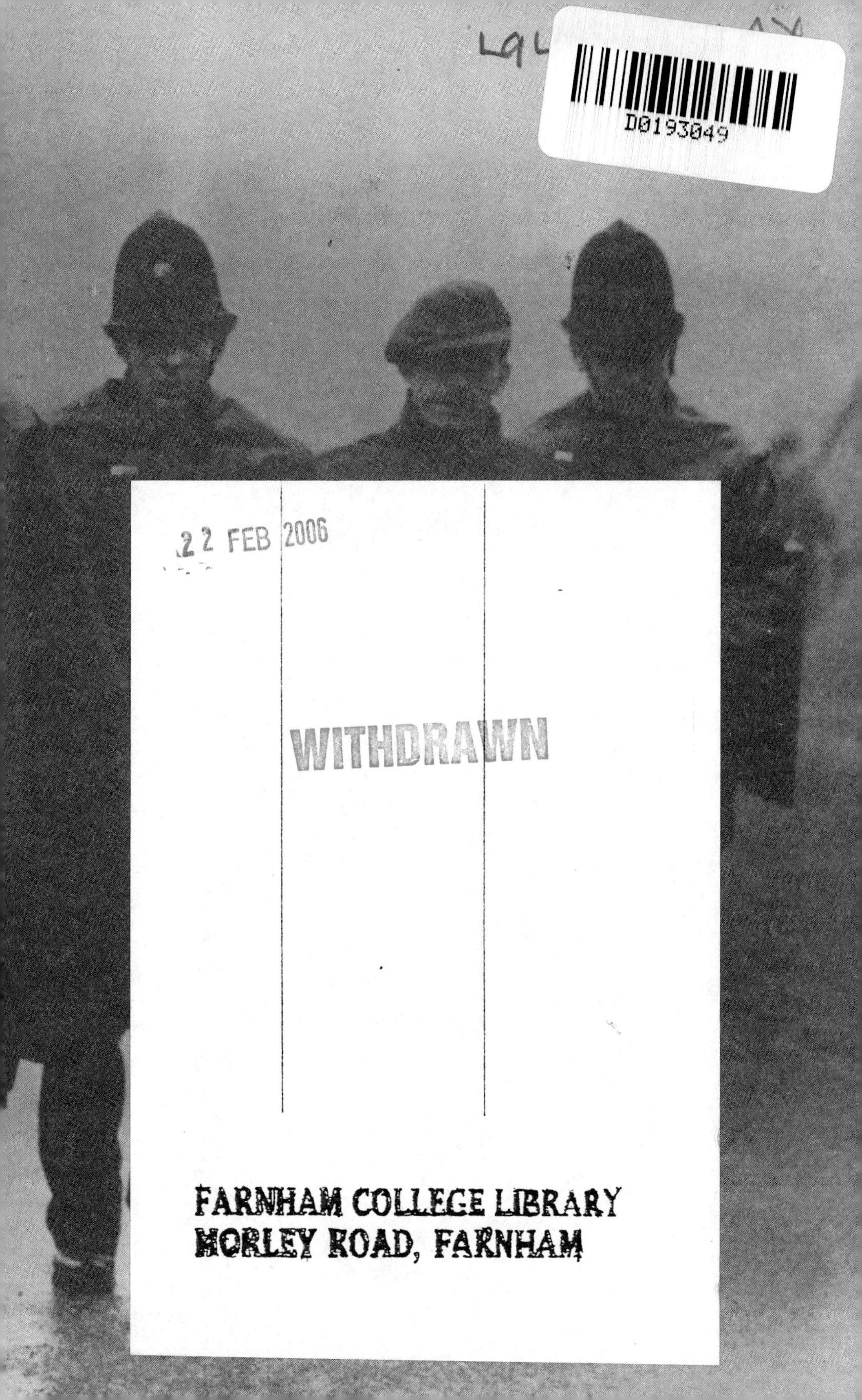

BRITAIN ON THE BREADLINE

To Rosemary, Peter and Elizabeth

BRITAIN ON THE BREADLINE

A SOCIAL AND POLITICAL HISTORY OF BRITAIN BETWEEN THE WARS

KEITH LAYBOURN

ALAN SUTTON

First published in the United Kingdom 1990
Alan Sutton Publishing · Brunswick Road · Gloucester

First published in the United States of America 1990
Alan Sutton Publishing Inc. · Wolfeboro Falls · NH 03896–0848

British Library Cataloguing in Publication Data

Laybourn, Keith
Britain on the breadline.
1. Great Britain, 1910–1945
I. Title
941.083

ISBN 0-86299-490-X

Library of Congress Cataloging in Publication Data applied for

Typesetting and origination by
Alan Sutton Publishing Limited.
Printed in Great Britain

CONTENTS

CONTENTS

SECTION III: POLITICS IN THE AGE OF
UNEMPLOYMENT

ACKNOWLEDGEMENTS

I owe a great debt to many fellow historians, librarians and archivists who have assisted me over many years. Although it is impossible to mention them all by name, I must express my thanks to David James, Elvira Wilmott, Brett Harrison, and to Dr Alan Betteridge. In addition my colleagues at Huddersfield Polytechnic, particularly Dr David Wright, have been rather more supportive and helpful over the years than they probably realize. But above all I must pay thanks to the late Jack Reynolds whose support and inspiration have encouraged most of my research.

I must also thank the West Yorkshire Archives departments at Leeds and Bradford for permission to reproduce the photographs which are included in this publication. It was David James and Brett Harrison who particularly directed me towards the more valuable photographic evidence in these archive deposits. Other photographs have been provided by courtesy of the Communist Party of Great Britain.

ABBREVIATIONS

BUF: British Union of Fascists

CPGB: Communist Party of Great Britain

ILP: Independent Labour Party

NAC: National Administrative Council (of the ILP)

NEC: National Executive Committee (of the Labour Party)

NUWM: National Unemployed Workers' Movement

PAC: Public Assistance Committee

PLP: Parliamentary Labour Party

TUC: Trades Union Congress

UAB: Unemployment Assistance Board

LIST OF TABLES

INTRODUCTION

Unemployment was the dominating issue of British society during the inter-war years, creating social problems, determining the social policies of governments, and shaping the politics of the age. As a result of Britain's loss of export markets and her industrial decline in the staple industries, unemployment levels were rarely less than the 'intractable million' and reached more than three million, about a quarter of the insured workforce, in 1931. Such horrendous levels of unemployment created difficulties at every level of society and influenced all aspects of life during years – the 'locust years' and the 'long weekend' – when Britain, according to some, survived on the breadline. The title of this book, *Britain on the Breadline*, is, of course, contentious for while there was severe depression and unemployment at this time there was also evidence of rising living standards, especially in those regions of the country which were not dependent upon Britain's staple industries of coal, textiles, engineering and shipbuilding. Certainly, B.W.E. Alford,[1] John Stevenson, Chris Cook,[2] and others, maintain that the quality and quantity of life improved for the majority of families throughout the period. That may be true for the majority of workers but for many workers the standard of living did not improve and, using modern concepts of relative poverty and John Boyd Orr's[3] contemporary observations, it is clear that by the mid-1930s there may have been at least half the population of Britain existing at a standard of living which was insufficient to maintain healthy life. At least, as the social investigations of Rowntree and others reveal, unemployment had risen as a cause of poverty.[4]

1

This book seeks to contribute to the debate about the quality of life in Britain during the inter-war years, examining the views of Charles Webster and Margaret Mitchell,[5] who are pessimistic about the condition of working-class life, ranging them against the more optimistic views of those who believe that the inter-war period was one of transition, which saw substantial improvements in living standards for the vast majority of working-class families.[6] But, in addition, it will examine the pressures which unemployment and industrial depression placed upon other aspects of social and political action.

Unemployment conditioned many aspects of working-class life, made decisions for working people about the housing which they could afford, determined their physical health and affected their willingness and ability to reproduce.[7] Not surprisingly, social policy, housing policy and population growth, or lack of it, reflected the impact of unemployment.

Even the General Strike of 1926, the most important industrial dispute that has ever occurred in British history, can be seen within the context of rising unemployment and falling monetary wage rates. It occurred against the background of falling wage rates and the frequent attempts of employers and governments to further reduce wages in order to improve the competitive ability of British industry. The whole episode has to be seen within the context of unemployment and the methods by which British industry could become more effective.

No general election in these years, other than that in 1918, was fought without some major discussion on how to deal with unemployment. In the early 1920s the Conservatives looked towards protection, while both the Liberal and Labour parties advocated the revival of international trade as the solution to unemployment. The latter view prevailed – one which suggested that it was futile of governments to spend money to tackle unemployment when an anticipated revival in world trade would put the unemployed back to work. This, indeed, was the economic philosophy adopted by Philip Snowden, Chancellor of the Exchequer in the first Labour government of 1924, and the policy pursued by Stanley Baldwin's Conservative government between 1924 and 1929.

When the second Labour government was formed in May 1929 its emergence was not so much a product of the new socialist policies which it offered, which in any case were much less advanced in

2

dealing with the unemployed than those offered by David Lloyd George and the Liberals,[8] as much as it was due to the failures of the Conservative government to deal with the unemployed in a humane fashion. The second Labour government collapsed in August 1931, not because it failed to stem the rise of the unemployment from one million to three million but because it attempted to reduce unemployment benefit by 10 per cent. Indeed, the provision of unemployment benefit and the 'dole', in all its forms, occupied the attention of all inter-war governments as they struggled to keep the unemployment fund afloat, to end the poor law, and to deal with the long-term unemployed.

Unemployment encouraged the formation of new political parties to challenge the existing British two-party parliamentary system. Indeed, it was unemployment and depression which forced Oswald Mosley to leave the Conservative Party for the Labour Party and, subsequently, to leave the Labour Party in the early 1930s to form the British Union of Fascists. Although it was hidden from view by its conflicts with the Communist Party and the Jews, it should not be forgotten that the British Union of Fascists emerged to deal with unemployment and to instigate the economic renaissance of Britain.

According to A.J.P. Taylor, the only major issues of the inter-war years, other than unemployment and the General Strike, were the Spanish Civil War and the rise of European fascism. The Spanish Civil War, in particular, provided the opportunity for those who were frustrated with the events at home to rid themselves of their feelings of impotence. For the vast majority of those who did not go to Spain it gave them the opportunity to contribute to the defence of 'democracy' and to make their own personal and financial statement of position. Paradoxically, the events in Spain and the rest of Europe engendered a defence of political citizenship by many of those very people who had been denied economic citizenship in Britain by virtue of unemployment and poverty.

This book attempts to examine the social life of Britain during the inter-war years and seeks the answers to six main questions. First: how pervasive and protracted was unemployment? Second: did the standard of living of the working class rise or fall? Third: did the health of the nation improve or deteriorate during the inter-war years? Fourth: how did the social problems of the period, particularly unemployment, affect the politics of the age? Fifth: what impact, if any, did unemployment exert upon the pattern of industrial relations? Sixth: why did the British people, normally so insular in their attitude to international politics, take great interest in the Spanish Civil War?

It will be argued that while social conditions improved substantially after 1918, compared with before 1914, there was some falling away of living standards throughout the inter-war years among large sections of the working class in the old declining industrial areas. Yet this was not always perceived by the various inter-war governments who were either not aware of the full extent of poverty or were preoccupied with the, apparently, exigent need to balance the budget. Consequently, the social policies of inter-war governments evolved slowly, population growth rates declined rapidly, and a substantial section of the working class came to dread the Household Means Test, the Public Assistance committees, and the Unemployment Assistance boards. A.J.P. Taylor once asked the question, 'which was the more significant for the future – over a million unemployed or over a million private cars?'[9] He implied that the obvious answer was a million private cars. Yet, to the millions of people who lived in acute poverty and in a state of undernourishment, this is an inadequate answer and it it fatuous to suggest that the acute poverty of millions can be so lightly dismissed.

NOTES

1. B.W.E. Alford, *Depression and Recovery? British Economic Growth 1918–1939* (London, Macmillan, 1972).
2. J. Stevenson and Chris Cook, *The Slump* (London, Jonathan Cape, 1977).
3. J. Boyd Orr, *Food, Health and Income* (London, Macmillan, 1936).
4. B.S. Rowntree, *Poverty and Progress: A Second Social Survey of York* (London, Longman, Green & Co., 1941).
5. C. Webster, 'Healthy or Hungry Thirties', *History Workshop Journal*, 13, Spring, 1982; M. Mitchell, 'The Effects of Unemployment on the Social Conditions of Women and Children in the 1930s', *History Workshop Journal*, 19, Spring 1985.
6. Stevenson and Cook, *The Slump*; H.W. Richardson, *Economic Recovery in Britain* (London, Weidenfeld and Nicolson, 1967); D.H. Aldcroft, *The Inter-War Years 1919–1939* (Batsford, 1970).
7. J. Stevenson, *British Society 1914–1945* (Harmondsworth, Penguin, 1984).
8. *Britain's Industrial Future, being a Report of the Liberal Industrial Inquiry of 1928* (London, Ernest Benn, 1928, 1977).
9. *Observer*, 21 March 1971, quoted in Stevenson and Cook, *The Slump*, p. 4.

SECTION I:
THE IMPACT OF UNEMPLOYMENT: SOME PROBLEMS AND ATTEMPTED SOLUTIONS

CHAPTER 1

THE ECONOMY AND UNEMPLOYMENT 1918–39

Unemployment was the most persistent problem facing British governments during the inter-war years. Throughout the 1920s it averaged more than 10 per cent of the insured working population and rose to nearly 25 per cent during the early 1930s. Therefore, between one and three million workers were unemployed at any one time. Not surprisingly, it was a major political issue and its solution became the keystone of the policies offered by the leading political parties of the day. In turn, these varied policies were influenced and shaped by the common perception of the causes of unemployment, the traditional values of the individual parties, and the pressure exerted by the Treasury in pushing forward its economic orthodoxy. It was this unique blend of forces which produced the free-trade orthodoxy of the 1920s and paved the way for the protectionist solutions of the 1930s. Throughout these years the economic orthodoxy of the day prevailed and governments persisted in their attempts to balance the budget. Those individuals, such as Oswald Mosley and J.M. Keynes, who demanded determined and direct action to deal with unemployment, which called for expenditure well beyond income, were marginalized from the mainstream of economic and political thinking.

7

The Causes and Distribution of Unemployment

The causes of inter-war unemployment were many and complex. There was obviously the problem of seasonal unemployment and casual work, which always occurred. There was unemployment which was caused by the cycle of boom and slump and amplified by the loss of trade which occurred during the First World War. Indeed it was not until the mid-1920s that world trade began to recover to anything approaching the pre-war levels. And even this limited recovery was swept away by the collapse of world trade following the Wall Street Crash of October 1929. But it was structural unemployment which was the major cause of the persistent long-term unemployment which occurred in these years; the old staple industries were declining and shedding their surplus labour as they lost their markets to both domestic and foreign competitors.

The problem had begun before the First World War when British industry – particularly textiles, engineering, iron and steel and shipbuilding – began to face stiff foreign competition from France, Germany and the United States. But the whole situation was aggravated by the First World War, which saw a decline in British exports and the rise of domestic production in some participating nations, most particularly in Japan whose rapidly rising industrial productivity and output permitted her to capture some of Britain's former Far Eastern markets.

Table 1.1 *Percentage Unemployment in the Staple Trades Compared with the National Average*[1]

	1921	1929	1932	1936	1938
Coal		18.2	41.2	25.0	22.0
Cotton		14.5	31.1	15.1	27.7
Iron and Steel	36.7	19.9	48.5	29.5	24.8
Shipbuilding	36.1	23.2	59.5	30.6	21.4
Average of all industries		9.9	22.9	12.5	13.3

By the end of the war, in 1918, Britain had lost the industrial leadership that she had previously enjoyed. Even as British industries recovered in the early 1920s, it was soon evident that they had lost about one-fifth of their old markets. War and the immediate post-war inflation made it difficult for Britain's staple export industries to compete with the, often subsidized, foreign industries. Consequently, unemployment rose sharply in Britain's staple industries.

8

Table 1.2 *Unemployment Figures for Insured Workers*[2]

Date		Total	Date		Total
December	1920	691,000	December	1929	1,334,000
March	1921	1,355,000	December	1930	2,500,000
June	1921	2,171,000	December	1931	2,500,000
December	1921	2,038,000	January	1932	2,850,000
December	1922	1,464,000	January	1933	2,950,000
December	1923	1,229,000	January	1934	2,400,000
December	1924	1,263,000	January	1935	2,290,000
December	1925	1,243,000	January	1936	2,130,000
December	1926	1,432,000	January	1937	1,670,000
December	1927	1,194,000	January	1938	1,810,000

Since most of the staple industries were to be found in the North, Scotland, Wales and Northern Ireland, it is hardly surprising that unemployment was a regional problem. It was the north and west of Britain, rather than the Midlands and the South East, which were most afflicted. In the 1920s, unemployment rates of 20 and 30 per cent were not uncommon and even in the textile districts of the West Riding of Yorkshire, which was never an unemployment blackspot, levels of between 10 and 25 per cent were not unusual. The complete disintegration of the world markets between 1929 and 1932 and the move throughout the industrial world to autarky added to the problem. The *Yorkshire Observer* contended that 'to describe 1930 merely as the blackspot period in post-war history was a completely inadequate description of the wool industry's tragic experience.'[3] Conditions throughout the textile districts of the West Riding of Yorkshire in the early thirties were distressing. In all the of the major industries unemployment rose to about 28 per cent of the insured workforce during the 1930s, and this figure was not reduced below 9 per cent until the level of effective demand rose substantially as Britain prepared for the Second World War.

The fact is that the woollen and worsted industry of Yorkshire was in structural decline. In 1922 about 206,000 were employed in textiles; by 1939 this figure had been reduced to 184,000, a loss of 22,000. The woollen and worsted industry was already technologically backward and cloth manufacturers were forced to exploit the high quality market, the last refuge everywhere of declining textile industries.

Table 1.3 *Unemployment in the Yorkshire Textile District, 1929–36*

Year	Unemployment	Year	Unemployment
1929	13.9	1933	13.2
1930	24.0	1934	16.0
1931	25.3	1935	12.9
1932	20.8	1936	10.1

Yet the problems of the Yorkshire textile industry were nothing compared to those of the declining engineering, shipbuilding and coal industries. It is well known that Jarrow, Maryport, Merthyr, and other towns in the North, Scotland and South Wales, faced unemployment levels which were well in excess of 50 per cent during the 1930s. Indeed, Ellen Wilkinson wrote:

> Jarrow in that year, 1932–33, was utterly stagnant. There was no work. No one had a job, except a few railwaymen, officials, the workers in the co-operative stores, and a few workmen who went out of the town to their jobs each day. The unemployment rate was over 80 per cent. 'Six thousand are on the dole and 23,000 on relief out of a total population of 35,000', was the estimate given at the time by the Medical Officer of Health.[5]

The official figures indicate that, in 1934, 67.8 per cent of the insured workers were unemployed in Jarrow and 61.9 per cent in Merthyr. These high levels contrast markedly with those experienced in the southern half of England. As the car industry expanded in the Midlands and the consumer industries boomed in the South East so unemployment levels fell to between 4 and 8 per cent in these regions. The contrast between the declining North and the prosperous south was most accurately documented by the Pilgrim Trust investigators in their report *Men Without Work*. Studying six communities – Rhondda Urban District, Crook in County Durham, Blackburn, Leicester, Deptford and Liverpool – they maintained:

> Everybody knows that there are at present in England prosperous districts and 'depressed areas'. The case of a prosperous district is described by conditions in Deptford, where about 7 per cent of the industrial population were unemployed in November 1936; the Rhondda U.D. is part of a depressed area, and 35 per cent of the industrial population were out of work. This description is inadequate to describe the differences in conditions. Not only are the number unemployed in Deptford very much

10

smaller . . . than they are in the Rhondda, but they represent entirely different types of unemployment. Only 6 per cent of the Deptford unemployed were long-term unemployed men, but 63 per cent in the Rhondda. The inclusion of the ins-and-outs in the unemployment figures must produce an entirely false picture of the differences in unemployment conditions in various parts of the country. Between prosperous and depressed districts there are two differences. The queues in the Rhondda are far longer than in Deptford, for example at the same time among them the proportion of 'really' unemployed men is far higher. Among every 1,000 workers, 4 in Deptford but 280 in Rhondda have failed to get a job for at least a year. This gives an idea of the unevenness in the distribution of the long term unemployed over the country. The difference between a prosperous and a depressed area is thus not in the neighbourhood of 1:7 but of 1:70. In a depressed there are 70 long-term unemployed men, where there is a prosperous community of the same size there is one.[6]

Indeed, these types of divisions were a regular feature of the unemployment figures of any year. For instance, at the bottom of the severe depression of 1932, when the annual rate of unemployment was in the region of 25 per cent and when all districts were experiencing high levels of unemployment, the percentage of unemployment ranged from 13.5 per cent in London to 36.5 per cent in Wales.[7]

For many workers, especially those in one industry towns which had depended upon the old staple exporting industries, the consequence was long-term unemployment. It was this problem which created most concern amongst social investigators. Many, including D. Caradog Jones, *The Social Survey of Merseyside* (1934), Hilda Jennings, *Brynmawr* (1934), and Herbert Tout, *The Standard of Living in Bristol, a Preliminary Report*, exposed this problem. In addition, George Orwell's *The Road to Wigan Pier* (1937), J.B. Priestley's *English Journey* (1934), and Wal Hannington's *Unemployed Struggles 1919–1936: My Life and Struggles amongst the Unemployed* (1936) examined the personal impact of unemployment upon the unemployed.[8]

Such unemployment varied from area to area and depended upon the industry, the area, and the age of the worker. Hilda Jennings was one of investigators who noted that once men in depressed areas reached their forties they would often find themselves made redundant and be out of employment for the rest of their lives.[9] The lives of the long-term unemployed were desperate. Their condition meant that they lacked income and therefore suffered a poor diet and ill-health. Inevitably, as G.C.M. M'Gonigle and J. Kirby found in their famous study of the health of the working class in Stockton-on-Tees, this meant that death rates increased dramatically among those families afflicted by long-term unemployment. As they noted, it was income, not housing or environment, which was vital to good health.[10] As will be suggested in the next chapter, low income meant poor nutrition and ill-health. In addition, the long-term unemployed faced a constant struggle for survival, made even more difficult by the uncertainties imposed by the Household Means Test and the other financial tests which they faced after their unemployment relief was exhausted. As Orwell noted, in *The Road to Wigan Pier*, this meant the break up of families as aged parents were forced to leave the household as their pittance of a pension or unemployment relief was included in the assessment of household needs. Hilda Jennings elaborated upon the concerns of the long-term unemployed in her study of Brynmawr:

> While some effects of unemployment are general, individual men and their families of course react in different ways, and out of some six hundred families normally dependent upon unemployment benefit probably no two have precisely the same attitude to life and circumstances. The unemployed men must register twice a week at the Exchange; he must draw his pay there on Fridays. If he has been out for some time, each Friday he will have a short period of sickening anxiety lest the clerk should single him out out and tell him that he is to be sent to the 'Court of Referees', then will follow a few days consequent dread lest his benefits should be stopped and he be cast on to the Poor Law, have to do 'task work' for his maintenance, and to take home less to his family in return for it. Having received his 'pay', duly contributed his 'Penny' to the Unemployed Lodge of the Miners' Federation, and conversed with his fellow unemployed, he returns home. The wife awaits his return in order that she may do the weekly shopping, and in many cases almost all of his unemployment pay, with the exception of a little pocket-money for 'fags' goes straight to her.[11]

Not all the long-term unemployed were men over the age of forty. There were, indeed, many young people affected, as was indicated in *Disinherited Youth*, a survey conducted by the Carnegie Trust and published in 1943, which examined the effects of unemployment upon young people in South Wales. It noted that the impact of unemployment affected the able and ambitious young man more than someone who had little ability and ambition, but stressed:

The central problem of the lives of most of these young men is one of maintenance of self-respect. Rightly, they feel a need to take their places in society, achieving in their own right the means of living. Much of their conduct, irrational and unreasonable . . . becomes understandable if regarded in its perspective, as part of the struggle for the retention of self-respect.[12]

The very fact that such regional variations persisted well into the 1930s, that such misery, depression and desperation continued throughout the inter-war years, and that long-term unemployment remained a problem, calls into question the effectiveness of government policies. What is clear is that all inter-war governments failed to create the climate for increased employment as they attempted to pursue an economic orthodoxy which demanded that budgets be balanced even if free trade and the gold standard could not be retained.

Government Policies on Unemployment: The Gold Standard, Free Trade and Protectionism

1918–29 – Until the early 1930s the fundamental problem of all governments facing unemployment was that they generally accepted the need to return to the gold standard, which had been suspended during the First World War, for that would signify Britain's return to free trade. It was believed that such action would persuade other governments to return to free trade, world trade would be stimulated and unemployment would wither away. This commitment to free trade was only abandoned during the economic and political crisis of 1931, when the second Labour government collapsed and a National government was formed under the leadership of Ramsay MacDonald.

The desire to return to the gold standard and free trade clearly persisted among political and financial leaders who had been forced to abandon such policies during the First World war. But the view was further encouraged by the report of the Cunliffe Committee on Currency and Foreign Exchanges after the War, which outlined the need for and conditions of returning to the conditions of the pre-war world, which included a return to the gold standard. It advocated a battery of actions, including the balancing of the budget, the legal limitation of note issue and the repayment of the national debt.[13] The balancing of the budget, which would strengthen the pound, was, however, seen as crucial to the return to gold.

The economic orthodoxy of the day accepted that there was a reciprocal relationship between the gold standard and balanced budgets. It was believed that a return to gold would act as an automatic check to inflation, for it was assumed that governments would then be able to only issue money equivalent to their gold and bullion reserves. If the economy did well exports would increase, gold would flow in, governments could issue more currency and prices would rise. The consequent price rises would reduce exports and attract imports. producing a balance of payments deficit. Governments would then be forced to reduce the supply of money, since gold and bullion would have flowed out of the country to pay international debts. This would force domestic prices down, make the goods of the country more competitive, raise exports and increase the flow of gold and bullion into the economy, thus raising domestic prices. The point was that the gold standard was envisaged as a self-regulating mechanism for the economy which would force governments to balance their budgets. The immediate post-war British governments accepted this philosophy without demur. Interest rates rose, the currency in circulation was reduced by 10 per cent between September 1920 and September 1921, and the budget was balanced thereafter. In effect British governments were also attempting to achieve other objectives as well. The deflation caused by their economic policies would force down prices and thus make British industry more competitive. In addition, if prices were reduced and trade recovered, government expenditure would be reduced. To this end, also, governments sought to pay off the National Debt, which had risen to more than £6,500 million and which was costing £325 million in interest charges, almost one-third of the yield from taxation.

Such policies had immediate consequences for the level of unemployment: official figures rose from 700,000 (6 per cent of the insured workers) in December 1920 to 2,200,000 (18 per cent) in June 1921 – although factors other than government policy were also at work.[14] In effect, the economic orthodoxy of the day forced successive governments – Coalition, Labour and Conservative – to contribute significantly to unemployment by the deflationary policies which they pursued. Those same policies prevented governments from taking significant long-term action to tackle unemployment. Nevertheless, the urgency of the problem forced all governments to recognize the need for some limited action.

A Treasury Committee, known as the Unemployment Grants Committee, was created under the chairmanship of Viscount St David in 1921. However, it was initially allocated a mere £3 million a year to ease unemployment, with this it attempted to support those local authorities which brought forward labour-intensive projects. Such relief programmes proved entirely inadequate to deal with the problem, even after the Committee was given increased funding. Between 1921 and 1929, the St David's Committee assisted various local authorities to the tune of £115 million but was never able to provide more than 40,000 unemployed people with direct employment at any one time. The impact of these projects was never very substantial and, indeed, diminished throughout the 1920s; an average of only 57,000 people were employed under this scheme between 1921 and 1926, a figure which fell significantly to about 7,000 in 1927 and 1928.[15]

Other short-term schemes were equally ineffective. In 1928, for instance, Baldwin's Conservative government inaugurated the Industrial Transference Scheme, by which the St David's Committee offered special grants to areas of low unemployment capable of absorbing transferees. At least 50 per cent of the men employed on any project approved under the terms of this scheme had to be transferees. This was the Government's response to the uneven geographical distribution of unemployment and was particularly devised to help miners. It was supposed to deal with the 200,000 miners who were surplus to requirements in the industry. However, by 1929 only 42,000 men had been transferred, and the Industrial Transference Board observed that many of the transferees were failing to retain their jobs, that there was a change in the quality of men coming forward for transfer, and that many of them had been unemployed for years.[16] These various short-term government schemes were to be no solution to unemployment, but this was hardly surprising given the prevailing belief in the gold standard, free trade and the balanced budget. Sir Alfred Mond, of the chemical firm Brunner–Mond, reflected upon the difficulty of getting the government to take unemployment seriously when he commented upon the speech of one politician in 1925. He argued:

. . . he seems to be still in the atmosphere of the period which I remember so well, when I was chairman of a Cabinet Unemployment Committee, and when the orthodox view seemed to be that you were still with a state of things in which unemployment went up automatically in autumn and came

15

down automatically in summer; that if you could device some scheme to get over the trouble from October to March, or April, you were dealing with the problem; and if you had any scheme which lasted longer than six months you were gravely informed that it was a very unwise thing to do, because probably by the end of that time there would be no unemployment. That delusion has been going on for three or four years. Had the great schemes which were outlined three or four years ago been started, they would be today in operation. I remember an important scheme for building a canal from the Forth to the Clyde which was turned down on the grounds that by the time it was finished there would be no unemployed. That scheme would almost be completed today. It would have employed 100,000 men. [17]

The problem was that both politicians and economists were besotted with the idea of returning to the gold standard, which they believed would return Britain to some golden age of industrial expansion and prosperity. This was not to be, for when Britain returned to the gold standard in 1925 she found that the world conditions had changed and that other nations were not willing to offer the level of international agreement which would have been necessary in order to make such a system work.

John Maynard Keynes had already suggested as much in the early 1920s, reflecting that the deflationary policies needed to get back to the gold standard would cause a significant rise in unemployment and that there was no guarantee of international cooperation. Regardless of such informed advice, Churchill, in his Budget speech of 28 April 1925, declared that Britain would return to the gold standard, adding:

> A return to the gold standard has long been a settled and declared policy of this country. Every expert Conference since the war . . . has urged in principle the return to the gold standard. No responsible authority has advocated any other policy. [18]

He added to this the need to raise the level of sterling from $4.40 to the pound to $4.86, thus raising the value of the pound by 10 per cent to the pre-war level and thus, commensurately, increasing the cost of British exports. [18] Keynes was provoked into producing *The Economic Consequences of Mr. Churchill* (1925), [19] a pamphlet which criticized Churchill's actions. He considered that the return to gold with the apparent over-valuing of the pound would be greatly damaging to the British economy and the export trade.

Although Keynes' views were not widely accepted, there was some support to be found for them within the Labour Party, the Independent Labour Party (ILP) and the Liberal Party.[20] But even in these areas, such support was limited in 1925. Within the Labour Party, Philip Snowden's emphasis upon economic orthodoxy marginalized the supporters of the more reflationary views of Keynes.[21]

In recent years it has become fashionable to support Keynes' criticism. Robert Skidelsky delivered a blistering attack upon Snowden and the Labour Party's economic policy in his seminal work *Politicians and the Slump; the Labour government 1929–1931* (1967) in which he argued that Labour politicians were generally orthodox in their economic thinking and devoid of economic understanding and originality.[22] Sydney Pollard endorsed this view shortly in introducing and editing an excellent collection of essays, which included Keynes' 1925 pamphlet. The gist of his argument is that the return to the gold standard was a 'bankers policy not directly concerned with industry at all' and that the government had been pushed into it hastily by Montague Norman, the irresponsible Governor of the Bank of England.[23] However, more recently, economic historians have been re-examining the return to the gold standard which took place in 1925. K.G.P. Matthews has argued that the 'sterling exchange rate of $4.86 did not amount to an overvaluation to the degree which economists and historians, from Keynes to Pollard, have hitherto argued.'[24] This view is, however, rejected by M.E.F. Jones who believes that the overvaluation sterling added to the regional problems of the 'outer areas' of Britain, such as South Wales, west-central Scotland and the North East.[25] J. Redmond had taken the middle line by suggesting that, while there was overvaluation of the pound in 1925, it did not persist — even though the precise level cannot be measured accurately.[26]

Yet, whatever the state of the current debate, it is clear that the immediate return to gold was little short of disastrous for the British economy. The fact is that British exports declined quickly, that the staple industries stagnated further, and that unemployment worsened in the wake of the return to gold at the new parity rates. As already indicated in Table 1.2, unemployment rose by an average of at least 100,000 between 1925 and 1929, before the international collapse of world trade following the Wall Street Crash, which more than doubled the official unemployment figures in Britain. The balance of trade situation worsened considerably from 1925 to 1930 and the only major beneficiary was the City, as indicated by the rise in invisible earnings.

Table 1.4 *Balance of Trade and Balance of Payments*
(£ million)

	Balance of trade			Invisibles	Balance of payments
Year	Imports	Exports	Balance		
1924	1291	953	−338	410	72
1925	1331	940	−392	438	46
1926	1253	790	−463	449	−14
1927	1226	839	−386	469	83
1928	1206	842	−353	475	122
1929	1229	848	−381	484	103
1930	1053	666	−387	413	27

The prosperity which orthodox economists felt would follow the return to gold eluded the British economy as the export trade of its principal export industries declined. The belief that Britain was experiencing a temporary cyclical depression was no longer tenable. Nevertheless, Conservative and Labour governments alike stuck faithfully to the gold standard, encouraged by the City bankers. Alternative schemes to deal with unemployment were summarily dismissed. The suggestion of developing an imperial tariff system received short shrift, particularly from Philip Snowden, Chancellor of the Exchequer in the second Labour government, who saw it as a form of protectionism. The Liberal Party, under the leadership of David Lloyd George, offered a long-term plan to deal with structural unemployment and a short-term scheme to tackle the immediate problem in its report, *Britain's Industrial Future*, published in 1928. This was followed by *We Can Conquer Unemployment*, its manifesto for the 1929 general election, which suggested that the government could borrow £300 million from the unused banking deposits of the nation, the 'idle savings', to generate work without causing inflation.[27] Similar schemes were put forward in the ILP's programme 'Socialism in Our Time' and *The Living Wage* and by Oswald Mosley in the 'Mosley Memorandum' and the

'Mosley Manifesto'.[28] But they were all rejected despite their obvious relevance to the problem.

Instead, Baldwin's Conservative government continued a policy of deflation and made it increasingly difficult for the unemployed to obtain benefits. The problem was that the National Insurance Act of 1920 had extended the insurance scheme to industries employing about twelve million workers at a period of relative prosperity. In addition, uncovenented benefit, better known as the 'dole', was provided for those workers, including many people who had returned from the war and could not find employment, who had not paid sufficient contributions to be entitled to benefit. The onset of depression, however, created financial difficulties for the unemployment insurance fund, which ran into debt, and for the government which was faced with underwriting the accumulating debt and contributing the 'dole'. The precise details of arrangements were altered through a variety of acts – there were indeed[28] insurance acts introduced between 1920 and 1938 – and the 'dole', or extended benefit as it became known, was increased under the Labour government of 1924. Since the Labour government's insurance act expired in 1926 Baldwin's Conservative government set up the Blanesburgh Committee to examine the problem of national insurance for the unemployed. It reported in 1927, suggesting that since unemployment was falling the differences between 'standard' and 'extended' benefit should be abolished and that those who had been unemployed longest should receive 'transitional benefit'. These suggestions were incorporated within the Unemployment Insurance Act of 1927 which, with the Blanesburgh Committee, was hostile to the idea of relief being readily available to those outside the insurance scheme. There was also a determined effort by the Conservatives to reduce the cost of unemployment benefit and to provide only for the 'genuine' unemployed. As a consequence the Conservative government attempted to reduce unemployment expenditure, a policy which fitted in well with its attempt to balance the Budget. The prospects for the unemployed grew worse.

1929–31 – Both Baldwin's Conservative government of 1924 to 1929 and MacDonald's Labour government of 1929 to 1931 pursued, to coin a phrase used of Philip Snowden, economic orthodoxy and deflation 'with almost ghoulish enthusiasm'.[29] Despite the mounting evidence that economic orthodoxy was failing there was almost a blind faith in the need for such policies from the majority of economists and politicians. This was possibly because the Treasury, Snowden, Churchill and other prominent economic experts were massaging economic beliefs which were effectively the shibboleths of British economic thought and accepted by the British public. It was only the economic events of 1930 and 1931 which shook this faith in economic orthodoxy, although they did not inaugurate a more expansive attitude towards dealing with unemployment.

The economic crisis of August 1931 was largely the product of the Wall Street Crash of October and November 1929, which led to an abrupt decline in international trade and the worsening of the already serious structural decline of Britain's staple industries. Official unemployment figures in Britain rose quickly, reaching 1,537,000 in January 1930 and 2,753,000 − practically a quarter of the insured workforce − in June 1931.

Philip Snowden's domination of financial matters ensured that the options to deal with this situation were limited. Tariffs and protective measures for specific industries were not to be entertained and Snowden informed his Cabinet colleagues, on 26 June 1929, that he would no longer support any more 'safeguarding of industries' measures that is, protectionist arrangements applied to specific industries which had first appeared in the early 1920s and had been the basis of the Conservative Party's electoral programme in 1929.[30] Also, the vast public works schemes advocated by the Liberal Party were anathema to Snowden.

In the new Labour government, J.H. Thomas was given the task of developing schemes to deal with unemployment through the Unemployment Committee, better known as the 'Thomas Committee', but soon found that his committee was ineffectual due to departmental and Treasury opposition. Oswald Mosley, a member of that committee, struck out on his own and issued the 'Mosley Memorandum', which circulated government circles between December 1929 and February 1930, proposing that free trade should be set aside in favour of import controls in order to encourage the home market to expand. In addition, Mosley advocated that there should be increased government expenditure to pay for public works, a scheme for early retirement and that the school-leaving age should be raised. It was no surprise that Mosley's ideas were quickly dismissed in Cabinet, and some surprise that they were only narrowly defeated at the October 1930 Labour Party Conference in Llandudno.[31]

The Labour Party and the Labour government remained almost

slavishly loyal to Snowden and acquiescent to his economic strategy. They accepted, with little demur, his determinedly deflationary 1930 Budget and increased tax from 4s to 4s 6d (20p to 22p) in the pound. Given Snowden's increased determination to balance the budget there was little scope for increased expenditure to finance unemployment schemes, especially at a time when the rapidly rising levels of unemployment were raising the cost of unemployment benefits and building up a budget deficit. As a result, Snowden came under increasing pressure from the opposition parties to curb the escalating cost of unemployment.

At this time unemployment provision essentially consisted of three types of benefit. First, there was insurance benefit paid out of an Unemployment Insurance Fund to anyone who had paid thirty contributions in the previous two years. Secondly, there was the so-called 'transitional benefit', paid out by the Exchequer to those who were not entitled to unemployment benefit but who had made contributions to the Fund. Thirdly, there was Public Assistance which was paid to those who had depended upon the Poor Law until the late 1920s. This cost was borne partly by the state and partly by the local authority, and paid through a Public Assistance Committee.

By 1930 the Labour government was faced with an exhausted insurance fund, the mounting payment of 'transitional benefits', and the rapidly rising cost of Public Assistance Committee expenditure. Ramsay MacDonald had to avert an impending financial crisis. In June 1930 he took over the special responsibility for unemployment from Thomas and set up a committee of five economists under J.M. Keynes to report to him on the matter. In October 1930 they suggested that unemployment benefits should be restricted, that public work schemes should be financed and that a general tariff should be introduced.

Snowden was clearly opposed to tariffs, and hesitant about public works, but agreed with the need to restrict unemployment benefits. The task of examining the whole issue of unemployment and the financing of the Unemployment Insurance Fund was left to a royal commission set up under Judge Holman Gregory in December 1930. When it reported in June 1931 it argued that the Unemployment Fund should be balanced by a 30 per cent cut in benefits, that 'anomalies' should be eliminated, that unemployment should be rigidly confined to twenty-six weeks per year, and that applicants for 'transitional benefit' should be means tested. Given the political sensitivity of these issues within the Labour Party, all the Labour government did was introduce a bill to deal with the 'anomalies', allowing for variations in the conditions, amount, and period of benefit for casual, seasonal, and short-time workers and for married women.

Notwithstanding the Labour government's retreat from the Gregory Report, the reduction of unemployment benefits was now central to British politics. The events of early 1931 had made the issue of unemployment even more significant than it had been in 1930. The financial crisis worsened and Snowden only avoided parliamentary censure in February 1931 by accepting a Liberal amendment committing the government to setting up an all-party committee of inquiry into the financial crisis. It was headed by Sir George May and was to advise Snowden on how to reduce national expenditure in such a way as to ensure a balanced budget. In the meantime, Snowden produced an interim Budget for 1931.

The May Committee Report was available by June 1931, was discussed by the Cabinet and published the following month. Its main finding was that there would be a budget deficit of £120 million for 1931–2 and that £97 million should be saved by tax increases and savings. The savings, of about £67 million, were to come from increases in unemployment insurance contributions, by limiting benefit to twenty-six weeks in a year, reducing the standard rate of benefits by 20 per cent and by the introduction of a means test for 'transitional benefit'. This report was being discussed at a time when there was declining international confidence in the pound, despite high interest rates, resulting in an out-flow of money and gold from London. On 24 July Snowden was warned by officials that the 'gold exodus is unprecedented . . .. Unless we take such steps as are open to us to rectify the situation, there is a real danger of our being driven off the gold standard.'[32] Snowden's priority now became the securing of an £80 million loan from New York and Paris to help the City bankers. In order to secure this loan he supported the Treasury view, which happened to be his own, that the Budget had to be balanced.

As the dominant member of the Economy Committee of the Cabinet, set up at the end of July to consider the May Report and to deal with the economic crisis, Snowden ensured that his colleagues were aware of the necessity of balancing the budget, maintaining Britain on the gold standard and in a state of free trade. Throughout the early weeks of August, through lengthy and detailed negotiations, he forced the Economy Committee to accept a package of cuts worth £78 million. However, the full Cabinet, when it met on 19 August, was reluctant to accept these cuts, jibbing at the reductions in unemployment insurance which were set to be £43,500,000 in the full package. It came up with its own package which, at £56,250,000, was more than £20 million less than that recommended by the Economy Committee.[33]

During the next four days, Snowden pressured the Cabinet, using the Treasury and the New York bankers to support his argument for balancing the budget. He did not inform them that the New York bankers were no longer demanding that the £50 million Sinking Fund payment, to help pay off the National Debt, should be paid nor that the Treasury was no longer advising high levels of tax increases as they had done previously.[34] Stressing that the opposition leaders were dissatisfied with the small scale of the cuts agreed to by the full Cabinet he, and MacDonald, forced a decision on cuts in unemployment benefit at the Cabinet meeting on 23 August 1931. On this occasion eleven ministers supported MacDonald, and thus the demand for a 10 per cent cut in standard unemployment benefit, eight opposed him and one was absent.[35] It was agreed that the Cabinet could not continue and that MacDonald would offer their resignation to the king. The second Labour government had effectively come to an end and, subsequently, Ramsay MacDonald earned the epithet 'traitor' when he emerged from meetings with the king and opposition leaders to form a National government.

In terms of broad economic policy, this was the turning point in British history for, in the wake of the collapse of the second Labour government and the formation of a National government, the gold standard had to be abandoned in September 1931 and protectionist economic measures were imposed throughout 1931 and 1932.[36] But protectionism, although it did not necessarily impose the same deflationary pressures as were imposed to return to and operate the gold standard, brought little relief for the unemployed.

1931–1939 – The most obvious point to make about the National governments headed by MacDonald (1931–5), Baldwin (1935–7) and Chamberlain (1937–40) is that while they were protectionist, and though they allowed interest rates to fall, they retained many orthodox ideas on the management of the economy. Roger Middleton has recently noted:

23

During the 1930s Britain alone among the major western industrial economies eschewed 'resort to a policy of budget deficits to promote internal recovery'; instead reliance was placed on active monetary policy, tariff protection, devaluation, and specific intervention at a micro-economic level. The role accorded to a budgetary policy as a stabilization instrument was limited. The principal objective was the maintenance of domestic and international confidence in the authorities' economic policies, and this dictated adherence to balanced budgets and orthodox financial principles. Consequently budgetary operations were potentially destabilizing, for the contemporary practice was to attempt to balance revenue and expenditure with little regard for autonomous fluctuations in economic activity.[37]

Effectively, as Middleton suggests, the National governments were extremely orthodox in their economic policies. At first they attempted to defend the pound and the gold standard and imposed cuts in the pay of teachers, the police, the armed forced and civil servants as well as imposing the 10 per cent cut in unemployment benefit. In other words, MacDonald's National government imposed the cuts which had been discussed by the second Labour government. Even when Britain was driven off the gold standard, in September 1931, it continued to apply these policies and did not restore the salary cuts until 1934. Indeed, these were in no way disturbed by the emphasis which it placed upon constructing new tariff barriers throughout 1931 and 1932, nor by the emphasis which it placed upon constructing a system of Empire free trade both before, during, and after the Ottawa Conference of 1932. Given its new priorities and its adherence to balanced budgets MacDonald's National government was never likely to stimulate the economy and reduce unemployment.

The unemployed could expect little direct help from the National governments which dominated British politics from 1931 to the Second World War. In the first place, in September 1931, the government introduced the 'Household Means Test' on the 'transitional payments', paid to applicants once the twenty-six weeks of standard benefit had expired. Subsequently, it indulged in the rhetoric of offering to undertake action in the winter months, when unemployment was high, and did nothing in the summer months, when unemployment was low due to seasonal factors. The various National governments adopted a policy of reducing competition in the staple industries by closing the more inefficient units and amalgamating firms. They did this in the mining and cotton industries and, most dramatically, in the shipbuilding industry, where National Shipbuilders Securities Ltd., financed by an offshoot of

24

the Bank of England, closed down numerous shipyards, including Palmers of Jarrow. Although such a policy might have been rational for these industries as a whole they did not help the one-industry towns such as Jarrow, which suffered unemployment levels well in excess of 70 per cent in the mid-1930s.

When the National government took action to deal with the problem of high levels of regional unemployment it offered little financial assistance. This was apparent partly in the limited provision for, and interest in, the Juvenile 'Instruction' or 'Unemployment' centres, usually known as the 'dole schools' which emerged in the 1930s.[38] It was particularly evident in the case of the Special Areas Act of 1934, which established special-area status for southern Scotland, the North East, West Cumberland and South Wales, and appointed two commissioners to spend £2 million a year to help local authorities carry out amenity schemes and to attract firms to their areas – although the figure was increased in 1936 and 1937 to allow the commissioners to spend £17 million in 1938.

From the outset, the Cabinet was aware of the delicate nature of their policy and attempted to project it as being a policy of 'experiment and research'.[39] It was also recognized that there might be difficulties over the initial amount of money available for the scheme and it was suggested that it was not possible to estimate in advance the amount of money that would be required but:

the Government desired the commissioners to enter upon their work free from any immediate financial difficulties; that that end would be attained by the provision of the sum of £2,000,000 and that of as a result of experience more money was found to be required, Parliament would be invited to vote for it.[40]

Yet the limited nature of these proposals was ridiculed by David Lloyd George's amusing biblical reference to the scheme in the House of Commons on 6 December 1934:

The age of miracles is past. You cannot feed the multitude with two Commissioners and five sub-commissioners. The new Commissioners are being sent on their apostolic mission not without purse and script, but pretty nearly that – just with a little bit of cash to deal with a problem costing £100,000,000 a year.[41]

Not surprisingly the results were disappointing and it has been estimated that in the North East fewer than 50,000 jobs were created in areas where over 350,000 were registered as being unemployed in January 1935.[42]

This neglect of the interests of the unemployed was also evident in the policy of the National governments towards the application of the 'Household Means Test' on transitional payments. This issue raised resentment, as already indicated by Orwell's evidence. From the start, these governments were anxious to keep expenditure low. Neville Chamberlain, the Chancellor of the Exchequer in Mac-Donald's National government, was first of all concerned to control the Public Assistance committees, which had been set up by local authorities to replace the Poor Law, since some of them were considered to be generous in the assessments they made in their provision of government money to those claiming 'transitional' benefit. Secondly, he wished to distinguish between the short-term and long-term unemployed. In these endeavours he was supported by the Royal Commission on Unemployment Insurance, chaired by Holman Gregory, which, in 1932, reported on the need for a reorganization and rationalization of unemployment relief. The Unemployment Act of 1934 reflected these concerns. Part I of the Act put the Unemployment Insurance scheme on a sounder footing and established the Unemployment Insurance Statutory Committee to act as a supervisory body. This was to deal with the short-term unemployed and, first of all, restored the benefit cuts of 1931 and subsequently increased dependants' allowances. Part II of the Act set up the Unemployment Assistance Board which took responsibility for the long-term unemployed who had exhausted their benefit. It effectively replaced the Public Assistance committees of the local authorities and acted as a centrally-based body operating a means-tested system of benefits. However, there was such protest at the benefit rates being offered by the new body that a Standstill Act was introduced for two years, allowing the long-term unemployed to choose whichever benefit was the higher – that of the UAB or the PAC. The scheme was not actually introduced until 1937.

As for the immediate needs of the unemployed, the National governments became more liberal in their provision of relief as time went on and provided a modest amount of special aid to overcome some of the worst excesses of regional mass unemployment. Yet, as Middleton suggests, this was achieved within the confines of balanced budgets. There was little evidence that they were ever seriously interested in introducing the more expansionary policies of

J.M. Keynes or in adopting the budget deficit policies adopted by other countries. Indeed, according to recent research, it remains debatable as to whether or not Keynesian ideas could have solved the economic and unemployment problems of the 1930s even if the various National governments had adopted them.[43]

It seems likely that factors other than government policy helped to improve employment prospects and reduce unemployment. The fact that Britain became protectionist certainly helped the general climate of the British economy by increasing domestic demand for British products and by the stabilizing impact it exerted upon the value of the pound – due to the fact that the Exchange Equalization Account was formed in 1932 in order to buy and sell in the foreign exchange. In addition, protection meant that interest rates could be reduced because the bank rate was at 2 per cent from June 1932 until the Second World War, no longer geared to the need to defend the pound in the international markets. Whatever the intention of the government, this 'cheap money' policy resulted in cheap mortgages, which encouraged the housebuilding boom of the mid-1930s and enabled consumers to borrow more easily in order to purchase the new consumer items which were becoming increasingly available. In consequence, the new car and electrical industries of the Midlands and the South East flourished. Other factors, such as rearmament in the mid- and late 1930s, also contributed to the revival of the economy and the fall in unemployment.

What is clear is that none of the inter-war governments made any determined effort to tackle unemployment and that their policies often contributed significantly to raising its overall level. Indeed, it was often factors outside the direct control of governments which alleviated the problem from time to time. Therefore, the majority of the long-term unemployed had little prospect that their situation would be improved by the action of any government. Most accepted their situation in silence, weighted down with the problems of surviving from day to day. But a few made a determined effort to draw their plight to public notice.

The National Unemployed Workers' Movement, the Hunger Marches and Attempts to Organize the Unemployed

George Orwell wrote in *The Road to Wigan Pier* that:

> By far the best work for the unemployed is being done by the NUWM –
> the National Unemployed Workers' Movement. This is a revolutionary
> organization intended to hold the unemployed together, stop them
> blacklegging during strikes, and give them legal advice against the Means
> Test. It is a movement that has been built out of nothing but the pennies
> and the efforts of the unemployed themselves. I have seen a good deal of
> the NUWM, and I greatly admire the men, ragged and underfed like the
> others, who keep the organization going. Still more I admire the tact and
> patience with which they do it; for it is not easy to coax even a penny-a-
> week subscription out of the pockets of the people on the PAC . . . In
> many towns the NUWM have shelters and arrange speeches by Communist
> speakers.[44]

In a few short sentences, Orwell had summarized the work and achievements of the most effective organization involved in the defence of the unemployed during the inter-war years, although it must be recognized that their activities were always marginal to the experience of the vast majority of the unemployed. The fact is that the NUWM was simply the largest and most confrontational of the many small and largely ineffective groups which emerged to defend the unemployed.

It emerged from a similar London organization which was formed in 1920 by Wal Hannington, Percy Haye and Jack Holt, who were all active members of the Communist Party, and brought together many unemployed men who were often ex-servicemen. In April 1921, a national conference brought together seventy or eighty similar organizations to establish the National Unemployed Workers' Committee Movement (later to drop the word Committee from its title), with a national administrative committee as its governing body. Its members took an oath 'never to cease from active strife until capitalism is abolished', which they felt was the only way to end the 'horror of unemployment', and it was clearly a socialist and Communist body from the outset – although its leaders, such as Hannington, were often in conflict with the official Communist position. The London district had begun its own journal *Out of Work* in March 1921 and this became the official organ of the NUWM. In November 1921, a further and more representative national conference was held and Wal Hannington was appointed national organizer.

Immediately, the organization moved onto the offensive and began to seek representation at the TUC, and local unemployed committees were told to apply for affiliation to their trades councils, to arrange local trade union conferences on unemployment and to take action to prevent overtime working in local factories. Indeed, *Out of Work* carried in its next few issues reports of raids by the unemployed on factories which were working overtime – actions which were occasionally successful. The NUWM also urged that the trades union movement and the TUC should join in the efforts to improve the situation of the unemployed. Indeed, throughout 1923 the NUWM successfully negotiated with the TUC to form the Unemployment Advisory Committee, with representatives from both the NUWM and the TUC, to take action to deal with the unemployed. As Hannington wrote, in *Out of Work:*

> The General Council has taken up the challenge. It cannot now turn back without black disgrace and bankrupt prestige . . . .. Our movement will strive to keep the Trade Union movement in the front line in our and their struggle. The United Front is an important and hopeful phase in the struggle and should enormously strengthen the NUWCM.[45]

Yet the TUC always kept the NUWM at bay, rejecting its attempt to affiliate with the TUC in March 1923, and failed to develop the work of the Unemployment Advisory Committee.[46] Relations between them worsened when the Communist Party, which greatly influenced the NUWM, strongly attacked the TUC in the wake of the unsuccessful General Strike of 1926. The trades unions kept their distance from the NUWM, which was attempting to be the trade union of the unemployed, by virtue of the fact that they did not need to act if the NUWM prevented the unemployed from blacklegging and thus undermining the employment conditions of trade unionists.[47]

The close association of the NUWM leaders with the Communist Party proved to be an unsurmountable difficulty in its work. And the sins of the NUWM were compounded when its candidates stood with Communists against Labour candidates at the 1929 General Election. But how strong was the link between the NUWM and the Communist Party?

H.J.P. Harmer has argued that the Communist link with the NUWM was stronger than has often been supposed. He maintains:

> The NUWM was intended to politicise the unemployed, to provide a point of contact between the Communist Party and a section of the working class. The unemployed were to be educated to understand the reasons for their condition and to go on from then to accept a need for revolutionary socialism.[48]

Given the fact that the mass of the unemployed and employed working class, as well as working-class institutions, did not accept either the NUWM or the Communist Party it is hardly surprising, to Harmer, that the Communist scheme failed. The problem appears to have been that most of the NUWM agitational activities were related to 'the wider tactical needs of the Communist Party than to the everyday needs of the unemployed themselves.'[49] Where the NUWM was most effective, in its representation of the cases of the unemployed before the PACs and the umpires, the Communist Party was less supportive of its activities favouring the more confrontational tactics of the hunger marches.[50]

Harmer is probably right; the Communist Party intended to use the NUWM as one of its major means of arousing revolutionary sentiments amongst the working classes. Yet even his own evidence suggests that there was always argument and resentment against the Communist Party's attempt to manipulate the NUWM. Other recent writers, particularly R. Hayburn have played down the direct influence of the Communist Party on the NUWM, while admitting that it did exert a good deal of influence over the movement at the national level.[51]

Yet, whatever the degree of Communist direction, the image which the wider British Labour movement received was one which suggested that the NUWM was some type of puppet organization of the Communist Party. Indeed, while it is true that local organization often operated independently of the national leadership, the Communist Party did manipulate the NUWM's national policy. It was partly responsible for the organization of the hunger marches, the fluctuating interest in various campaigns, and, at various times, Hannington's removal from the Communist leadership. There were clearly struggles between the competing interests of both organizations, as illustrated in the *Memorandum on the policy of defending claims before the Unemployment Insurance Authorities*. This was produced by Sid Elias, E.G. Llewelyn and W. Hannington as a report of the National Administrative Council meeting of the NUWM, 25–26 January 1930. It reveals that the NUWM had fought off the suggestion that it should not work on defence of claims for unemployment benefits in order to concentrate its efforts towards building up the mass membership of the movement. Clearly, as the *Labour Monthly* reflected later, 'What the Party [Communist] and Movement found difficult to accept was that the unemployed

30

wanted so little and felt, or at least expressed, so little anger.'[52] The fact is that the NUWM was forced to recognize that the bread and butter business of representing the unemployed in their claims for increased benefits outweighed some of the wider ambitions of the Communists.

The authorities suspecting the NUWM of being a subversive Communist organization maintained a close surveillance of its activities and blighted its efforts. Indeed, there was a remarkable degree of police surveillance at NUWM meetings, of its 'Hunger March' activities, and of its leaders, several of whom were frequently imprisoned.

There were many other problems which reduced the possibility of the NUWM adequately representing the interests of the unem-ployed, much less preparing the ground for revolution. Local relations with the Communist Party were not always easy. Tiffs, such as the one in Liverpool between Jack and Bessie Braddock and the Communists, lost the movement members and support.[53] Finance was always limited and membership was transitory and small; 13,356 members in 1923, 10,000 in 1929, 17,062 in 1932 20,409 in 1935 and down to a mere 10,301 in 1938.[54] Although NUWM influence amongst the unemployed was obviously greater than its numbers would suggest, these figures were infinitesimal when compared with the three million or so unemployed in 1931. The fatalism of the unemployed, the fluctuating unemployment levels, and the disparate nature of the NUWM all militated against its success. Nevertheless, it was the only significant body which drew the attention of the nation to the plight of the unemployed.

Apart from setting up soup kitchens for the unemployed the NUWM was involved in a variety of other activities. The introduc-tion of the 'Household Means Test' in 1931 created the opportunity for the organization to attract wide support throughout the country as it organized numerous demonstrations to oppose the means test. It held meetings outside local Labour exchanges, which often led to clashes with the police. It launched a campaign to obtain one million signatures for a petition against the means test which it intended to present to parliament. In fact many Labour-dominated PACs, such as that at Rotherham, were illegally ignoring many aspects of their duties under the new arrangements and the NUWM was, in these areas, often superfluous to the debate between the PACs and Whitehall.[55] In September 1932, faced with the need to

31

revive its efforts against the means test, the NUWM led the marches on the local unemployment offices of the Public Assistance Committee at Birkenhead, which were followed by several days of rioting. It was also involved in similar disturbances at Liverpool and with the rioting at Belfast in October, which followed a demonstration by unemployed men working on a relief scheme.[56] Throughout the 1930s the NUWM took up the case work of individuals who were coming before the PACs and the umpires – although, for instance, the number of appeals to the umpires was never larger than 8 per cent of the total and fell to between 3.3 and 4.5 per cent of the total between 1934 and 1936 and the success rate was generally lower than the overall average.[57] Perhaps its greatest success was in mounting opposition against the new Unemployment Act of 1934, which created the Unemployment Assistance Board, where it exposed the fact that claimants in some areas would get increased benefits while others, particularly those in South Wales, Durham and Glasgow, would find their benefits reduced. The Cabinet had been impressed by the savings which would be brought about by the creation of the UAB but had not anticipated the level of local opposition which the NUWM and other bodies raised against it, eventually forcing it to introduce the Standstill Act.[58]

From 1937 to 1939 the NUWM made the issue of additional 'Winter Relief' the focus of its campaign. Under the Poor Law and the PACs extra winter relief had been provided for the unemployed. As Hannington recalled, this was not to be provided on the same scale by the new UAB, in what he referred to as 'The Winter Relief Fraud', for 'only a very small number of claimants were granted extra allowances' by the Winter Adjustment Regulation which was introduced.[59] Amongst the many incidents connected with this campaign was an occasion when a group of unemployed men sought tea in the Ritz, only to be ejected by the police, and the occasion on 31 December 1938 when the NUWM carried a coffin in a mock procession from Trafalgar Square to St Paul's – on the sides of the coffin was written 'He did not get Winter Relief'.[60] The atmosphere of these times is captured by Ernie Trory's emotional recollections of these events. Among the chants and slogans which he recalls was the following:

> One, two, three, four. Who are we for?
> We are for the working-class. DOWN with the ruling class.
> Mary had a little lamb whose fleece was white as snow,
> Shouting the battle-cry of TREASON.[61]

32

Max Cohen also remembered the slogans of one demonstration:

> Work or full maintenance!
> Not a penny off the dole
> Not a man off benefit!
> Down with the Means Test![62]

There is no doubting the strong economic and political commitment which the NUWM engendered in its day-to-day and routine activities. Nevertheless, it was the hunger marches for which it will be best remembered.

They began in 1922 when the NUWM mounted a national hunger march to London in which about 2,000 people made their way to the capital from the depressed areas of the country. This was followed by other marches, such as that of the South Wales miners to London in 1927, and the national hunger marches, on London, of 1932, 1934 and 1936. In addition, there were numerous local marches including those at Belfast, Birkenhead and Liverpool in 1932. Most did not receive the approval of the Labour Party or the TUC. It should also be stressed that it would be stretching a point to include the famous Jarrow March of 1936 in this type of activity since it was a small march of 200 men, organized by the Labour Party, who walked to London to demand that the government set up a steel works in Jarrow to replace the, then defunct, Palmer's shipbuilding yard. Unlike the NUWM marches, it received some support from all the major political parties.

The 1932 'Great National Hunger March against the Means Test', which brought together eighteen contingents of marchers from all over the country to meet in London on 27 October 1932, was possibly the most dramatic of the hunger marches organized by the NUWM. Once in London, the 2,000 marchers were to invade Whitehall and present a mass petition of one million signatures to parliament protesting at the means test and demanding the restoration of the 10 per cent cut in unemployment benefits of 1931. They intended to present the petition themselves and not through the good offices of Labour MPs.

Recent evidence has revealed the full extent of police surveillance and harassment. The Glamorgan contingent of marchers were, for instance, subjected to close surveillance, to such an extent that files on individual marchers, noting their tendency to be 'easily led' or 'Communist and prone to violence against the police', were passed on to the Metropolitan Police and Special Branch.[63] There was, indeed, much violence between the marchers and the police as they moved to London, and the marchers were in frequent conflict with the authorities since they claimed and were often refused casual relief as they moved to London.

The situation was little better once they arrived in London for the authorities made a determined effort to ensure that the petition could not be presented. There were reports that the marchers, and their London supporters, were armed with all manner of weapons. The welcoming demonstrations for the marchers, at Hyde Park on the 27 October, was marked with baton-charges by the police, and other disturbances occurred. On 1 November, Wal Hannington was arrested at the NUWM headquarters in Great Russell Street and taken to Brixton prison and other leaders, such as Sid Elias, were followed by the police.[64] Over several days, the petition was moved around London and the marchers were finally forced to abandon their efforts and leave London on 5 November. Subsequently, on 8 November, Hannington was finally convicted on a charge of causing disaffection, for which he was given three months imprisonment.[65]

The 1934 and 1936 hunger marches were far less dramatic and attracted some support from Labour MPs, most notably Nye Bevan, Edith Summerskill and Ellen Wilkinson. Bevan, indeed, asked 'Why should a first class piece of work like the Hunger March have been left to the initiative of unofficial members of the Party, and to the Communists and the ILP?'[66] He subsequently greeted the 1936 marchers at a welcoming rally in Hyde Park.

However, the National governments remained determined in their efforts to discourage such marches. In February 1934, the Cabinet reaffirmed its decision not to greet the hunger marchers and Ramsay MacDonald, the Prime Minister, was to make a statement that the meeting of a deputation of the hunger marchers would serve no useful purpose and would 'merely encourage and recognize the exploitation for political ends of the legitimate grievances of the unemployed.'[67] In the case of the 1936 hunger march, due to arrive in London on 8 November, there were also two other similar marches by the Jarrow marchers and 250 blind persons due to arrive on 31 October. The Cabinet felt that it could not distinguish in its treatment of all three, although it was more sympathetic towards the last two, and clearly felt that the parliamentary system was the correct way in which to influence British politics. In addition it was decided to:

. . . arrange, probably through the National Publicity Bureau, for selected
journalists to be interviewed and given material for exposing the uselessness
of the hunger marches.[68]

The NUWM, for a variety of reasons, received scant recognition
from the Labour Party and the TUC. Its influence was always
marginal and restricted. Yet, it did leave its mark on British society
during the inter-war years. Hannington believed that the NUWM
managed to influence the course of government legislation, especially over the delay in introducing total central control over benefits
by the Unemployment Assistance Board, though Stevenson, Cook
and Harmer have their reservations about the extent to which the
NUWM influenced government policy towards the unemployed.[69]
Indeed, it may well have been the case, as David Lloyd George
noted, that the government unemployment benefit system acted as
an effective 'fire insurance' against the prospect of significant
disturbances among the unemployed.[70]

In any case, the role of the NUWM disappeared as the Second
World War swallowed up the unemployed in the war effort. There is
little doubt that its influence upon government policy was limited.
Nevertheless, a highly partial Hannington maintained, in his
autobiography:

When the NUWM closed down there were no golden handshakes! – but
there was a history of which we were proud . . .. It is to the credit of the
Communist Party that it consistently encouraged the NUWM and
cooperated with it in its bitter struggles to improve the conditions of the
unemployed.[71]

The pity is that its influence was so restricted by force of circumstance.

The fact is that there were many small organizations dealing with
the unemployed but they rarely exerted much influence beyond a
small locality. In Bradford, for instance, there were several such
bodies, apart from a local branch of the NUWM. The most
prominent was the Drummond Street Occupational Centre which
ran both allotments for the unemployed and set men to work to
producing their own textile goods. But such efforts could hardly
tackle the large numbers of unemployed, even in areas where
unemployment was normally close to the national average, and the
production of textile goods could have only added to the difficulties
of a slowly declining trade.[72]

In Leeds there were also several similar organizations. The St John's Unemployment Association was formed by Revd Hurst, the Vicar of St John's Church in cooperation with Roundhay Church, on 17 January 1933 at Alma Hall, Newtown, Leeds. It attempted to offer the unemployed work experience.[73] The Leeds Trades Council also set up its own Unemployment Association in 1933 to work on behalf of the 39,000 registered unemployed and 21,000 on poor relief in the city of Leeds.[74] These bodies did what they could for the unemployed, opposed the means test and expressed concern at the limitations being imposed by the National government on the PACs. But in the end they, like the NUWM, could do little to alleviate the plight of the unemployed, to influence government policy or to organize the vast majority of those affected by unemployment.

Conclusion

Posterity is still not sure whether anything could have been done to improve the economy and to tackle the mass unemployment which occurred during the inter-war years. Quite clearly, it would have been very difficult for any economic system to have dealt with the massive rise in unemployment which occurred as a result of the intense world slump of the late 1920s and the early 1930s. Nevertheless, it is possible that both cyclical and structural unemployment may have been tackled more effectively by the introduction of the more expansionary policies advocated by Keynes, the Liberal Party and by some sections of the Labour Party and the TUC. This is certainly the view which Skidelsky presented more than twenty years ago and which some historians are still suggesting. On the other hand, Glynn and Booth, as well as other historians, have questioned the validity of this view and suggested that Keynesian or expansionary policies might not have made much difference. In their view, the economy did as well as could be expected and, in any case, the expansionist policies of Keynes and others were unlikely to be introduced.

Nevertheless, although the fine detail of debate will continue, it cannot be doubted that the deflationary policies of the inter-war governments contributed significantly to the high levels of unemployment. Even though the abandonment of the gold standard in 1931 helped to ease some of the deflationary pressures on the economy, governments still attempted to balance the Budget and there was never any serious effort made to use the Budget as a financial weapon to expand the economy. At the very least, inter-war governments failed to direct the market forces towards a more expansionary outlook. Instead they let unemployment take its own course, except when the defence of the nation demanded greater expenditure on rearmament in the mid-1930s. Successive governments lacked the vision which was necessary to tackle the problem of mass unemployment and the various National governments of the 1930s, bolstered up by their overwhelming parliamentary majorities, were powerful enough to ignore both the demands of the 'expansionary' economists and the organized unemployed. In the final analysis, there was no serious attempt to tackle unemployment and the social and economic problems of the depressed areas continued to blight the lives of millions of working-class families.

In 1937, Wal Hannington wrote:

> There can be no doubt that, unless something very effective is done to grapple with this problem of the Distressed Areas, the present feeling of unrest against the Government over the question will assume still greater proportions in the political life of this country; it may become the main issue in domestic policy that will hasten the end of any Government which fails to solve it.[75]

Events proved him to be over-optimistic in his estimation of the political potentiality of unemployment. Nevertheless, there was no denying the social distress which unemployment created, and the health of the nation did become a key issue of debate during the inter-war years.

NOTES

1. J. Stevenson, *British Society 1914–45* (Harmondsworth, Penguin, 1984), p. 271.
2. Variety of sources, including C.L. Mowat, *Britain between the Wars 1918–1940* (London, Methuen, 1968 edition), pp. 273–5.
3. *Yorkshire Observer*, Trade Review, 5 January 1931.
4. *Report on Wages, Hours and Work in the Wool Textile Industry in Yorkshire, 1936.* Also quoted in J. Reynolds and K. Laybourn, *Labour Heartland: A history of the Labour Party in West Yorkshire during the inter-war years 1918–1939*

(Bradford, Bradford University Press, 1987), p. 11.

5. E. Wilkinson, *The Town that was Murdered: The Life-Story of Jarrow* (London, Gollancz, 1939), pp. 191–2; B.D. Vernon, *Ellen Wilkinson* (London, Croom Helm, 1982).

6. The Pilgrim Trust, *Men Without Work* (Cambridge, Cambridge University Press, 1938), pp. 13–14.

7. Stevenson, *British Society*, p. 271.

8. D. Caradog Jones, *The Social Survey of Merseyside* (London, Liverpool University Press & Hodder and Stoughton, 1934.); H. Tout, *The Standard of Living in Bristol* (Bristol, Bristol University Press, 1934); G. Orwell, *The Road to Wigan Pier* (London, Gollancz, 1937 and Harmondsworth, Penguin, 1962); J.B. Priestley, *English Journey* (London, Heinemann, 1934, 1968, 1976).

9. H. Jennings, *Brynmawr*, pp. 138–142.

10. G.C.M. M'Gonigle and J. Kirby, *Poverty and Public Health* (London, Gollancz, 1936), especially ch. vii, xv and p. 273.

11. Jennings, op.cit., pp. 138–42.

12. Carnegie Trust, *Disinherited Youth* (Edinburgh, Carnegie UK Trust, 1943). Also quoted in J. Stevenson, *Social Conditions in Britain between the Wars* (Harmondsworth, Penguin, 1977), p. 248.

13. First Interim Report, Cunliffe Committee on Currency and Foreign Exchange after the War reproduced in *The Gold Standard in Theory and History* (London, Methuen, 1985), ed. B. Eichengreen, pp. 169–83.

14. S. Constantine, *Unemployment in Britain between the Wars* (London, Longman, 1980), p. 48.

15. K.J. Hancock, 'The reduction of unemployment as a problem of public policy, 1920–1929', *Economic History Review*, xv, December 1962, reproduced in ed., S. Pollard, *The Gold Standard and Employment Policies between the Wars* (Methuen, 1970).

16. Idem.

17. Idem.

18. Hansard, 28 April 1925.

19. A copy can be found in S. Pollard, op.cit.

20. Oswald Mosley was one of the prominent in the ILP who contributed to what became the 'Socialism in Our Time' programme, although his individual views differed somewhat from the precise programme adopted by the ILP in 1926.

21. K. Laybourn, *Philip Snowden* (Aldershot, Temple Smith/Gower/Wildwood, 1988).

22. R. Skidelsky, *Politicians and the Slump; the Labour Government 1929–1931* (London, Macmillan, 1967).

23. S. Pollard, op. cit.

24. K.G.P. Matthews, 'Was Sterling Overvalued in 1925?', *Economic History Review*, xxxix, no. 4, November 1986, p. 587.

25. M.E.F. Jones, 'The Regional Impact of an Overvalued Pound in the 1920s', *Economic History Review*, xxxviii, 4, November 1984.

26. J. Redmond, 'The Sterling Overvaluation in 1925: A Multilateral Approach', *Economic History Review* xxxvii, 4, November 1984.

27. Constantine, op.cit., pp. 58–60.
28. Skidelsky, op.cit.
29. Ibid., p. 69, quoting Bob Boothby.
30. PRO, Cab. 23, report of Cab. 24 (29), 26 June 1929, 11 a.m.
31. T. Jones, *Whitehall Diary*, vol. II 1926–1930, (ed.) K. Middlemass (London, Oxford University Press, 1969), p. 259, 20 May 1930.
32. D. Marquand, *Ramsay MacDonald* (London, Jonathan Cape, 1977), p. 608.
33. PRO, Cab. 23, report of meeting 19 August 1931.
34. B.C. Malament, 'Philip Snowden and the Cabinet Deliberations of August 1931', *Society for the Study of Labour History*, autumn 1980, p. 32.
35. H. Berkeley, *The Myth that will not die: The formation of the National Government 1931* (London, Croom Helm, 1978), p. 83.
36. Revenue tariffs of 1931 and 1932 and the Ottawa Conference of 1932 confirmed this trend.
37. R. Middleton, 'The Constant Employment Budget Balances and British Budgetary Policy, 1929–39', *Economic History Review*, xxxiv, 2 May 1981, p. 278.
38. R. Pope, ' "Dole Schools": The North-East Lancashire Experience, 1930–1939', *Journal of Educational Administration and History*, vol. ix, no. 2, July 1977, pp. 26–33.
39. PRO, Cab. 23, Report of meeting 24 October 1934.
40. Ibid., Report of Meeting 14 November 1934.
41. Hansard, 6 December 1934.
42. Constantine, op.cit., p. 70.
43. S. Glynn and A. Booth, 'Building Counterfactual Pyramids', and W. R. Garside and T. J. Hatton, 'Keynesian Policy and British Unemployment in the 1930s', *Economic History Review*, xxxviii, 1, February 1985.
44. Orwell, op.cit., pp. 74–5.
45. *Out of Work*, 49, January 1923, quoted in H.J.P. Harmer, 'The National Unemployed Workers' Movement in Britain 1921–1939: Failure and Success', unpublished PhD, London School of Economics and Political Science, 1987, p. 82.
46. Harmer, op.cit., particularly ch. 4.
47. S. Shaw, 'The Attitudes of the Trade Union Congress towards Unemployment in the inter-war period', unpublished PhD, University of Kent, 1979.
48. Harmer, op.cit., p. 2.
49. Ibid., p. 3.
50. Ibid., particularly ch. 8.
51. R. Hayburn, 'The National Unemployed Workers' Movement 1921–1936; A Re-Appraisal', *International Review of Social History*, vol. xxxviii, part 3, 1983, and R.H.C. Hayburn, 'The Responses to Unemployment in the 1930s, with particular reference to South-East Lancashire', unpublished PhD, University of Hull, 1970.
52. *Labour Monthly*, May 1932, quoted in Harmer, op.cit., p. 223.
53. J. & B. Braddock, *The Braddocks* (London, MacDonald, 1963), passim.
54. Harmer, op.cit., appendix B, pp. 387–8.
55. Ibid., p. 241, and PRO, Cab 24/230 (CP 186), Minister of Labour to

Cabinet, 'Administration of Transitional Payment', 10 June 1932.
56. Harmer, op.cit., pp. 176–8.
57. The success rate of cases taken to the umpires by the NUWM, was markedly below the national average in 1930, at 12.7 per cent compared with 28.4 per cent, was marginally below the average thereafter. In 1935 it was 42 per cent compared with 45 per cent and in 1936 34 per cent compared with a national average of 35 per cent. Being supported by the NUWM did not necessarily argur well for the applicant to the umpire.
58. Ibid., ch. 10.
59. Stevenson and Cook, op.cit., pp. 169–73; W. Hannington, *Ten Lean Years* (London, Gollancz, 1940), pp. 50–69.
60. Hannington, *Ten Lean Years*, pp. 206–20; W. Hannington, *Never on Our Knees* (1967), pp. 324–8.
61. E. Trory, 'Between the Wars: Recollections of a Communist Organizer', p. 27.
62. M. Cohen, *I Was One of the Unemployed* (London, Gollancz, 1945 and E.P., Wakefield 1978), p. 20.
63. Society for the Study of Labour History, Bulletin 38, Spring 1979, contains documents from the Glamorgan police about individual marchers and an interview with Sid Elias.
64. Idem.; Stevenson and Cook, op.cit., p. 177.
65. Stevenson and Cook, op.cit., p. 158.
66. J. Campbell, *Nye Bevan and the Mirage of British Socialism* (London, Weidenfeld and Nicolson, 1987), pp. 59–60.
67. PRO, Cab. 23,, Report of Meeting, 21 February 1934.
68. Ibid., Report of Meeting, 14 October 1936.
69. Stevenson and Cook, op.cit., p. 194; Harmer, op.cit., introduction.
70. C. Cross (ed.), *Life of Lloyd George: The Diary of A.J. Sylvester 1931–45* (London, 1975), p. 78.
71. Hannington, *Never on our Knees*, p. 329.
72. Bradford Archives, West Yorkshire Archives Service, 22 D77/3/2/8.
73. *Leeds Citizen*, 3 February 1933.
74. Ibid., 10 March 1933.
75. W. Hannington, *The Problem of the Distressed Areas* (London, Gollancz, 1937), p. 12.

CHAPTER 2

POVERTY AND ILL-HEALTH DURING THE INTER-WAR YEARS

Recently, Charles Webster has argued that:

> With more than a sideways glance at Engels, Harry Pollitt proclaimed:
> 'The stark reality is that in 1933, for the mass of the population, Britain
> is a hungry Britain, badly fed, badly clothed and housed' . . . .. The
> Secretary General of the Communist Party of Great Britain thus unleashed
> a fierce debate among contemporaries, and even now the issue remains
> unresolved and contentious. Were the '30s characterised by severe social
> deprivation or was this idea a myth assiduously cultivated by a
> mischievous minority for the sake of political advantage.[1]

Webster's own view is that while general standards might have
improved, the health of many of those who were in poverty, due in
many cases to unemployment, probably deteriorated – though he
shows more equivocation than did Pollitt. The clear implication is
that unemployment was responsible for a rise in ill-health and death
rates. More recently Margaret Mitchell has tended to endorse
Webster's view that health problems were rooted in the economic
disadvantage which was caused by unemployment.[2] Yet these views
are in variance with those presented by C.L. Mowat, D.H. Aldcroft,
John Stevenson and Chris Cook in what has been referred to as the

41

'received opinion'.[3] Aldcroft, indeed, presented their alternative case most effectively when he wrote:

> . . . not only was there a significant increase in real incomes and real wages but, partly as a result of the improvement and together with the extension of community services, the nation generally was better fed and clothed, and was housed in better conditions than those prevailing before the war. The statistics again point to an improvement in the national health and physical well-being of the population. Death rates declined, children were on average fitter and healthier than their parents, and the worst forms of malnutritional diseases, such as rickets . . . had all but disappeared by the Second World War.[4]

Contemporary politicians and government officials also held such views and denied that there was any connection between unemployment and ill-health. For instance, on 7 July 1933 Sir E. Hilton Young, Minister of Health, stated in the House of Commons that 'there is no available medical evidence of any general increase in physical impairment, sickness or mortality as a result of the economic depression and unemployment.'[5] This official comment reflected the view of Sir George Newman, the Chief Medical Officer at the Ministry of Health, who started 'Taking the country as a whole the evidence appears to point to the conclusion that . . . there has been no general excess of sickness, ill-health or physical incapacity attributable to unemployment.'[6] More recently, in a climate of rapidly increasing unemployment, Dr Gerard Vaughan, Conservative Minister of Health, informed the House of Commons on 20 October 1981 that the link between unemployment and illness was not 'scientifically proven'.[7]

These comments undoubtedly demonstrate the political need of governments to deny the possible link between economic depression, unemployment and ill-health. The possibility that unemployment might actually reduce food intake and increase ill-health, a logically sensible possibility, was never to intrude into official government and political thinking during the 1930s, nor, it would seem, in more recent times. In general, medical officers of health throughout the country tended to endorse such a viewpoint and, along with various specialist reports, recorded the impression that malnutrition, high rates of infant mortality and rises in maternal mortality were entirely due to other factor – such as abortion and the poor management of the family budget. Governments and officialdom were determined to deflect criticism of continued ill-health and death away from the depression, unemployment and the level of unemployment benefits towards other factors.

Historians and politicians are thus deeply divided upon the true extent of poverty and ill-health during the the inter-war years. Ideological and political differences have conditioned their varying approaches, and debate has been fuelled by the contradictory nature of the evidence.

Yet there is some common ground. Both extremes agree that the general standard of living, and thus the general health of the nation as a whole, probably increased during these years. Even a contemporary critic such as B.S. Rowntree suggested that living standards in York rose by about 30 per cent between 1889 and the mid-1930s.[8] There is little doubt about the downward direction of many of the vital statistics. The disagreement arises from two lines of argument developed by Webster and Mitchell. First, they challenge the accuracy of the official statistics which they feel underplay the true extent of ill-health. Indeed, they suggest that governments applied pressure on Medical Officers of Health, and others to ensure that the true extent of poverty and ill-health was under-recorded. Secondly, they believe that the common experience of the large proportion of the working class, particularly those living in the old industrial centres, which were declining, was much worse than suggested by the national average statistics of ill-health produced by government departments. They offer a powerful battery of criticisms with which to attack the 'received opinion'. It is, therefore, vital to examine the detailed nature of the evidence before even a tentative conclusion can be offered to such questions as 'Did poverty decline during the inter-war years?', 'Was the health of the nation much improved during the 1920s and 1930s?' and 'Was unemployment responsible for ill-health?'

Poverty

Until recently, historians have generally accepted that poverty diminished during the inter-war years. More than twenty years ago, C.L. Mowat argued that all suggestions to the contrary were sedulously nurtured by Wal Hannington, the Communists and the left, whose political purpose outweighed their judgement.[9] Stevenson and Cook, and others, have also maintained that the condition of

43

the majority did improve.[10] Their judgements are based upon the Booth, Rowntree, Bowley and Llewellyn Smith surveys which, cumulatively, suggested that, from calculations drawn from studies of York, London, Reading, Northampton, Warrington, Bolton and Stanley (County Durham), families were on average probably 30 per cent better off in the 1930s than they had been in the pre-war years.[11] Such evidence, however, rests upon a relatively narrow range of material and it is important to be aware of its limitations.

It is quite clear that during the late nineteenth century the first surveys lacked the statistical comprehensiveness and objectivity to provide the basis of any sound analysis of the level of poverty which existed throughout the nation. Charles Booth's *Life and Labour of the People of London*, which was produced in two volumes in 1889 and 1891, drew heavily from the notebooks of school-board visitors, who cross-checked their information with the clergy and charitable workers who claimed a familiarity with the households examined. As E.P. Hennock has suggested:

> What Booth was counting were impressions, carefully cross-checked with other impressions insofar as these were available. One of his collaborators was to describe the Poverty Survey very accurately as 'a statistical record of the impressions of the degrees of poverty'.[12]

Rowntree, by way of contrast, in his study of York in 1899 obtained information on household income and used this to calculate the number of households in primary poverty – that is poverty caused by an income inadequate to meet the physical needs of a household as opposed to secondary poverty which was caused by wasteful expenditure. However, much of this information, particularly on secondary poverty, was impressionistic in similar ways to that of Booth. In addition, neither the Booth nor the Rowntree study could be easily applied to the national situation – even though one of Rowntree's intentions was to make comparisons and to establish the general level of poverty throughout the nation. He found that 28 per cent of the population of York lived in poverty, compared with the 30 per cent which Booth's survey had found for the East End of London, and projected that probably between 25 and 30 per cent of the population of the United Kingdom lived in poverty. To Rowntree, York was 'a typical provincial town'.[13] The problem was that his detailed study of York could hardly establish such a claim.

Although the pre-war poverty surveys of London and York were faulty, the pre-war work of A. L. Bowley provided the way forward for meaningful comparative work. By using a method of random sampling and standard deviation he was able to examine not one but several towns. In 1912 he undertook a pilot study based upon a 5 per cent sample of working-class households in Reading and then, in 1913, made similar studies of Northampton, Warrington and Stanley. These were published in 1915 under the title *Livelihood and Poverty*. Another similar study, carried out in Bolton in 1914, was subsequently published in 1920. These various studies examined household incomes, housing conditions, rent levels, the composition of the household and the degrees of overcrowding. Bowley also attempted to relate his findings to those made by Rowntree and arrived at the conclusion that the main cause of poverty was the low level of wages paid to those in work. Calculating the percentage of all working-class households living in primary poverty, and comparing them with York, Bowley came to the conclusion that York was probably typical of most towns, being neither the best nor the worst of those studied: Reading 23.3 per cent, Warrington 13.4, York 12.7, Northampton 8.9, Bolton 7.6 and Stanley 6.0.[14]

What can be gathered from the pre-1914 studies as the basis of comparison with poverty studies of the inter-war years? It is clear that, apart from Bowley's work, surveys were quite inadequate as a basis for strict comparison – even though Bowley suggested that the York survey might have been fairly typical of poverty in provincial towns. The fact is that the pre-war attempts at poverty surveys were rather less sophisticated than the inter-war surveys and this might exaggerate the improvements which had occurred. Nevertheless, some features of the pre-1914 surveys are worthy of note. To begin with, levels of 12 to 15 per cent primary poverty were probably not untypical of provincial towns. Also the vast majority of the poor were probably in poverty as a result of low wages rather than unemployment. It would also appear that anything between 25 and 30 per cent of the total population of provincial towns might have been living in some form of poverty – both primary and secondary.

The inter-war surveys built upon these earlier attempts at estimating poverty, gradually changing the form and direction of their research. The 'poverty line', a prerequisite for measuring poverty and drawn up in various ways by all investigators, began to include more calculations of dietary requirements and became far more scientific in approach as the inter-war years progressed. There was also increasing acknowledgement that the standard requirement of healthy life was higher than the early investigators had suggested, thus implying that the true extent of the level of poverty of the pre-war years was grossly underestimated in the light of inter-war standards. Although the various social investigators adopted their own 'poverty lines', these new trends were reflected in the tendency to adopt the British Medical Association standard, first established in 1933. This laid down a food requirement of 3,400 calories per day for an average man, at a cost of 5s 11d (30p) per week. It was later adjusted for men in heavy and light work, and women and children of various ages. Rowntree used this as the basis of his second survey of York. Sir John Boyd Orr, however, in *Food, Health and Income*, adopted the much more generous standards compiled by Stiebeling for the United States Bureau of Economics, which suggested that a very active man required 4,500 calories per day and that the average calories per head of the population should be 2,810.[15] In addition, more detailed records were taken of the budgets of working-class household rents and other features of working-class expenditure.

Any attempt to compare pre-war with inter-war surveys is plagued with problems. Yet this did not prevent Bowley repeating his pre-war investigations, with M. Hogg, which were published in 1925 under the challenging title *Has Poverty Diminished?* Examining the same five towns which he had investigated before the war, it concluded that poverty had diminished, due largely to the increased real wages of the inter-war years and the fact that the birth rate was falling and that families were smaller. Only about 11 per cent of working-class families, based upon an expenditure of 37s 7d for a family of five, excluding rent, were considered to be in poverty in the towns which they studied. There were, however, many more who were living on inadequate and insufficient incomes.[16] Indeed, Bowley and Hogg wrote:

> The improvement since 1913 is very striking. The proportion [of families] in poverty in 1924 was little more than half that in 1913. If there had been no unemployment, the proportion of families in poverty in the towns would have fallen to one third and of persons to a little over a quarter, of the proportion in 1917. All the towns except Stanley show an improvement in nearly the same ration: and it is found for both sexes and all ages.[17]

46

Other surveys made much the same point. Llewellyn Smith's *The New Survey of London Life and Labour*, conducted in the 1920s and published in 1934, attempted to make a comparison with Booth's survey, and suggested that poverty had fallen by about two-thirds; the Eastern Survey, which more or less covered the East End of London, maintained that the number living in poverty had fallen from about 700,000 or 800,000 in the 1880s to around 250,000 in the 1920s.[18] Rowntree's investigation of York, conducted in 1935 and 1936, repeated his study of 1899 through a house-to-house survey. In 1899 he had found that 43 per cent of the working classes, about 28 per cent of the population of York, were living in poverty. Of these 15.5 per cent of the working class, just over 12 per cent of the total population, were living in 'primary poverty'. Using the same standard as he had used in 1899, he found that only 6.8 per cent of the working class were living in 'primary poverty'.[19] In fact, however, his standards had been altered to reflect the changing attitudes towards the physical need of labour. Using the calculation that a family of five needed 43s 6d (£2 17p) per week on a 'human needs' calculation, excluding rent, to enjoy even a basic standard of living he calculated that 31.1 per cent of the working classes, about 18 per cent of the total population of York, were living in poverty.[20]

Many other surveys, although they could not draw upon comparative evidence, claimed that the levels of poverty had fallen even though 25 per cent or more of the population of the towns they investigated were in poverty. Herbert Tout, for instance, found that 10.3 per cent of working-class families were living below the 'poverty line' in prosperous Bristol at the peak of the 1930s recovery. But, in addition, another 19.3 per cent of working-class families had insufficient income and rather more than a quarter of the Bristol working class as a whole were considered to be in utter destitution. The picture of poverty in prosperous Bristol was not quite as rosy as is often supposed.[21] In his relatively short survey, Tout suggested that the drabness of working-class life on the poverty line, where three pairs of trousers were to last two years and where, 'The minimum standard makes no allowance whatever for sickness, savings, old age or burial expenses, holidays, recreations, furniture, household equipment, tobacco, drink, newspapers or postage.'[22] Similarly, the Merseyside survey suggested that 16 per cent of working-class families were living in poverty, though about

47

30 per cent of them fell below a 'human needs' standard similar to the calculation made by Rowntree.[23] These figures compare favourably with the 10 per cent indicated by the London survey, where again there were many people living on the fringes of poverty.

Although these various surveys are not strictly comparable, the weight of evidence suggests that poverty, where it could be adequately compared, had fallen during the inter-war years. This may have been due to the rise in wages brought about by the First World War and the fact that, by the 1920s, the majority of male workers were covered by health and unemployment insurance, and that the dole – uncovenented benefits, transitional payments and extended benefit – was available to alleviate at least the worst excesses of poverty. In the 1930s, the Public Assistance Committee and the Unemployment Board, regardless of the fluctuating levels of benefits offered, undoubtedly exerted some impact in reducing acute poverty.

Yet the really depressed urban areas were rarely examined in a similar fashion to York, London, Bristol and the other investigated towns. For Jarrow, Stockton-on-Tees, Brynmawr and other unemployment disaster areas, it is only the reports of medical officers of health and the unemployment statistics that hint at the full extent of poverty which, in these communities, may have affected between 30 and 80 per cent of the working-class families in the worst years of the 1930s, not the approximately 20 per cent recorded in the various social investigations already mentioned. How much more pervasive and debilitating must poverty have been in the really depressed industrial areas of the North, Wales and Scotland than in relatively prosperous York and London?

The scale of poverty might be open to question, but what were its major causes? Despite their limitations the surveys of those few relatively prosperous areas which were properly investigated do indicate the major causes of poverty and the changes which had occurred over time. They suggest that chronic sickness, old age, low pay and large families remained significant causes of poverty, as they had been before the First World War, but that unemployment had risen as a cause of poverty. Stevenson suggests that unemployment was not the only cause of poverty, but it should be remembered that unemployment was undoubtedly a bigger factor in those areas which were not surveyed, many of which faced three or four times the level of unemployment as York, Reading or London.[24]

Rowntree's investigation of York in 1935–6 included both an assessment of unemployment as a cause of poverty and a comparison between the 1899 and 1936 surveys. The results of these investigations are presented in the tables below. What they show is that unemployment was much more significant as a cause of poverty than it had been in 1899, even in a city which was not particularly afflicted by unemployment compared with other industrial towns in the North, Wales and Scotland.

Table 2.1 *The Causes of Poverty, York, 1936*[25]

Causes of poverty	% in poverty
Unemployment of chief wage earner	28.6
Inadequate wage of workers	32.8
Inadequate earnings of other workers	9.5
Old age	14.7
Death of husband	7.8
Illness	4.1
Miscellaneous	2.5

Table 2.2 *Proportion of the Working-Class Population in Primary Poverty due to Various Causes in 1899 and 1936*[26]

	1899 (%)	1936 (%)
Death of chief wage earner	2.42	0.61
Illness or old age of chief wage earner	0.79	1.60
Unemployment	0.36	3.04
Irregularity of work	0.44	0.40
Largeness of family – i.e. more than 4 children	3.43	0.54
In regular work, but low wages	8.03	0.63

Tout's Bristol survey arrived at similar conclusions. Unfortunately no comparison could be made with the pre-war situation.

Table 2.3 *Causes of Poverty in Bristol*[27]

Causes	% of all families below the standard (poverty line)
Unemployment	32.1
Insufficient wages	21.3
Old Age	15.2
Absence of an adult male earner	13.3
Sickness or incapable	9.0
Self-employment and hawking	6.5
Other	2.6
	100.0

One of the most disturbing aspects of these investigations is the fact that they revealed that a very large proportion of children in working-class families were living in poverty. Indeed, Rowntree found 52.5 per cent of the working-class children under one year of age, and 39 per cent of those between 5 and 15, living below his minimum standards.[28] And in the Bristol survey it should be remembered that while only 9 per cent of families had three or more children such families contained 41 per cent of all the children, many of whom were living in acute poverty. Child-rearing obviously placed many families into poverty, as Rowntree suggested in his poverty-cycle argument, and very large families tended to keep them there longer. Also, recent research has suggested that Rowntree and other investigators, who tended to treat children as requiring two-thirds the expenditure of adults, clearly underestimated the cost of child-rearing which, after the age of ten, might be more expensive than maintaining an adult.[29]

The problem of child poverty is graphically described by Frank Cousins, a prominent trade union leader of the post-1945 era. Remembering a young couple with a child who were walking from South Shields to London in search of work, he wrote:

> They came into the cafe and sat down, and they fetched a baby's feeding bottle, and it had water in it. They fed the baby with water, and then lifted the kiddy's dress up – it was a small baby – and it had a newspaper for a nappy on. They took this off and wiped the baby's bottom with it and then they picked up another newspaper and then put that on for a fresh nappy.[30]

Old age was clearly a contributory factor since any couple aged over seventy would have a joint pension of only £1 a week. Without other income, highly unlikely amongst working-class families, old age meant acute poverty on whichever 'human needs' scale was used. The situation, as George Orwell made clear in *The Road to Wigan Pier*, was obviously worse for single pensioners on 10s (50p) per week who, even if they had been supported by their families might be ejected from the home after the introduction of the Household Means Test.

Although the various social investigations have assessed the extent of poverty and examined its causes they do not attempt to recreate the lifestyle of the poor. It is only recently that the detailed reconstruction of working-class life has been attempted through the work of Nigel Gray, Jerry White, Elizabeth Roberts and Carl Chinn.[31] What they indicate is the extent to which the poor operated the self-help social network of the neighbourhood and the street in order to survive. Above all, they emphasis the importance of the married women who fought to keep their families fed and clothed in the face of innumerable difficulties. Carl Chinn has particularly focused upon the importance of the married women of the poor in organizing the family finances against the extremes of destitution. It was they who operated the finances of their families in order to purchase the Provident Clothing cheque, with which to purchase clothes, and manipulated the system of credit (tick) operated by most shopkeepers in working-class districts. They also made regular trips to the pawnbrokers and many took in washing, or sweated labour in the home, in order to provide for their families. As Chinn states:

> The impoverishment of the lower working class did not dissipate with social change; it remained to haunt and hinder the attempts of women at improvement. The effects of poverty were everywhere apparent. So too were its symbols; the pawnshop; the money-lender; the 'strap' at the corner shop; a poor education, and ill-paid jobs and unemployment.[32]

Similar observations have also been well-illustrated in the politically-committed socialist writings of Jerry White. His work on Campbell Bank, a London community between the wars, reveals the extent to which poverty and destitution could drive the poor to crime, albeit often in the form of class war. Although one might suspect that the class conflict within such working-class groups is contrived to meet a political viewpoint it is clear that White offers some insight into the self-dependence of many of the poor and the value of the extended family connection to stave off starvation:

> The people of the Bunk had many things in common, things which tended towards a collective response to mutual problems. We have seen that many people in Campbell Road were desperately poor, scratching a precarious living standard, living outside normal society. The street was known as perhaps the poorest in Islington, and it was no stranger to the most pitiable neglect and even starvation. The solidarity of the very poor was strengthened by their reliance on the internal economy of the Bunk, and by a largely hostile world represented by enforcers – policeman, relieving officer, school-board man, debt collector. Kinship patterns, too, helped reinforce the self-contained and supportive community – the Taylor/Payne family could count 40 relatives in the 1930s, for example.[33]

As White suggests, the immediate survival of the family was always the vital consideration and the community was always at hand to help out. Borrowing off neighbours to tide the family over an immediate crisis was a common feature of the life of the lower working class, and White records the instance of the son of a building worker being sent to the wife of a railwayman, three doors along the street to say:

> 'Mum said, "Don't be offended, can you lend 'er 'alf-a crahn t'see 'er froo the week?"' Now, half-a-crown. I run up to the baker's. I get three pennorth of stale bread, which came to anything up to twelve loaves. I get three pennorth of bacon bones and a sixpenny ham bone . . .. Now that last us for two or three days. In between time, we get paraffin oil for penny-farthing, that's for our lighting. And a pennorth of tea, two ounces of tea a penny. And probably ha'porth of jam . . .. Oh, and seven pound of coal. We'd pay it back the end of the week, soon as got hold of a bit of money. He might do a day's work – back goes the half-crown.[34]

Those in poverty were more resilient, cooperative, and independent than the social investigators of the inter-war years implied in their research, even though their poverty was often acute.

To return to the main theme, however, despite the difficulties of making meaningful comparisons between the pre-war and inter-war years, poverty was probably less marked during the 1920s and 1930s than it had been previously. Monetary wage levels were higher due to the First World War and, despite the attack upon wages in the 1920s, referred to in a later chapter, it is evident that deflation meant that real wages rose on average throughout the inter-war years. Indeed, as already suggested, Rowntree felt that living standards had risen by about 30 per cent between 1899 and 1936. But it should be recognized that the improved general situation hid a tremendous amount of poverty and suffering, about which Rowntree rightly felt the nation should not be complacent. There is no contradiction in improved living standards occurring alongside acute poverty, and even worsening standards of life for a substantial minority of the nation. Yet it is difficult to accept that standards had improved substantially when the worst areas of unemployment, a factor of increasing importance in causing poverty, were barely surveyed. And ranged against over-optimism is the fact that Sir John Boyd Orr was, by the mid-1930s, suggesting that half the nation was undernourished and that some Medical Officers of Health were reporting that conditions of health were deteriorating. There is now even evidence that the biological statistics of health may not be the impartial record which they have been presented as being.

Health

In 1932, against the tide of official evidence, A. Fenner Brockway wrote Hungry England. In this book he conducted a survey of the living conditions of the towns of Lancashire, the Black Country and Birmingham, the Tyne and Tees, the docks and valleys of South Wales, Glasgow and Clydeside. It lacked the depth of sophistication of the social surveys produced during the inter-war years but it did challenge the view that the health of the nation was improving. Offering details of budgets and social conditions, Brockway argued that malnourishment existed in Britain, that wages were too low, that high infant mortality still existed and that working-class families had no margin with which to protect themselves against unemployment, sickness and old age. He wrote, of his book:

> This is a plain first-hand account (the result of personal investigation, interviews, the examination of budgets, etc.) of how a large percentage of the population is living. The facts themselves are shameful, whatever the causes, and whatever the solutions, and they are facts which no decent person can ignore.[35]

Brockway's book foreshadowed similar ones by George Orwell, J.B. Priestley and Alan Hutt[36] Harry Pollitt's introduction to Hutt's book, in fact, made a similar point to that made by Brockway: 'The stark reality is that in 1933, for the mass of the population, Britain is a hungry Britain, badly fed, clothed and housed.'[37] Although the views of these authors, with some justification, were regarded as being politically inspired it is clear that they provided an alternative view to the official attitude that conditions were improving. The seeds of debate were sown.

The views of Orwell, and other pessimists, were generally ignored during the 1930s and given short shrift by historians of the post-war years, particularly by C.L. Mowat, who wrote of the 'myth, sedulously propagated later, of the "hungry thirties". The reality was rather different.'[38] Stevenson and Cook, and Winter, have supported Mowat.[39] But, in the 1980s, Charles Webster and Margaret Mitchell revived doubts about the scale and nature of the improvements which occurred during the inter-war years.[40]

The thrust of Webster's argument is that there is sufficient detailed research to question the view that health was improving across the board and clear evidence that the biological statistics were not reliable. On the second point, he maintains that reliance placed upon the general fall of infant mortality blinded medical experts to the reality of what was going on:

A radically different perspective results from finer analysis of the mortality data, together with proper appreciation of the importance of data relating to morbidity. Fuller exploitation of the available demographic and epidemiological evidence suggests that the persistence of gross disparities between the sexes, or between social classes and occupational groups constitute the dominant features of the inter-war pattern of health. For those substantial sections of the population in a position of disadvantage it is difficult to maintain that the inter-war period was marked by any meaningful improvement in health. Advances in one direction were likely to be offset by deterioration in another. In view of the impressive body of evidence suggesting that the health problems experienced during the '30s were rooted in economic disadvantage, it is possible to argue that the inter-war economic depression was free from adverse repercussions on standards of health.[41]

The point is well made, for death rates and infant mortality figures did vary greatly from region to region, from town to town, and from ward to ward. Tables 2.4 to 2.8 indicate the enormity of the range in infant mortality, the number of children born alive who died before they reached their first birthday. Infant mortality in England and Wales fell considerably during the inter-war years. Indeed, Sir George Newman noted, in 1932, that no county in England and Wales had recorded an infant mortality rate of over 100 per 1,000 live births and argued that this rate was now approaching an 'irreducible minimum'.[42] Yet this report hid a much higher level of suffering for those in the old declining industrial areas where the levels of infant mortality were generally much higher than the national average. In the depressed North East, for instance, the general level was often 20 to 30 per cent higher than the national average. Within those markedly depressed areas the situation, in fact, was often worse, with infant mortality levels of up to 170 and more per thousand in some industrial towns. Even after some of these people were rehoused on modern housing estates, as at Mount Pleasant in Stockton-on-Tees, infant mortality normally remained over 100 – a factor which suggested to M'Gonigle, the Medical Officer of Health for Stockton-on-Tees, that income was rather more important than environment in determining illness and death rates.

The rising level of unemployment of 1930 and 1931 also contributed to low income, raised poverty and clearly increased infant mortality rates as indicated in Tables 2.4 and 2.6. M'Gonigle and Kirby also emphasized that death rates were 50 per cent higher amongst the unemployed of Stockton-on-Tees than among the employed, and that death rates were inversely proportionate to income levels.[43] The fact is that, despite the attempts of the Ministry of Health to prevent M'Gonigle from advertising his embarrassing findings, the true plight of the unemployed in Stockton-on-Tees, and other towns, in a period of economic depression could not be hidden from public view forever. The suggestion that the working class contributed to the continued high levels of infant mortality is just not tenable in the light of the contemporary work on family budgets conducted by Sir John Boyd Orr and the more recent research by Carl Chinn and N.J. Leiper, which suggest that working-class mothers did their best to ensure that their families were well fed.[44] The problem which they faced was that their incomes were simply not up to the task.

55

Table 2.4 *Infant Mortality in England and Wales and Specific Yorkshire Towns 1920–38*[45]

	Deaths per 1,000 births				
Year	England & Wales	Bradford	Halifax	Huddersfield	Leeds
1920	88	93	97	80	105
1921	80	109	98	85	96
1929	74	80	74	78	96
1930	60	75	62	56	66
1931	66	71	75	59	76
1932	65	75	81	52	88
1933	64	75	81	52	88
1934	59	62	77	53	71
1935	57	64	69	44	64
1936	59	82	68	63	65
1937	58	69	63	61	67
1938	53	58	57	66	64

Table 2.5 *Mean Infant Mortality Rates per 1,000 Live Births for England and Wales, Stockton-on-Tees and Districts of Stockton-on-Tees*[46]

	England and Wales	Stockton-on-Tees	Housewife Lane	Riverside
1923–27	71.8	91.8	172.6	173.2
			Mount Pleasant	
1928–32	66.2	78.8	117.8	134.0

Table 2.6 *Infant Mortality Rates in Lancashire's Industrial Towns, 1930 and 1931*[47]

(a) County Boroughs

	1930	1931		1930	1931
Bolton	67	80	Oldham	67	106
Burnley	76	86	Preston	68	89
Bootle	79	86	Rochdale	66	66
Bury	69	73	St Helens	79	88
Liverpool	81	94	Salford	75	101
Manchester	79	85	Stockport	57	79
Warrington	65	100	Wigan	106	103

(b) Municipal Boroughs and Urban Districts

Ashton-in-Makerfield	70	87	Leigh	57	98
Atherton	61	82	Middleton	46	99
Colne	51	110	Newton-in-Makerfield	65	79
Darwen	70	82	Prestwich	77	86
Eccles	64	85	Radcliffe	48	80
Farnworth	70	84	Ramsbottom	64	96
Haslingdon	69	95	Royton	87	120
Hindley	69	115	Widnes	55	82

Table 2.7 *Infant Mortality Rates in 1931, in Various Wards in Liverpool and Manchester*[48]

(a) Working-class Wards

Liverpool		Manchester	
Everton	113	Ardwick	120
Exchange	117	Colleyhurst	120
Abercromby	133	Bradford	101
		Collegiate	143
		New Cross	121
		St Clements	120

(b) 'Residential' Wards

Wavertree	68	Didsbury	49
Woolton	50	Levenshulme	44

There were also marked differences in the levels of infant mortality between classes and occupational groups. According to R.M. Titmuss, as indicated in Table 2.8, the families of coal miners, dock labourers, and general labourers, for instance, experienced high levels of infant mortality compared with the rest of the population. Indeed, in some cases the differences had widened between 1911 and 1931. These social differences were noted in other ways and for Lancashire, in 1931, infant mortality rates ranged from 31.3 for social class I to 78.9 and 93.3 for social classes IV and V.[49] A marked level of social inequality persisted during the inter-war years, even though the overall level of infant mortality was declining.

Table 2.8 *Infant Death Rate per 1,000 Legitimate Births by Social Class of Father in Separate Occupations, % of the Death Rate for all Classes (all classes = 100)*[50]

	% of all classes	
	1911	1930–2
Agricultural labourers	78	96
Coal miners	130	134
General labourers	134	132
Bricklayers	90	89
Bricklayers' labourers	117	113
Dock labourers	138	137

Nevertheless, not all the biological statistics were improving as is indicated by the maternal mortality statistics which rose by 22 per cent between 1923 and 1933.[51] These figures were, of course, subject to immense regional variation. In 1936 the level was 2.57 in the South East of England, compared with 4.36 in the North and 5.17 in South Wales.[52] Even in less depressed areas, such as the West Riding of Yorkshire, the figures were susceptible to great fluctuation, and this was particularly the case in Bradford, as suggested in Table 2.9. In other moderately depressed areas such as Lancashire, figures rose well above the rate of 5 per 1,000, which was considered bad. In Bolton an average of 5.2 from 1923–9 rose to 6.7 in 1930 and 6.5 in 1931. In Rochdale, the equivalent figures were 7.0, 9.6 and 7.4.[53]

58

Table 2.9 *Maternal Mortality Rates; Bradford and England and Wales, 1930–38*[54]
(Per 1,000)

Year	Bradford	England and Wales
1930	5.01	4.40
1931	4.68	4.11
1932	5.59	4.25
1933	4.65	4.51
1934	5.43	4.60
1935	2.66	3.93
1936	4.64	3.65
1937	2.62	3.23
1938	4.15	3.08

Nowhere was the contemporary debate over health, unemployment and poverty more vehemently fought than in the discussion of maternal mortality. Since maternal mortality rates were those which were most clearly rising successive governments were sensitive to their causes. The official line was that such rises were not due to the depression and unemployment. This assessment was partly supported by the work of J. Munro Kerr and P.L. McKinley on Scottish maternal mortality rates which suggested that the impact of insufficient means and housing problems was minimal.[55] In 1934, the National Government also decided to stave off possible criticism by announcing that the Ministry of Health would conduct two special reports on the problem in England and Wales.[56] When published in 1937, both reports denied any link between unemployment and maternal mortality. Indeed, they blamed criminal abortions, the changing age structure and the poor budgeting of working-class mothers for increases in maternal mortality.[57] Yet as N.J. Leiper's recent work on health and unemployment in Glamorgan makes clear, both reports, and particularly the Welsh one, studiously avoided the logical thread of connection between depression, unemployment, malnutrition and maternal mortality. After carefully examining the evidence on the Welsh 'special areas' of high unemployment, as available in the Welsh Report, Leiper concludes:

> It can therefore be argued that despite the denials of the government and the official Ministry of Health reports there does appear to be some kind of link between the level of unemployment in Wales and the rate of maternal

mortality. The facts are clear that as Wales is divided into more industrial areas and especially those hardest hit by recession, the risk of maternal mortality rises and also the strong correlation between the unemployment and mortality rates does provide yet another contributory piece of evidence. It is possible to question the credibility of the official reports due to ignorance and the need for political acceptability.[58]

Not surprisingly, death rates as a whole reveal similar regional and local variation in response to economic conditions. For England and Wales standardized death rates fell from an average of 13.5 per 1,000 in 1910–14 to 9.7 in 1931–4, and to 9.3 in 1937.[59] Yet, once again, figures were much higher outside London and the South East. In Bradford, the crude death rate for 1911 to 1915 was 15.5, and fell to 14.1 during the years 1921–5. Thereafter it never fell below that level until 1938, actually rising to 14.9 in 1936. In other words there had been only a marginal improvement in the death rates for Bradford in the early 1920s and some fallback in the 1930s.[60] The situation in Jarrow was broadly the same, while that in Stockton-on-Tees was probably marginally better.[61] M'Gonigle and Kirby's study of Stockton, however, suggests that there were areas of the town where, due to unemployment and low income, the standardized death rate, which calculates death rate according to the age structure, was four times as high as it ought to have been. The 'expected' standardized mean death rate for the new Mount Pleasant Estate should have been 8.12 per 1,000 of the population for the period 1928 to 1932. It was actually 33.15.[62]

Table 2.10 *Crude Death Rates for England and Wales, Scotland and Bradford, 1911–40*[63] *(Deaths per 1,000)*

	England and Wales	Scotland	Bradford
1911–15	14.3	15.7	15.5
1916–20	14.4	15.0	16.0
1921–5	12.1	13.9	14.1
1926–30	12.1	13.6	14.2
1931–5	12.0	13.2	14.1
1936			14.9
1937			14.6
1938			13.8
1936–40	12.2	13.6	

The fact is that when standardized to eliminate differences due to age structure, it is clear that real differences between the prosperous and depressed areas begin to emerge. Death rates in most industrial centres were at least a quarter and sometimes up to half again the average for the whole of England and Wales: 1.44 the average in the Rhondda, 1.31 in Blackburn and 1.3 in Jarrow and South Shields. At the other end of the scale, the standardized death rates for Buckinghamshire, Hertfordshire and Surrey were all about 20 per cent less than the average.[64]

The statistical evidence suggests that national death rates declined during the inter-war years but that in many depressed areas there was barely any significant improvement and, in some cases, a significant increase in the factors contributing to the overall death rate. It is clear that the main thrust of the argument presented by Webster and Mitchell is strongly supported; there were significant disparities between the national and local pictures suggests that millions of working-class people were no healthier during the inter-war years. There was also a wealth of supportive survey and campaign material for their viewpoint.

There were also many surveys and campaigns which examined and criticized various aspects of health during the inter-war years. The Women's Health Inquiry Committee, set up by Dame Janet Campbell in 1933, provided both qualititative and quantitative evidence of the plight of women who were often out of sight of any medical provision unless they were pregnant.[65] R.M. Titmuss conducted his critical survey which emphasized the degree of social inequality which emerged in health statistics.[66] The survey of Stockton-on-Tees emphasized the appallingly high death rates which occurred when statistics were standardized and stressed that unemployment and low income were largely responsible for these situations.[67] Yet, two other investigations stand out. The first was Sir John Boyd Orr's survey of budgets and diets in the early and mid-1930s and the second was the work of Lady Williams and the National Birthday Trust Fund in the Rhondda during the early 1930s.

Orr's investigation made the biggest impact since it maintained:

. . . a diet completely adequate for health, according to modern standards, is reached at an income level above that of 50 per cent of the population. This means that 50 per cent of the population are living at a level of nutrition so high that, on the average, no improvement can be effected by increased consumption.[68]

61

This was a controversial conclusion to research conducted by the staff of the Rowett Institute in cooperation with the staff of the Market Supply Committee, written up by Orr, and published in the face of government hostility in 1936. The purpose of this work was to discover what people ate. To facilitate this, 2,640 family budgets were gathered, of which 1,152 were used, in order to determine what was consumed by families on different income levels. These were used to refine calculations made on the average income per person and average expenditure on food, drawn from national statistics, and then related to the relatively high dietary requirements adopted by Stiebeling for the Government Bureau of Home Economics, USA. Form this information and analysis, Orr produced the controversial conclusion that half the population of the country were undernourished and produced tables of the varying diet and income levels of the six groups into which he divided the British population – indicated in Table 2.11.

Table 2.11 *Classification of the Population by Income Groups and Average Food Expenditure per Head in Each Group*[69]

Group	Income per head per week	Estimated average expenditure on food per week	Estimated numbers	Population %
I	Up to 10s	4s	4,500,000	10
II	10s to 15s	6s	9,000,000	20
III	15s to 20s	8s	9,000,000	20
IV	20s to 30s	10s	9,000,000	20
V	30s to 45s	12s	4,500,000	20
VI	Over 45s	24s	4,500,000	10
	Average 30s	9s	–	–

What Orr emphasized was that families would move from group to group at different stages of their life experiences, falling to the lower groups as children were being raised and rising as children began to work and contribute to the family income. In addition, his report produced tables which indicated the variation in diet between the various groups, noting the different mineral intakes and varying consumption levels. For instance, group VI consumed almost 70 per cent more iron, about 90 per cent more phosphorous, and 260 per cent more calcium than those in group I.[70] Group I drank less fresh milk, ate less butter, meat, cheese, fruit, vegetables and fish than the other groups but consumed more margarine, bread and flour and as many potatoes.[71] Not surprisingly the physical development of those in the lower categories was less than those with more income to spend on a better diet.

Critics of Orr, and particularly the National Government, suggested that his standards were too high since they were more exacting than those suggested by the British Medical Association, which meant that far more people fell into the categories of the undernourished. The Ministry of Health was particularly critical for it found it difficult to reconcile its own claim that malnutrition was a thing of the past with a nutrition expert's claim that half the British population was in a state of undernourishment. Orr's report was also criticized by A.L. Bowley, who argued that Orr had not taken sufficient account of the differing needs of women and children.[72]

The work of Lady Williams, in the Rhondda, tended to endorse the type of conclusion being arrived at by Orr. What it did was to link high maternal mortality with malnutrition. In 1933, responding to the growing concern over the high maternal death rate in the Rhondda, the National Birthday Trust Fund and the local authority carried out an extensive scheme to improve medical services. Despite their efforts, maternal mortality rose to the staggeringly high rate of 11.29 per thousand in 1934. It was then decided to provide expectant mothers with food through the clinics. Maternal mortality then fell to 4.77 in 1935. The scheme was then extended to five adjoining towns of a similar type and these also experienced a fall in maternal mortality, from 6.65 to 3.75 in the first six months of 1936.[73]

The government was benighted in its response. When the Medical Officer of Health for the region sent a report of Lady Williams' results to the Ministry of Health pointing out that economic conditions were the most important factor in maternal mortality, its response was that, 'The Minister did not desire any lengthy reference to Lady Williams' speculations.'[74]

Although the schemes like those in the Rhondda were unusual it should not be forgotten that there was concern at the rising level of maternal mortality in other areas. In 1921 very nearly half the midwives in the West Riding of Yorkshire were untrained; by 1928 that proportion was down to about a sixth. Bradford, whose Labour group had pushed through the transformation of the Poor Law Hospital to a Municipal Hospital, where internationally acclaimed research work was being done, provided more maternity beds than any other place in the country. Yet the figures for maternal deaths, as indicated in Table 2.9, refused to budge downwards very far – much to the consternation of medical authorities and to the acute embarrassment of a government reluctant to acknowledge the connection between deprivation through poverty, however caused, and high mortality rates.[75]

There was similar concern in Leeds, where maternal mortality remained a stubborn problem and where infant mortality remained high until, as indicated in Table 2.4, the mid- and late 1930s. Although the Public Health Department of Leeds City Council was making the public aware of the problems of tuberculosis it appears that the main thrust towards improving the health of the population of Leeds did not occur until about 1934. At that time a campaign for immunization against diphtheria was being mounted, new housing was being built and the Empire Marketing Board, or 'E.M.B.', posters on health matters, such as the 'Healthy Children' campaign concerned with maternity and child welfare, were being displayed outside Killingbeck and many other Leeds hospitals. Leeds, at this time, was taking up the work of the Central Council for Health Education.

Nevertheless, the wealth of evidence suggests that there was significant ill-health in many of the depressed and marginally depressed areas of the country and that this became more acute at times of very high unemployment, particularly in the early 1930s. Webster argues that this did not always show up in official reports because of the under-reporting, for a variety of reasons, of health problems. The Minister of Health had a vested interest in getting medical officers of health to emphasize the freak nature of some of their worst statistics, and Webster notes that many of the vital health statistics were not published until after the Second World War. In addition, some health statistics were highly subjective. The apparent disappearance of rickets was found to be grossly over-optimistic and the estimates of malnutrition among schoolchildren, by school doctors and visitors, were clearly influenced by the type of people who conducted the checks. When the Ministry of Health recommended that medical Officers should check upon child malnutrition it was suggested that they gauge it by the clinical procedure of: examining the 'state of the skin, the lustre of the hair, the appearance of the eyes, the colour of the mucous membranes, and the alertness and attitude of the child.'[76] These produced some farcical results in areas of acute unemployment. And the situation was no better when the school medical officers reported upon the situation. Webster concluded:

> The anomalies were bizarre and ridiculous. It was noted for example that rates for comparable areas in Northumberland varied from 0.5% to 7.5%; and that the rate for Bootle was 12 times that for Liverpool. Small and prosperous cathedral towns reported high malnutrition rates, while small impoverished towns reported low rates; the agricultural counties of Wales appeared to suffer from appalling malnutrition, while the mining areas seemed virtually free from the problem. . ... A widely reported experiment conducted by Dr W.F.W. Betenson, the County Medical officer of Breconshire, demonstrated complete lack of uniformity in the assessment of levels of malnutrition by three male and three female medical officers. The male observers noted only three cases of pronounced malnutrition, while the female observers recorded 17 among the 100 children examined. One of the women recorded 47 cases of subnormal malnutrition, while one of the men found only 13.[77]

There is no doubt that the official health statistics did not offer a full and accurate picture of the health of the nation during the inter-war years and that they consequently give an exaggerated impression of the improvements in the nations' health.

Conclusion

For the nation as a whole, poverty and ill-health were less pronounced during the inter-war years than they had been before 1914. Nevertheless, it is clear that in areas where there was high structural unemployment, and in all those districts which suffered high cyclical unemployment in the early 1930s, that poverty and ill-health were probably more rife than they were before 1914. In industrially depressed towns, such as Jarrow and Brynmawr, there can be little doubt that the conditions of working-class families were much worse than they had been in the pre-war years when unemployment was less pronounced; the hunger marches of the 1930s were not vacuous statements of the plight of the unemployed. It is also clear that even in the generally more prosperous towns, which were subject to detailed investigation, that high levels of poverty and ill-health existed; there are no equivalent studies to that on York for the really depressed towns of Britain. In the final analysis, the views of Webster and Mitchell seem fair; far too many people lived in acute poverty, due particularly to unemployment, for their plight to be swept away by some statistical average which might be subject to distortion. And even if the general health of the nation did improve there were many areas where health conditions remained poor, often as a result of the economic depression and the consequent high levels of unemployment.

NOTES

1. C. Webster, 'Healthy or Hungry Thirties?', *History Workshop*, 13, Spring 1982, p. 110.
2. M. Mitchell, 'The Effects of Unemployment on the Social Conditions of Women and Children in the 1930s', *History Workshop*, 19, Spring 1985, pp. 105–27.
3. C.L. Mowat, *Britain between the Wars, 1918–1940* (London, Methuen, 1968); D. H. Aldcroft, The Interwar Economy: Britain, 1919–1939 (London, 1970); J. Stevenson and C. Cook, *The Slump* (London, Jonathan Cape, 1977).
4. Aldcroft, op.cit., p. 375.
5. Sir E. Hilton Young, Hansard, Commons Debates, 7 July 1933, vol. 280, cols 657–658.
6. Ministry of Health, Annual Report, 1932, pp. 21–2, quoted in N.J. Leiper, 'Health and Unemployment in Glamorgan 1923–1938', unpublished M.Sc., University College of Wales, Aberystwyth, 1986, p. 1.
7. Dr G. Vaughan, Official Report Sixth Series Parliamentary Debates, 20 October 1981, vol. 10, cols. 154–6, quoted in Leiper, op.cit., p. 1.
8. B.S. Rowntree, *Poverty and Progress: A Second Social Survey of York* (London, Longman, 1941), p. 453.
9. Mowat, op.cit., pp. 31–53.
10. Stevenson and Cook, op.cit., pp. 31–53
11. B.S. Rowntree, *Poverty: A Study of Town Life* (London, Longman, 1901); Rowntree, *Progress and Poverty*, p. 433; A.L. Bowley and Burnett-Hurst, *Livelihood and Poverty* (1915); H. Llewellyn Smith (ed.), *The New Survey of London Life and Labour* (London, P. S. King, 1974), 3 vols.; A.L. Bowley and M. Hogg, *Has Poverty Diminished?* (London, P.S. King, 1925).
12. E.P. Hennock, 'The measurement of poverty: from the metropolis to the nation, 1880–1920', *Economic History Review*, xl, May 1987, p. 208.
13. Rowntree, Poverty, p. 356.
14. Bowley and Burnett-Hurst, *Livelihood*.
15. J. Boyd Orr, *Food, Health and Income* (London, Macmillan, 1936), p. 12.
16. J. Stevenson, *Social Conditions in Britain Between the Wars* (Harmondsworth, Penguin, 1977), p. 67.
17. Bowley and Hogg, op.cit., p. 16.
18. Loc. cit., pp. 6–8, 124–5.

19. Rowntree, *Progress and Poverty*, pp. 108, 120, 145.
20. Ibid., p. 34.
21. H. Tout, *The Standard of Living in Bristol* (1938); also quoted in S. Glynn and J. Oxborrow, *Inter-war Britain: a Social and Economic History* (London, George Allen and Unwin, 1976), p. 35.
22. Tout, op.cit., p. 19.
23. University of Liverpool, *The Social Survey of Merseyside* (Liverpool and London, Liverpool University and Hodder and Stoughton, 1934), vol. 1, p. 156.
24. Stevenson, *Social Conditions in Britain Between the Wars*, p. 68.
25. Rowntree, *Progress and Poverty*, pp. 38–9
26. Ibid., p. 116.
27. Tout, op.cit., pp. 44–6.
28. Rowntree, *Progress and Poverty*, p. 156.
29. Margaret Wynn, *Family Policy* (1970), ch. 3.
30. *The Listener*, 26 October 1961, quoted in Stevenson and Cook, *The Slump*, p. 36.
31. N. Gray, *The Worst of Times: An Oral History of the Great Depression in Britain* (London, 1985); J. White, *The Worst Street in North London; Campbell Bunk, Islington, Between the Wars* (London, 1986); E. Roberts, *A Woman's Place. An Oral History of Working-Class Women 1890–1914* (Oxford and New York, Oxford University Press, 1984); C. Chinn, *They Worked All Their Lives; Women of the Urban Poor in England, 1880–1939* (Manchester and New York, Manchester University Press, 1988).
32. Chinn, op.cit., p. 166.
33. J. White, 'Campbell Bunk: A Lumpen Community in London between the Wars', *History Workshop*, 8, autumn 1979, p. 21.
34. Ibid., p. 22.
35. A. Fenner Brockway, *Hungry England* (London, Gollancz, 1936).
36. G. Orwell, *The Road to Wigan Pier* (London and Harmondsworth, Gollancz and Penguin, 1937 and 1962); J.B. Priestley, *English Journey* (London, Heinemann, 1934); A. Hutt, *The Condition of the Working Class in England* (London, 1933).
37. Hutt, op.cit., p. xii.
38. Mowat, op.cit., p. 432.
39. Stevenson and Cook, *The Slump*.
40. Webster, op.cit., Mitchell, op.cit.
41. Webster, op.cit., p. 125.
42. Ministry of Health Report 1932, p. 223.
43. G.C.M. M'Gonigle and J. Kirby, *Poverty and Public Health*, pp. 267, 273.
44. Chinn, op.cit.; Leiper, op.cit.; and Orr, op.cit.
45. Medical Officer of Health, Report for various towns from 1920 to 1938, quoted in J. Reynolds and K. Laybourn, *Labour Heartland: A History of the Labour Party in West Yorkshire During the Inter-war Years, 1918–1939* (Bradford, University of Bradford Press, 1987).
46. M'Gonigle and Kirby, op.cit., p. 114.
47. Hutt, op.cit., p. 114.
48. Ibid.
49. Ibid., pp. 85–6.

50. R.M. Titmuss, *Birth, Poverty, and Wealth* (London, Hamish Hamilton, 1943), p. 53.
51. Webster, op.cit., p. 117.
52. N. Branson and M. Heinemann, *Britain in the Nineteen-Thirties* (London, 1943).
53. A. Hutt, op.cit., pp. 82–3.
54. Bradford Medical Officer of Health, Report, 1876–1940, quoted in Reynolds and Laybourn, op.cit., p. 24.
55. J.L. Munro, *Maternal Mortality and Morbidity* (1933) and P.L. McKinley, *Journal of Hygiene*, 1929, vol. xxviii, no. 4, quoted in Leiper, op.cit., 89.
56. Ministry of Health Report on An Investigation into Maternal Mortality (1937), cmd 5422 and Ministry of Health, Maternal Mortality in Wales (1937), cmd. 5422.
57. Ibid.
58. Leiper, op.cit., p. 114.
59. Stevenson, *Social Conditions in Britain between the Wars*, p. 127.
60. Medical Officer of Health, Report for Bradford. Also quoted in Reynolds and Laybourn, op.cit., p. 22.
61. E. Wilkinson, *The Town that was Murdered* (London, Gollancz, 1939), pp. 236–49; M'Gonigle and Kirby, op.cit.
62. M'Gonigle and Kirby, op.cit., p. 113.
63. Variety of sources, including Reynolds and Laybourn, op.cit., p. 22.
64. Glynn and Oxborrow, op. cit., p. 201.
65. J. Campbell and M. Spring Rice, *Working Class Wives* (1939, also London, Virago, 1981).
66. R.M. Titmuss, *Birth, Poverty and Wealth* (London, Hamish Hamilton, 1947), pp. 32–3, 98.
67. M'Gonigle and Kirby, op.cit., p. 113.
68. Orr, op.cit., Foreword, p. 5.
69. Ibid., p. 21.
70. Ibid., p. 37.
71. Ibid., pp. 24–8.
72. A.L. Bowley (ed.), *Studies in the National Income 1924–1938* (1944), pp. 118–19.
73. M. Mitchell, op.cit., p. 115.
74. Ibid.
75. Reynolds and Laybourn, op.cit., pp. 23–4.
76. Webster, op.cit., p. 118.
77. Ibid., p. 119.

CHAPTER 3

SOCIAL POLICY AND HOUSING

Unemployment, poverty and ill-health caused serious problems for the social policy of all governments during the inter-war years. The scale of social deprivation was so great, attitudes towards the poor so much changed from the nineteenth century, and politics much more open, that no government could afford to ignore the necessity of improving the lot of the poor. There was therefore a degree of conflation in the type of policies which were pursued by all governments, whatever their political colour, although there still remained some degree of variation in approaches to dealing with unemployment, health, old age, education, poverty and housing. What is also clear, however, is that all these policies were limited in their degree of effectiveness, and that changes were often more cosmetic than real. Except in the field of housing, which hardly offered a solution to the plight of those with a limited income, governments failed to offer policies which effectively tackled the social difficulties faced by the poor. The actions of inter-war governments were far less than what Beveridge and the post-war Labour governments contemplated in the 1940s and early 1950s. Yet many have seen the inter-war period as one of transition, when successive governments recognized the need for wider and more pervasive state intervention.[1]

69

Social Policy

The nineteenth century was dominated by the attempt of governments to operate a 'destitution' policy, whereby the poor law operated to prevent starvation; the early twentieth century was dominated by 'selective' social policies; and the post-Second World War period by the debate between 'selectivity' and 'universalism'. During the inter-war years, and more generally from 1906 to the Second World War, there was a clear tendency for legislation to select certain groups of the population as being in need of support on criteria other than destitution. The problem with this policy, as it has always been, is that some sections of society feel that a particular provision, be it extended benefit or health insurance, is abused by those who do not wish to go out to work to earn their living. Consequently, there was often fluctuation between Conservative, National and Labour governments on the generosity, or otherwise, of social provisions. The view was held within large sections of society that poverty, if not destitution, needed to be genuine – a factor which, connected with the financial problems of the time, led to the Household Means Test being applied by the National government in 1931 and which forced the second Labour government to introduce the Anomalies Bill. There was great concern that the 'scrounger' and the 'parasite' should not benefit from the system of social provision and, consequently, it was not unusual for the state to be blamed for over-indulging the poor and unemployed:

> The dole system which makes it easy to exist when increased effort is required tends to encourage laziness in those of weak moral fibre and increases the number of parasites at the bottom end of the scale. It depreciates character when character is already weak and already under temptation to give into circumstances, and at the same time diverts huge sums of money from productive industry, which provides the nation's sustenance and finds work for people, to the maintenance of an army of unemployed who are required to render no service whatever in return for what is given to them.[2]

Similar comments could be found in newspapers published everywhere in Britain, and attitudes like that expressed above were common among the working class as well as the middle class.

Yet, in the face of such anger and annoyance, both central and local governments were faced with the need to deal with the rising levels of unemployment and poverty in a more generous spirit than was common in the nineteenth century. Indeed, this is reflected in the rise of the net contribution of government expenditure on poor relief, health, insurance, old-age pensions and unemployment insurance, which rose from £22 million in 1913–14 to £179 million in 1921–2 and £204 million by 1934.[3] The problem, of course, was to keep the overall level of expenditure down – a factor which accounts for some of the major conflicts of this period.

Nevertheless, it was evident to all that the social security structure of the nineteenth century was, within the context of the new attitudes of the inter-war years, inadequate to meet the needs of a society faced with high levels of unemployment. Forced by circumstance and the need for expediency, rather than by some overall strategy, inter-war governments reshaped social security by a succession of acts which removed the Poor Law, extended and modified insurance provision, altered old-age pensions, and extended health provision.

The Poor Law

The most fundamental change was the ending of the Poor Law in its traditional form. Even at the beginning of the 1920s, determined efforts were being made to keep the poor law true to the principles of 1834. And, indeed, it was stressed by the Ministry of Health that, 'The amount of relief given in any case, while sufficient for the purposes of relieving distress, must of necessity be calculated on a lower scale than the earnings of the independent workman who is maintaining himself by his labour.'[4] However, faced with horrendously high levels of unemployment and poverty, guardians attempted to stretch regulations to ensure that improved scales of relief were given to the 350,000 to 400,000 unemployed, 1,500,000 in 1926, who normally received outdoor relief. In offering such benefits, and often refusing to apply a means test, conflict between some boards of guardians and the government became inevitable. This is best illustrated by the case of the thirty Labour guardians and councillors of the district of Poplar, in London, who were imprisoned in 1921 for dealing with the unemployed through generous relief scales and for ignoring the rules and regulations governing the provision of relief.

As Noreen Branson has explained, there were many other issues which were subsumed under the title of 'poplarism', and the fight against low benefits and the household means test, plus the demand for the equalization of rates throughout London to help the poor boroughs of London, lasted well into the 1920s and 1930s.[5] However, it was the events of 1919 to 1921 which attracted most attention.

In 1919 Labour gained control of the Poplar borough council and the local board of guardians. Immediately, the guardians ignored the specified relief rates and, in May 1920, agreed to set a minimum wage of £4 for all the lowest paid municipal employees, well above the previous minimum of £3 4s 0d. They felt that workers and the unemployed should have incomes sufficient for a healthy life. They also paid increased benefits for outdoor relief and refused to curb expenditure despite the inadequacy of finance and the problems of levying rates. For more than a year there was protracted debate over financial matters within Poplar and with government departments before matters came to a head with legal action which finally led to the arrest of the councillors and guardians in September 1921. They refused to compromise in prison and, after six weeks, were released. In a subsequent London conference to deal with the problem of equalizing the burden of poor relief,they successfully obtained an arrangement whereby the richer London boroughs contributed more to a fund, the Metropolitan Poor Fund, than the poorer boroughs who would then be able to spend on outdoor relief a sum agreed by the Minister of Health, Sir Alfred Mond. In fact Poplar, as a result of this arrangement, found her rates concerning Poor Law expenditure reduced by 33.2 per cent.[6] The Poplar councillors and guardians had been victorious in their demands for the better treatment of the unemployed and in their belief that the burden of Poor law costs resulting from an increase in unemployment should be shared between the rich and the poor boroughs of London.

The fine detail of the events at Poplar are exceedingly complex. Nevertheless, what they demonstrated was that the Poor Law was no longer capable of effectively dealing with the problem of high unemployment. It was also obvious to the government that, in an increasingly democratic age, it was quite possible for the electorate and their representatives to flout the law in an atmosphere which recognized the need to be generous to the unemployed. Indeed, by 1927 the Ministry of Health had come to realize how difficult it was for guardians to ignore the plight of the unemployed and the poor:

> . . . there has been a great increase in the proportion of the population
> applying for assistance to the Guardians of the Poor. There has also been,
> in view of the size of the problem and the comparative difficulty of any
> other means of dealing with it, a new and general tendency on the part of
> the Guardians themselves to grant, even to able-bodied persons,
> unconditional allowances of outdoor relief, in amounts which often
> approximate to, and may even exceed, the normal earnings of the applicant
> when he is in full work.[7]

Even worse for the government, it was clear that boards of guardians
in some areas were deliberately providing high levels of relief to the
families of strikers during industrial disputes, and provision for
those who were probably not entitled to relief. These abuses became
obvious during the General Strike and the coal lock-out of 1926 and
provoked Neville Chamberlain, Minister of Health in Baldwin's
1925 to 1929 government, to take action.

The General Strike of 1926 had increased enormously the
demands on the Poor Law, particularly from the families of the
800,000 or so miners who were locked out. In the months before the
coal lock-out and the strike, it had been made clear to all boards of
guardians that they must not make provision for those who were
effectively on strike and that any provision made to their families
must be according to the restricted scales which it had advised. In
the event, this advice was ignored by a number of local Guardians
and, as a result, Neville Chamberlain took action to replace these
guardians in West Ham, Chester-le-Street and Bedwelty, under the
Guardians Default Act of 1926. However, Chamberlain felt that the
whole Poor Law was in need of an overhaul and that it had to be
fitted more closely into attempts to rationalize unemployment
insurance.

The traditional structure of the Poor Law was dismantled in 1929
and 1930. Chamberlain's Local Government Act of 1929, plus a
similar act for Scotland, and the 1930 Poor Law Act ended the
existing Poor Law arrangements. As a result, Poor Law Unions and
the boards of guardians were replaced by local authority bodies
known as Public Assistance Committees (PACs) for the relief of the
destitute and the poor. The Poor Law hospitals were also handed
over to the local authorities in this transfer of responsibility.

Although it might appear that the government was making the
Poor Law system more representative, in fact the whole tone of this
legislation was directed at ensuring that government exerted greater

control than it had hitherto been able to achieve, since the 1930 Act, for instance, laid down the conditions upon which outdoor relief might be applied. In addition the government provided about 50 per cent of the expenditure, which meant that it could control the level of overall expenditure to a greater degree than it was previously able to do. Indeed, the PAC system of relief must have appeared even more draconian than that offered by the Poor Law system, with the widespread application of the Household Means Test by relieving officers who, in most cases, were those who had previously operated the Poor Law.[8]

At first the work of the PACs was varied, for the new body provided for the unemployed, the old and the young. But eventually, as already indicated, PACs gradually lost their responsibility for the unemployed with the creation of the Unemployment Assistance Board in 1935. At that time the UAB was supposed to take over responsibility for the 800,000 able-bodied unemployed maintained by the PACs and the 200,000 in receipt of poor relief. But the new regulations were delayed until 1937. Thereafter the PACs relieved only about 70,000 applicants.[9]

Unemployment Insurance and Benefits

The dismantling of the old Poor Law structure was, of course, closely related to the development and changes which had occurred in unemployment insurance and the provision of the 'dole', already outlined in Chapter 1. There it was suggested that National Insurance Act of 1911 was the basis of government attempts to deal with unemployment. During the First World War and afterwards, the contributory insurance scheme, which drew contributions from employees, employers and the state, was extended to cover most workers – about 12 million in all. Unfortunately, high levels of unemployment ensured that the unemployment fund, out of which benefits were paid, became exhausted as benefits exceeded contributions. In addition, the payment of an 'out of work donation', for those who could not claim from the fund, posed problems for governments who recognized the need to maintain such a provision in the face of rising expenditure and the hostility of those who felt that such benefits were being provided for the 'scrounger'. Additional expenses had been laid upon this system of unemployment relief by the 1921 Unemployed Workers' Dependants

(Temporary Provisions) Act, which provided additional benefits of 5s (25p) for a wife and 1s (5p) for each child.[10]

It was this system which, with changes in the level of benefit and nomenclature – the 'dole' being known as uncovenanted benefit (1921), extended (1924) and transitional benefits (1927) and then as transitional payments (1931) – which survived until the 1934 Act created the Unemployment Assistance Board and attempted to separate the long-term and the short-term unemployed.

In effect, then, inter-war governments dealt with the social problems of poverty, unemployment and ill-health through the Poor Law, unemployment insurance and the 'dole' during the 1920s and through the PACs, UAB, and unemployment insurance in the 1930s. Health insurance, however, provided one other way in which unemployed families could obtain relief, even though it formed no part of the official social net against destitution and poverty.

Health Insurance and Pensions

As Noel Whiteside has recently suggested, there was a steadily rising incidence of sickness and disability among working people which ran parallel to growing unemployment during the inter-war years in Britain, and economic factors helped to influence contemporary perceptions of sickness and health in such a way as to ensure that both those who were genuinely sick, as a result of unemployment, and those who regarded themselves as being so were able to obtain health insurance.[11] Indeed, he adds to the debate about the health of the nation in the inter-war years by noting that claims and payments in health benefit increased steadily throughout this period – though he qualifies this by stressing that such statistics might, as contemporaries commented, be only claims and that less than half the population was covered by health schemes in the late 1930s.[12] The thrust of his argument is that it is very difficult to distinguish between those genuinely suffering ill-health and those who were 'malingerers'; clearly unemployment caused ill-health, just as ill-health caused unemployment. However, there was a clear reluctance by the authorities to prevent unemployed people from applying for health relief, for this would have been a political 'hot potato', and a marked tendency for those who were unemployed to remain on health insurance since, 'The rights of the unemployed under the health insurance scheme were safeguarded. The rights of the long-term sick to statutory unemployment benefits were not.'[13] In addition, with the Anomalies Act and other actions against women who it was felt 'abused' the system of unemployment relief, many women felt safer on health, as opposed to unemployment, insurance. In other words, it is quite likely that some, possibly many, unemployed families used health insurance as an alternative to drawing the standard benefit offered by unemployment insurance, the various types of 'dole', or the Poor Law.

The health insurance which existed and expanded during the inter-war years was based upon Part I of the National Insurance Act of 1911, which remained largely unchanged. By 1920 the scheme was paying sickness benefit of 15s (75p) per week for men and 12s (60p) per week for women, with basic medical treatment for up to twenty-six weeks a year to all workers earning less than £250 per annum, in return for contributions from employers and employees. After six months, those who were still ill could claim disability benefit at half the previous rate. The system operated through approved societies, such as friendly societies, trade unions and industrial insurance companies, whose schemes had to be non-profit making. These bodies paid panel doctors to care for their members. The 1911 Act, and its amendments, therefore provided both insurance against loss of income due to ill-health and access to medical benefit.

Health insurance spread quickly, particularly during the inter-war years. The numbers involved in the scheme rose from 11.5 million in 1912, to 13.5 million in 1922, and 20.26 million out of a population of 47.5 million in 1938.[14] A significant number of women were also covered by the scheme, the figure rising from 3.68 million to 7.1 million between 1912 and 1938. But once unemployment rose sharply in the 1920s health insurance, like unemployment insurance, began to cost more than the contributions. Part of the reason for this was that, as with unemployment, 'temporary' solutions were found which allowed benefits to be paid for longer to those who could prove unemployment at the labour exchanges. As Whiteside notes, by the time unemployment peaked in the early 1930s the various approved societies were bearing the cost of six million members who were wholly or partly in arrears.[15] A Royal Commission on National Health Insurance had been set up by the Labour government in 1924, but its report in 1926, which suggested a system of National Health Insurance in which the government was a significant contributor, was ignored, on its own advice, until the financial situation improved.[16]

In many respects the health insurance scheme was good and effective in alleviating financial suffering due to ill-health, or ill-health caused by unemployment. But there is no doubting that it lacked administrative uniformity; there were, for instance, more than 7,000 societies and branches operating the system in the early 1920s.[17] These organizations offered different services, and sometimes different benefits, to their clients, since the 1911 Act simply provided minimum requirements. Access to a general practitioner was also guaranteed, although the quality of this could vary from area to area since many depressed industrial areas were short of doctors in comparison with more prosperous areas. But the biggest problem with the scheme was that there was no provision under health legislation for hospital or specialist treatment.

The Beveridge Report remarked upon this omission:

> Provision for most of the many varieties of need through interruption of earnings and other causes . . . has already been made in Britain on a scale not surpassed and hardly rivalled in any other country in the world. In one respect only . . . namely limitation of medical service, both the range of treatment which is provided as of right and in respect of the classes of person for whom it is provided, does Britain's achievement fall seriously short of what has been accomplished elsewhere.[18]
> The chief problem was that there was no adequate or effectively organised system of hospital or specialist treatment.

At this time, hospital treatment was unevenly distributed throughout the country and between the social classes. For the working class, by far the largest section of the community, there were about 137,000 beds available in the local authority and the Poor Law hospitals by the mid-1930s, many of the latter having been transferred to local authority control when the Poor Law system was dismantled, or indirectly transferred to their control through the formation of the PACs.[19] The current St Luke's at Bradford and St. Luke's at Huddersfield were in fact originally Poor Law hospitals. These were financed out of local rates. In addition, there were also the voluntary hospitals, with about 83,000 beds, which earned their income from patients fees, donations and legacies. Although there were also other special facilities for infectious diseases and the like, the total provision of hospital beds was low for the population and was not distributed in such way as to effectively tackle the health problems of the nation as a whole. It was this inadequate situation, and the problem of financing health insurance in a period of high unemployment, which contributed significantly to the debate which led Nye Bevan to force through his version of the National Health Service after the Second World War. This incorporated both the concepts of a free service and the state control of hospitals.

The state was far more organized and effective when it came to old-age pensions. The pension scheme which had been introduced in 1908 was non-contributory and, subject to means, 5s (25p) per week was paid to all persons reaching the age of seventy. In 1925 a contributory scheme was added which provided 10s (50p) per week without a means test to those reaching sixty-five and for the widows and orphans of insured men, of any age. Also, from 1926, the non-contributory pension was raised to 10s (50p) per week.

Yet even the most optimistic of assessments could not suggest that the state adopted any systematic and comprehensive scheme for distributing the wealth of the nation to the poor, the unemployed and the ill. Social security in Britain during these years was clearly an inadequate hotch-potch of ideas with little semblance of organization. In no way were the problems of the unemployed, for instance, tackled in any effective manner. It was this lack of clear organization which, undoubtedly, made the housing programme of central importance to the evolution of social policy, less effective than it might have otherwise been.

Housing

The expansion of house-building during the inter-war years is often considered to be one of the great achievements of this period, improving the condition of the housing stock and providing better accommodation for both middle-class and working-class families. As Stevenson has written:

> The improvement of housing conditions was one of the major social advances between the wars. Although large areas of slums remained in the major conurbations, there were remarkable advances in the field of housing . . . .. The inter-war period saw the completion of over four million houses, two and a half million for private sale and the rest for rent by local authorities. The bulk of this housing boom came in the thirties, when

78

nearly three million houses were built, mainly for private sale. Within twenty years, the housing situation was transformed; in 1918 there were 610,000 fewer houses than families while by 1918 there was a theoretical surplus of over 500,000 houses.[20]

Yet the pace of development was uneven between social classes, and it was the middle class, rather than the working class, who received the major benefits of new housing during the inter-war years. Contemporary critics amplified this point. Orwell, for instance, reflected:

'Housing shortage' is a phrase that has been bandied about pretty freely since the war, but it means very little to anyone with an income of more than £10 a week, or even £5 a week for that matter. Where rents are high the difficulty is not to find houses but to find tenants . . . in the industrial areas the mere difficulty of getting hold of a house is one of the worst aggravations of poverty. It means that people will put up with anything – any hole and corner slum, any misery of bugs and rotting floors and cracking walls . . . simply to get a roof over their heads.[21]

Similar comments were made by M'Gonigle and Kirby, who also noted that new housing was beyond the means of the poor.[22] It is clear that the very people who were most in need of improved living standards were not going to be the chief beneficiaries of housing improvements and there is much to suggest that official thinking on housing was not attempting to deal with their particular problems.

There is no doubt that both the quantity and quality of housing stock was better by the 1930s than it had been in pre-war years. At the beginning of the 1920s, it was estimated that there was a shortage of between 300,000 and 400,000 houses – due partly to the First World War which saw rent control and a practical suspension of house building – but this was quickly whittled away as the state and private builders tackled the problem. Throughout the 1920s it was the state which took the lead in tackling the problem through the provision of municipal housing; in the 1930s the vast majority of houses were built for private sale. By the late 1930s there was, allegedly, a surplus with, for the first time ever, more houses than families.[23]

The government attempted to tackle the shortage of houses through a variety of legislation. The Housing and Town Planning Act of 1919, usually referred to as the Addison Act, committed local authorities to surveying their housing needs and offered

79

government subsidies in order to encourage them to build houses and then to let them to the working class at the prevailing level of rents. Any loss of income they incurred as a result of this rent policy would be made up by central government, except for the proceeds of a 1d (O.4p) rate. In total, 213,800 houses were built under the legislation before the economy cuts of 1921 eventually brought the efforts of the 'spending minister' to a halt in 1922.[24] Subsequently, the Chamberlain Act of 1923 provided a subsidy of £6 towards the building of private and local authority housing for a period of twenty years and the Wheatley Act of 1924 which provided more generous subsidies of £9 and £12 for forty years, though there were more controls applied.[25] These two acts operated together until 1934 and added greatly to the overall stock of housing built during this period, as is indicated in Table 3.1.

Such legislation also contributed to an improvment the quality of housing by dictating that larger houses would be built, though the main contribution to the improvement in the quality of housing came from attempts to remove slums, particularly through the Greenwood Housing Act of 1930, which provided subsidies for slum clearance. As a result, about 273,000 houses were either demolished or closed as unfit between 1931 and 1939, and it is estimated that anything up to 700,000 houses or flats were built in their place to house slum dwellers and others.

Table 3.1 *House Building During the Years of the Chamberlain and Wheatley Subsidies: England and Wales, 1923–34*

	Private enterprise	Local authority	Total
Chamberlain subsidy	362.7	75.3	438.0
Wheatley subsidy	15.8	504.5	520.3
Unsubsidised	1085.8	–	1085.8
	1464.3	579.8	2044.1

Some of the most dramatic improvements in housing occurred in the West Riding of Yorkshire. In Bradford new housing estates were built in the 1920s and, in the early 1930s, there were schemes to clear 1,953 houses and to remove 6,617 people from the slum areas

80

of Exchange, Wapping and Broomfield.[27] These plans, drawn up under the Greenwood Housing Act of 1930, confirmed Bradford's position as a leader in social reform. But even Bradford's housing schemes paled into insignificance when compared with the rush of housing activity which occurred in Leeds under a Labour-dominated city council.

In many ways Leeds was backwards in housing activity until the 1930s. In the 1920s the city council had not taken full advantage of the various subsidies on offer. At the beginning of the 1930s it had been slow to react to the Greenwood Act. It did not produce the required housing survey and five-year plan for slum clearance and house-building until February 1931, although the Greenwood Act had demanded this by December 1930. When this survey was finally produced it was considered to be totally inadequate; merely advocating 2,000 demolitions and a commensurate rehousing programme.[28] Labour councillors were dissatisfied with the small scale of the programme and Councillor Revd C. Jenkinson (Labour) asked the Tory chairman of the 'Unhealthy Area Committee' to speed up his survey of Leeds – adding that there were 72,000 back-to-back houses in Leeds, 33,000 of which were concentrated in high densities of 70 to 80 per acre. He argued that at least 10,000 were in need of immediate demolition.[29]

Jenkinson's attack forced the city council to take action and to form a special committee to oversee the slum problem. But the response was purely cosmetic. The committee was formed in July 1931, met once in December 1931, and never met again. In January 1932, an Improvement Committee took over its functions but did nothing up to November 1932. Slum clearance and rehousing in Leeds was clearly going to be a slow and painstaking affair. As a result, Councillor O'Donnell (Labour) made a speech in council in November 1932 demanding the immediate clearance of 5,865 houses and outlining the woefully slow progress of the Tory administration. Feeling that further delay would be politically damaging the Tory administration announced its intention to clear 400 slum houses and to request tenders, by 30 June 1933, for 1,000 three-bedroomed houses.

After more than two years of delay the Tory council had taken action. But this was not enough to appease the Labour councillors who stressed that 54,000 houses had been built in Leeds before 1872 and that 37,500, 'are very old and back-to-back' – and that the

81

council's housing scheme would not touch the tip of the problem.[30] They argued that overcrowding and ill-health could only be avoided by the demolition of 15,000 or 16,000 houses over a five-year period and the construction of an even greater number of two and three-bedroomed parlour and non-parlour houses.

The city council's housing policy was one of the key issues fought out in the November 1933 municipal elections where Labour's demands for more slum clearance were met by Tory charges of the ruinous threat of 'Red finance'. Nevertheless, the Labour Party won a majority on the council and was committed to a more adventurous and challenging housing programme. Slum clearance was to be increased, more houses were to be built, houses were to be built in preference to flats and differential rents were to be charged.[31]

The new Labour administration acted quickly to raise the pace and change the character of the Leeds housing programme. There was a rush of activity. By January 1935, Councillor Revd Jenkinson had announced the slum clearance of more than 2,000 houses and plans to construct a similar number of houses.[32] Indeed, during the two-year period of Labour control about 6,000 houses were demolished and a similar number were constructed.[33] All of the demolished houses were subject to a survey by the Leeds Engineers Department in 1935 and 1936. The City of Leeds Health Exhibition, which ran from the 17 to 24 September 1934, also involved the construction of two of the new three-bedroomed houses near the Leeds Town Hall and in front of the town library in order to show the citizens of Leeds what new housing they could expect. Many of those living in Leeds today would recognize the design. There was a scheme to build council houses at Moortown and a decision to build houses according to the needs of the community; 10 per cent of the houses were to be built for the aged, 10 per cent were to be two bedroomed, 50 per cent three-bedroomed and 10 per cent four- or five-bedroomed houses.[34]

It was at this stage that the National government began to renew its attack both upon slums and overcrowding. At the beginning of 1933, it recognized that:

> Overcrowding was characteristically an evil associated with the central areas of large towns. New accommodation in the outskirts was no solution to the problem, involving as it does the uprooting of people from the neighbourhood they looked upon as their home, and moving them far from where they wished to work. What was needed was more rehousing on the

overcrowded and slum sites. In order that the rehousing in the central areas concerned might accommodate as large a population as possible, normally redevelopment was necessary, in order to make the best of the land, and more housing in flats.[35]

Shortly afterwards it accepted that new Exchequer support would be limited to schemes where:

the rehousing is effected on or near the central site by means of blocks of flats and should not be given in cases where the rehousing is effected by means or ordinary small houses erected on undeveloped land on the outskirts of the area of the local authority.[36]

Although this policy was later to be the subject of amendment, after discussion with the local authorities it is clear that it was partly responsible for the decision of the Leeds Council to move towards the building flats just before the Second World War.[37]

The Tories had regained control of Leeds City Council in November 1935, claiming as their own some of the schemes which the Labour Party had begun during its period of control. Indeed, the famous Quarry Hill scheme near the centre of Leeds, where 2,000 slum houses were demolished and 938 new flat dwellings built at a cost of £1,500,000, began life as an idea put forward by Labour Party activists and stimulated by the grant policy of the National government. Incorporated in the scheme was a day nursery for the children of the residents.

Nevertheless, the Tories introduced some changes. In particular, the Moortown estate, which would have bordered the houses of the wealthy, was replaced by a scheme to build a council estate at Cookridge.[38]

It was clear that many people, in Leeds and throughout the country, saw slum clearance and the construction of modern dwellings as a basis of a better future through the provision of an improved physical environment. In Stockton-on-Tees, and other depressed areas, there were similar schemes to those developed in Leeds and Bradford. But did these schemes, and the improvement in the supply of private housing, contribute to the improvement of the health of those in poverty and unemployment?

There is much to suggest that improvements in the quantity and quality of the housing stock did not greatly improve the lot of the unemployed and the poor. For a start, as George Orwell suggested, the cost of housing was often prohibitive to the poor. Consequently, they continued to live in relatively expensive and unhealthy slums. Orwell noted one of several such slums in Wigan, including the following:

> House in Greenhough's Row. One up, two down. Living-room 13 ft by 8 ft. Walls coming apart and water comes in. Back windows will not open, front ones will. Ten in family with eight children very near together in age. Corporations are trying to evict them for overcrowding but cannot find another house to send them to. Landlord bad. Rent 4s, rates 2s 3d, total 6s 3d[39]

Even when new council house estates were available they were often pitched at such a price that poor families could not afford them without reducing their already poor standards of nutrition. The result was that death rates among the poor did not notably improve as a result of new housing. This was particularly evident in Stockton-on-Tees. The residents of the Housewife Lane area, a slum area, paid rents and rates of 4s 8d per family per week in 1927 and the residents of Riverside area paid the almost identical sum of 4s 7d. In 1928, the rents of the Mount Pleasant Estate, to which many of the Housewife Lane residents had been transferred, were 9s per family per week. In other words, they were paying 4s 4d per week extra which had to come out of family budgets which had not changed. M'Gonigle and Kirby, reporting upon a survey that was conducted of the budgets of the families of the Mount Pleasant Estate and the slum Riverside area, concluded that the diet of families on both the new estate and the old slum area was deficient for the maintenance of healthy life.[40] Indeed, it has already been demonstrated, in Table 2.5, that infant mortality remained high on the new housing estate although it was lower than in the slums of Stockton-on-Tees. But for both the crude and the standardized death rate, which allows for age structure, the figures were higher than the old slum areas, death rate was actually higher – even though this may have something to do with the fact that unemployment rose during the late 1920s and the early 1930s. Table 3.2 indicates this particular situation, which was by no means uncommon; housing was clearly less important than income in improving the health of the poor and the unemployed. It was not, by itself, a solution to their condition. The point was emphasized further by M'Gonigle and Kirby:

The calculation made in Stockton-on-Tees in December 1933 showed that the economic rent and rate of houses built in the town, at the prices ruling then would be:

For a two-bedroomed house, 11s 8d

For a three-bedroomed house, 12s 10d

For a four-bedroomed parlour house, 14s 4d

. . . The larger the house the more people it can accommodate without overcrowding, but as the size increases so does the rent. It is unfortunate that income does not automatically correspond with the size of family. The large family requires a larger house than does a small family; it also requires more food and more clothing and therefore more income, but there is no sliding scale of wages to meet the increased need for commodities.

Many responsible and highly-placed individuals have stated publicly that an urgent need is that of houses suitable for the working-classes which can be let at an all-in rent not exceeding 10s per week. Unfortunately, these individuals have not realized that a rent of 10s per week is beyond the capacity to pay of a large proportion of the working classes.[42]

Table 3.2 *Crude and Standardized Death Rates in the Slums and the New Housing Estate of Mount Pleasant in Stockton-on-Tees*[41]

Crude death rate	
Housewife Lane area (slum)	18.75 per 1,000 for 1923–27
Riverside area (slum)	22.16 per 1,000 for 1923–27
Mount Pleasant Estate	
Population transferred from Housewife Lane	26.77 per 1,000 for 1928–32
Population transferred from Riverside	20.45 per 1,000 for 1928–32
Standardized death rate	
Housewife Lane area	22.91 per 1,000 for 1923–27
Riverside area	26.10 per 1,000 for 1923–27
Mount Pleasant Estate	
Population transferred from Housewife Lane	33.55 per 1,000 for 1928–32
Population transferred from Riverside	22.78 per 1,000 for 1928–32

This situation had been remarked upon by John Wheatley when, in a House of Commons debate in 1923, he reflected that the real problem of working-class housing was the shortage of suitable and reasonably-priced rented accommodation. In this circumstance, Chamberlain's scheme, which essentially provided a subsidy for private builders who were intending to sell the houses they built, was simply ignoring the problem.[43] However, Labour-dominated Leeds City Council understood the problem well and set-up a rent scheme in the mid-1930s based upon a means test and the careful use of government subsidies.

For those who could afford the higher, and largely unsubsidized, rents of new council houses the environment in which they lived was greatly improved – although there were complaints that many of the large estates, such as Norris Green on the outskirts of Liverpool, did not provide the shops, pubs and other facilities which were essential to the social fabric of any newly-created community. The new working-class houses were twice as large as those built in pre-war years and were normally provided with bathrooms and indoor water closets. Piped hot water, from a back boiler behind the fire, also became more common, as did the provision of electricity. For those who could not afford the new housing, or were struggling to do so, because of low income and unemployment, the situation in which they found themselves had improved little, if at all, since 1914.

Table 3.3 *Overcrowding in the Textile District of the West Riding of Yorkshire, 1921–1935*[45]

(Percentage of families in overcrowded conditions, i.e. more than 2 persons per room)

Borough	1921 %	1931 %	1935 %
Bradford	10.7	6.9	2.4
Dewsbury	18.0	13.85	8.0
Halifax	13.2	10.08	5.2
Huddersfield	13.6	7.82	4.6
Leeds	12.0	8.21	3.3*
Wakefield	14.0	8.25	3.7

* The survey in Leeds did not include 25,650 dwellings being dealt with in the slum clearance programme. It is estimated that if they had been included the percentage overcrowding would have been 5.5.

Most towns and cities had blackspot areas where a significant proportion of the population, inevitably the poor and the unemployed, congregated in overcrowded and insanitary houses. Conditions, as already suggested, were bad in Leeds, although in some other towns they were probably worse. In Glasgow and Birmingham, respectively, 200,000 and 68,000 people lived more than three to a room in the early 1930s.[44] The textile district of the West Riding of Yorkshire also provides further evidence of the appalling level of overcrowding, though it was by no means the most depressed of areas. And though conditions did improve it is clear that it was the unemployed and the poor who congregated in the slum areas.

Conclusion

In their desire to move away from the nineteenth-century commitment of dealing only with destitution and to develop a selective policy of tackling the problem of specific groups, successive inter-war governments had created a confused and complex pattern of social security which barely alleviated the condition of the vast majority of the unemployed and the poor. If the social security system which emerged improved the general conditions of the working classes, and offered a greater diversity of relief than had existed in the nineteenth century, it did little for the millions affected by long-term unemployment and acute poverty. This was despite the fact that governments increased their financial commitment to the working classes in the form of unemployment, old age, health and housing provision. The fact is that there was still a strong streak of hostility against the view that the unemployed and the poor should be treated in a generous manner just in case this reduced the incentive to work. Though the Poor Law, as an institution, disappeared in 1930 the mentality behind its operation – the view that it must be a final deterrent – lingered on in the Household Means Test, the Anomalies Bill and other legislation. The inter-war years revealed that the nation was not yet ready for the redistribution of income and wealth which was necessary if those in poverty were to be properly relieved. It was not until the Second World War that such a change of attitude came about. In the meantime, millions of working-class families, and particularly those of the unemployed, failed to benefit fully from the improvements in social provision which had occurred. Their benefits were means tested and their incomes did not permit them to enjoy the improvement in housing provision, which was central to the evolution of social welfare policies affecting the working-class standards of living. Partly as a consequence social and economic inequality persisted in British inter-war life, with some significant consequences.

NOTES

1. S. Glynn and J. Oxborrow, *Inter-War Britain; a Social and Economic History* (London, George Allen and Unwin, 1976), ch. 9.
2. J. Stevenson, *British Society 1914–45* (Harmondsworth, Penguin, 1984), p. 315.
3. Ibid., p. 306.
4. The Second Annual Report of the Ministry of Health, 1920–1.
5. N. Branson, *George Lansbury and the Councillors' Revolt: Poplarism 1919–1925* (London, Lawrence and Wishart, 1979).
6. Ibid., p. 108.
7. The Eighth Annual Report of the Ministry of Health, 1926–7.
8. In Halifax the relieving officers were the same under the PAC in 1930 as those employed by the guardians in 1928 and 1929.
9. Stevenson, *British Society 1914–1945*, p. 302.
10. Glynn and Oxborrow, op.cit., p. 250.
11. N. Whiteside, 'Counting the cost: sickness and disability among working people in an era of industrial recession, 1920–1939', *Economic History Review*, xl, no. 2, May 1987, pp. 228–46.
12. Ibid., p. 230, refers to 20.26 million, out of a total population of 47.5 million, being able to claim sickness and medical benefit.
13. Ibid., p. 237.
14. Ibid., p. 230.
15. Ibid., p. 231.
16. Report of the Royal Commission on National Health Insurance 1926, Majority Report, paragraph 151.
17. Social Insurance and Allied Services, (Beveridge Report), cmd. 6404, 1942, p. 24.
18. Ibid., p. 5.
19. Glynn and Oxborrow, op.cit., p. 264.
20. Stevenson, *British Society 1914–45*, p. 221.
21. G. Orwell, *The Road to Wigan Pier* (London and Harmondsworth, Gollancz, 1937, Penguin, 1962), p. 46.
22. G.C.M. M'Gonigle and J. Kirby, *Poverty and Public Health* (London, Gollancz, 1936), pp. 117–19, 206–13.
23. General Register Office, Census of England and Wales, 1951 Housing Report, table A, p. xxiii.
24. Stevenson, *British Society 1914–45*, p. 222.

25. Housing Act, 1923, paragraph 1a.
26. Glynn and Oxborrow, op.cit. pp.223.
27. *Bradford Pioneer*, 21 September 1934.
28. *Leeds Citizen*, 11 November 1932.
29. Ibid., 10 April 1932.
30. Ibid., 17 November, 2 December 1932, 3 March 1933.
31. City of Labour Party, Minutes, 19 July 1933.
32. Ibid., 3 January 1935.
33. *Leeds Citizen*, 6 December 1935.
34. *Bradford Pioneer*, 7 June 1935.
35. PRO, Cab. 23, Report of Meeting, 31 January 1934.
36. Ibid., Report of Meeting, 21 February 1934.
37. Ibid., Report of Meeting 31 July 1934.
38. *Leeds Citizen*, 13 March, 8 May and 18 September 1936.
39. Orwell, op.cit., p.47.
40. M'Gonigle and Kirby, op.cit., pp.117–23.
41. Ibid., pp. 110,112.
42. Ibid., pp. 207–9.
43. Hansard, 24 April 1923, debate in the House of Commons between N. Chamberlain and J. Wheatley.
44. Stevenson, *British Society 1914–45*, p. 227.
45. Census of England and Wales, 1921, 1931; Report on the Overcrowding Survey in England and Wales, 1936. Also, J. Reynolds and K. Laybourn, *Labour Heartland: A history of the Labour Party in West Yorkshire during the inter-war years 1918–1939* (Bradford, Bradford University Press, 1987), p. 28.

SECTION II:
THE ECONOMIC AND SOCIAL IMPACT OF UNEMPLOYMENT

CHAPTER 4

POPULATION DURING THE INTER-WAR YEARS

In 1942 Richard and Kathleen Titmuss wrote that:

> The present war is the first war the people of this country have waged with a birth-rate below replacement level. Although the 1914–18 war quickened the speed of the decline in fertility and resulted, during a loss of around 600,000 unborn children who would otherwise have been brought into the world, at no time did the rate touch the low level at which it stood in 1939. We entered this war with a little over 41,000,000 souls, or roughly 4,500,000 more than in 1914. Nevertheless we had over 2,000,000 fewer children under 14 to care for, but 2,500,000 more people over 60 to provide for, before the last war. We have even 1,500,000 fewer children than we had at the time of the Boer War . . ..[1]

This was just one of several anxious comments about the changes which had occurred in population during the inter-war years. G.F. McCleary's book, *The Menace of British Depopulation* and Eva Hubback's, *The Population of Britain* were other publications which were even more almost alarmist about the future viability of the British population.[2] The fear was that Britain's population would decline rapidly, that it would be dominated by an aged population with few people of working age coupled with a rapidly decreasing birth rate. In the final analysis there would be a dramatic decline in population, with deaths exceeding births – a foretaste of which had occurred in the early 1930s.[3] It appeared that, without changes in policy, Britain would be on the way to racial suicide. The contemporary concern was so great that a Royal Commission on Population was set up in 1944 to examine the problem of Britain's declining rate of population growth.[4] These concerns, of course, provoke many questions. What were the reasons for Britain's declining population growth rate? How justified were the alarmists in their doom-laden prognostications? What were the social and economic implications of the slow down in population growth? How important were the depressed economic conditions and unemployment in accounting for the slow down in population growth? Was it the prosperity of an acquisitive society prepared to forsake children, or the depression which accounted for the inter-war population trends?

The Pattern of Change

The concern about population trends emerged as it became evident that population growth was declining and that the birth rate, in particular, was falling rapidly. By the late 1930s, the birth rate was about three-quarters of what it had been at the end of the First World War. Death rates had also declined, though not as sharply, and had it not been for the inward migration of population in the 1930s the decline in population growth would have been more marked. In fact the population of Great Britain only increased by about four millions during the inter-war years, about half the level of growth which might have been expected had the rate of growth of the late nineteenth century continued. It appeared that the rapid growth associated with the British industrial revolution had come to an end and that the theory of demographic transition, which predicted a phase when death rates and birth rates fell to low levels, was correct.

In addition, it became clear that there was a substantial restructuring of population as regional migration occurred to the expanding light industry areas of the Midlands and the South East and from the declining industrial areas of Scotland, Wales and the North. The importance of this development has been the subject of some debate. John Stevenson feels that this urban migration was important in restructuring the population of Britain, although Glynn and Oxborrow argue that this internal migration was less marked than it had been in the nineteenth century – being about one third of its former level. Presumably, therefore, internal migration exerted no more impact, and probably less, on the British population structure than it had in the nineteenth century. Notwithstanding the reservations of Glynn and Oxborrow it is clear that population growth rates were less than one third of their nineteenth century peaks and the fact is that there was a substantial loss of population from the old industrial areas to the new ones. At least a million people of working age migrated to the the South East during the inter-war period, and Wales, as a whole, lost both its natural increase in population and an actual loss of about 450,000 people.[6] Other depressed areas also lost much, if not all, their natural increase in population. Internal migration, even at a relatively low scale, exerted a profound impact upon a British population which was slow to increase.

Table 4.1 *Population of Great Britain, 1881–1941*[7]

Date	Total population (in thousands)	Increase in previous 20 years (in thousands)	Increase as a % of population 20 years before
1881	29,710	6,582	28
1901	37,000	7,290	25
1921	42,769	5,769	16
1941*	46,605	3,836	9

* No census taken in 1941. The figures given are an estimate of the population defined in the same way as in previous census figure.

Table 4.2 *Natural and Actual Increase, Great Britain, 1871–1941*[8]
(thousands)

Period	Natural increase (excess of births over deaths)	Net gain(+) or loss(−) by migration	Actual increase
1871–81	3,895	−257	3,638
1881–91	4,137	−817	3,319
1891–1901	4,094	−122	3,971
1901–11	4,587	−756	3,831
1911–21	2,796	−858	1,938
1921–31	2,591	−565	2,026
1931–41	1,160	+650	1,810

Table 4.3 *Births and Deaths, Great Britain, 1871–1941*[9]
(*thousands*)

Period	Births	Deaths
1871–81	9,838	5,942
1881–91	10,147	6,010
1891–1900	10,438	6,344
1900–11	10,596	6,009
1911–21	9,466	6,670*
1921–31	7,935	5,334
1931–41	6,930	5,770

* Including the deaths of 651,000 non-civilians overseas in the 1914–18 war.

Table 4.4 *Birth and Death Rates in Great Britain, 1901–40*[10]

	Births per 1,000		Deaths per 1,000	
	England & Wales	Scotland	England & Wales	Scotland
1901–5	28.2	29.2	16.0	17.0
1906–10	26.3	27.6	14.7	16.1
1911–15	23.6	25.4	14.3	15.7
1916–20	20.0	22.8	14.4	15.0
1921–5	19.9	23.0	12.1	13.9
1926–30	16.7	20.0	12.1	13.6
1931–5	15.0	18.2	12.0	13.2
1936–40	15.9	17.6	12.2	13.6

Table 4.5 *Geographical Distribution and Changes, 1921–38*[11]

Regions	Population in 1938 (millions)	% change 1921–1938
South East	14.49	+18.1
Midlands	7.21	+11.6
West Riding	3.46	+ 6.0
E. Counties (R)	1.85	+ 3.7
Lancashire & Cheshire	6.16	+ 3.5
South West	2.08	+ 3.3
Northern rural counties	1.29	+ 3.1
Scotland	4.99	+ 2.1
Northumberland & Durham	2.20	− 1.0
Central Wales	0.68	− 4.8
South Wales	1.78	− 8.1

The Reasons for the Decline in Population Growth Rate

Only four factors can determine the rate of population growth – migration, the age of marriage, death rates and birth rates. By and large, the first three factors can be discounted for the inter-war years and it is clear that the most important factor was the decline in birth rate.

Migration may have been a factor in the 1920s, though the level of net migration from Britain was somewhat less than it had been in the previous two decades. In addition, for the first time in generations, as Table 4.2 indicates, there was an actual net inflow of population to Britain during the 1930s, a factor which would, of course, have increased Britain's population growth rate. And as a whole it is clear that the inter-war period saw Britain's population increase, rather than decrease, as a result of migration.

Equally, changes in the proportion of people married in particular age categories does not appear to have contributed to any significant decline in population increases. Broadly, there was stability in the marriage rates from the 1870s to the 1940s, although there appears to have been something of a minor dip in those getting married in the late 1920s and 1930s. It would appear that there was some increase in the marriage rates among those in their early twenties during the early 1920s, perhaps because of the delays caused by the First World War, and after 1934, when the domestic economy began to revive from the worst excesses of the slump.

Table 4.6 *Proportion of People of Each Sex Aged 45–54 Who Were or Had Been Married, Great Britain, 1871–1947*[12]

	Men	Women
1871	89.9	86.9
1881	90.0	87.1
1891	89.6	86.8
1901	88.5	85.7
1911	87.4	83.7
1921	87.4	83.2
1931	88.6	83.1
1939 (estimate)	90.1	82.9
1947 (estimate)	90.9	83.5

Table 4.7 *The Proportion of the Population ever Married by Sex and Age Group, England and Wales, 1871–1951*[13]

| Date | Age group | | | | | |
| | 20–24 | | 25–34 | | 45–54 | |
	Male	Female	Male	Female	Male	Female
1871	23.3	34.8	68.4	71.1	90.3	97.9
1881	22.3	33.5	68.3	70.7	90.4	88.1
1891	19.5	29.9	65.7	67.4	90.0	87.6
1901	17.4	27.4	64.1	66.0	89.0	86.6
1911	14.3	24.3	61.4	64.5	87.8	84.2
1921	17.8	27.4	65.9	66.3	88.0	83.6
1931	13.9	25.8	64.8	67.0	89.2	83.6
1939	17.4	34.4	66.3	71.0	90.5	83.3
1951	23.8	48.2	72.8	81.8	90.8	84.9

Since death rates also declined, and therefore more people were surviving into middle and old age, it is evident that population increases should have been higher. Death rate was not a significant or relevant factor in explaining the slow down of population growth. It is clearly birth rate which is central to any explanation of population trends during the inter-war years. The fact is that the birth rate declined by almost half between the 1900 and the late 1930s, and by an even higher proportion when compared with nineteenth-century levels. But why did it decline?

There are several possibilities. In the first place, the decline might simply be seen as an inevitable feature of the maturity of any industrialized society. The theory of demographic transition suggests that as nations move towards maturity that the decline in death rates, occasioned by higher living standards, will be followed by a decline in birth rates to a more or less similar level. In other words, there was something inevitable in this decline – although it must be noted that other industrialized nations, such as the United States, at a similar stage in their economic development have not necessarily followed the same pattern of development.

Alternatively, it is possible that the decline occurred because of the economic conditions of the inter-war years. The deep economic depression, particularly of the late 1920s and the early 1930s, may well have discouraged the continued raising of large families and encouraged the greater use of birth-control techniques. As Beatrice Webb wrote of birth control and the economic conditions:

> The practice arose in the last decades of the nineteenth century within the ruling class. Since the Great War, 1914–18, it has been practiced by wage-earners, suffering from long periods of unemployment and under-employment, so drastic that it seemed abject folly to produce children who could neither be adequately nourished nor sufficiently educated to secure a satisfactory livelihood. [14]

As a prominent socialist, Webb had a vested interest in explaining developments in the way she did. Nevertheless, there seems to be ample proof that the depression exerted some short-term downward impact upon birth rates, especially in the early 1930s at the height of the depression. And the 1949 Royal Commission on Population suggested that the struggle for security and social promotion in society, the 'Social Capillarity', as it was referred to, was a sufficient explanation of the downward trend in population growth since the mid- and late nineteenth century. [15]

Thirdly, it is also possible that the advances in birth control operating within the climate of an 'acquisitive society' might well have permitted couples to plan their family lives in such a way as to allow them to enjoy the consumer benefits of society. Put bluntly, it is possible that couples decided to 'have baby Austins rather than baby boys.'[16]

Now these alternative explanations are not exclusive of each other and, obviously, may vary from region to region. It is possible that against a long-term downward movement of population, perhaps sparked off by a variety of economic concerns, the economic depression helped to determine the immediate attitudes in some of the old declining industrial centres just as the prospect of prosperity, and the accumulation of consumer goods and property, may have stimulated a desire to control family size among the population of the expanding industrial centres of the Midlands and the South East.

In addition the development of birth-control techniques provided the opportunity for the above changes of attitudes to be encouraged. The pro-birth control movement had begun in the late nineteenth century with the formation of the Malthusian League and the trial and work of Annie Besant and Charles Bradlaugh, events which encouraged the dissemination of knowledge about birth-control techniques. Subsequently, millions of pamphlets were circulated on birth control. Eventually, in 1921 Marie Stopes opened the first birth control clinic. Her purpose was to establish a pilot project which might encourage the government to use its antenatal clinics and infant and maternal welfare clinics, of which there were more than 2,000, to distribute information on birth control and contraceptives; the Ministry of Health was by that time offering financial aid to the 400 local authorities who ran such clinics and could have forced them to become centres for birth control.[17] Stopes's fundamental conception of the role of the clinics led to a heated political debate during the inter-war years as the issue was fought within political parties and in parliament. Support was widespread in all the major political parties and among the MPs of all parties, though not initially sufficient in number to achieve Stopes's objective. The situation changed quickly.

By the late 1920s the activities of birth control groups ensured that the matter was openly discussed, the matter being almost a compulsory subject for discussion in the local meetings of the Women's Section of the Labour Party.[18] In 1928 Marie Stopes sent one of two horse-drawn caravans outfitted as birth control clinics into the mining areas of South Wales where the majority of workers were suffering from unemployment and reduced hours.[19] The second caravan was sent north and was burned by 'a disgruntled Catholic woman in Bradford.'[20] In addition the Workers Birth Control Group, led by Frida Laski, carried the message of family limitation to Wales and Durham.[21] Other groups were also attracted to support the gospel of family limitation. Eventually, in 1930, several local authorities, including Poplar and Shoreditch, began to instruct their medical officers to provide information on birth control. Shortly afterwards, the Ministry of Health suggested that birth control information could be given at maternal and child welfare centres on medical grounds.[22] From the summer of 1930 onwards, birth control facilities at least became more openly available, although they were often provided in a grudging and limited fashion.

At first the gospel of family limitation appears to have been spread most effectively among the middle classes before it percolated through to the working classes. Nevertheless, there is a question mark about how widespread such knowledge was among the

100

working classes. Did they in fact have access to the new birth-control methods or did they practice older nineteenth-century birth-control techniques, more suited to the pockets of the working class?

There is ample evidence that in the Victorian and Edwardian ages working-class women were knowledgeable about techniques by which they could control family size. Angus McLaren's study of the Lancashire textile workers, whose fertility was less than other working-class groups in the nineteenth century, suggests that many of the miscarriages which were reported, and many which were not reported, were probably the result of abortion achieved through the use of Epsom and Glauber salts or similar substances. Indeed, McLaren makes two main claims. The first:

> . . . knowledge of abortive techniques was widespread in factory districts and spreading due to the interchange of information in the mills, to increase in therapeutic abortions carried out by surgeons, and to the publicity of quacks for their abortifacients.[23]

The second point is that factory women were well versed in appraising the advantages and disadvantages of additional family members. Therefore, he suggests:

> . . . in contrast to the middle classes, in which by the second half of the century contraceptives were available and effectively used, abortion was becoming a 'back-up' method of birth control; in the case of working-class women, without safe contraceptives, it was a basic means of family planning. Working-class women had always had recourse to abortion; but in the case of the last century it was particularly likely, first, where married women workers worked outside the home and hence paid a key role in determining their families economic stability; and second, where the dependence of the family on the women's wage led to a reappraisal of family strategy. The demand for child labour in the textile areas could have been . . . an inducement for workers to aim for high fertility. What has not been adequately appreciated, however, is that a whole constellation of social forces – high infant mortality rates, loss of mother's income, the fluctuating utility of child labour – could equally well encourage fertility control.[24]

Similar views have been expressed by Patricia Knight who explored the subject of women and abortion in Victorian and Edwardian England. She suggests that abortion was probably the most prevalent form of contraception for working-class women before 1914.[25] She also notes that chemist shops sold quinine, which could be used as a spermicide or as a drug to procure abortion, that a wide variety of drugs were used to achieve abortion, and that advertisers offered many female pills, such as Widow Welch's Female Pills and Towle's Pills, which were, in effect, abortifacients.[26] If such knowledge and techniques were readily available in pre-war years then it is obvious that the same techniques were known about and used during the inter-war years. It may be true, as some suggest, that working-class budgets would not stretch to paying for the regular use of new birth-control methods but old, tried and cheap techniques might still be used. Even infant mortality figures, as implied by McLaren, may have partially reflected the need of working-class families to reduce their family size. Equally, the new ideas and advice offered by the Marie Stopes clinics and by the Family Planning Association, which was established in 1930 and had sixty-six clinics by 1939, would have been very limited.[27] Marie Stopes's books, *Married Love* and *Wise Parenthood* may have sold widely in the early 1920s but the main readers were almost certainly the middle class. Richard Allan Soloway's excellent study of the birth control movement between 1870 and 1930 may well reveal the extent to which these groups were concerned about the need to spread knowledge about birth control amongst the working classes but, it would seem, in the light of more recent research, that such concern was inappropriate. Soloway's comment that, 'The birth control groups found it difficult to persuade the middle and upper-class membership of the feminist organizations that access to the contraceptive methods was a genuine problem', seems both ill-founded and unnecessary.[28] Indeed, it seems highly likely that working-class families would have controlled family size through the old, rather than new, techniques.

The evidence of the 1949 Royal Commission on Population on the use of birth control techniques, recognized to be inadequate on the matter, suggests that only 40 per cent of women married between 1910 and 1919 used some form of birth control at some time in their marriage compared with 66 per cent of those married between 1935 and 1939.[29] In addition it was suggested that only about a quarter of the earlier sample of women had used birth control methods other than withdrawal compared with 57 per cent of the latter group. It seems unlikely, given the delicate nature of

102

such a survey, that the true extent of birth control would be revealed and hardly likely that those surveyed would own up to the use of abortion, an activity which had been illegal, though widespread, since 1803. Birth control was clearly more widespread than the Royal Commission could possibly reveal.

Birth rates began to decline for all social groups as a consequence of changing attitudes towards economic conditions and opportunities. In the case of the working class – possibly more than the middle class – the unemployment of families and the depressed economic conditions that prevailed during the inter-war years encouraged the reduction of family size, even though there were still many areas where the birth rate remained high or increased, almost oblivious of the economic conditions.[30] It seems doubtful, except in the case of the more prosperous areas, whether the acquisitive nature of society was as important to the working class as was the need to survive and adjust to the depression. Strikingly, however, the average size of manual worker's families exceeded that of non-manual workers by a large and consistent margin of just 40 per cent throughout the early twentieth century. All sections of British society were clearly reducing family size – though for varying reasons if one accepts Angus McLaren's analysis.

Table 4.8 *Estimated Average Size of Completed Family of Women Married 1900–29*[31]

Period of marriage	Average number of live births
1900–9	3.37
1910–14	2.90
1915–19	2.53
1920–24	2.38
1925–29	2.19

Table 4.9 *Estimated Average Size of Completed Family, Manual and Non-Manual Workers, According to Period of Marriage*[32]

Date of marriage (1)	Non-manual workers (2)	Manual workers (3)	Ratio of (3) to (2) (%) (4)
1900–9	2.79	3.94	141
1910–14	2.34	3.35	143
1915–19	2.05	2.91	142
1920–24	1.89	2.73	144
1925–29	1.73	2.49	144

The Alarmists and the Consequences of the Decline in Population Growth

Richard and Kathleen Titmuss attempted to assess the economic and social consequences of the changes they had noted. In dramatic form they suggested:

> As some industries become redundant others will be required to expand. Arm-chairs and bedroom slippers instead of children's foods is one extreme instance of the change-over from the requirements of youth to those of old age. The demand for basic necessities, such as bread, will diminish as the need for the semi-luxuries of old age rises. Educational requirements will decline as the burden of old people increases. In fact, innumerable changes will result affecting agricultural, housing, medical, clothing and amusement policies. Broadly, we may say that industry will have to be far less rigid; indeed much more flexible in adapting itself to change than it has been for the past twenty years.[33]

Others predicted that the population of Britain would fall to around 18 to 20 million by the end of the century, with catastrophic effects as a diminishing workforce was burdened with a rapidly increasing number of old-age pensioners. It was deeply felt that the economy would no longer be viable and that demand would decrease since the aged would be unable to afford the type of demand required to sustain industry.

Many of these predictions were, of course, irrational and some economists, most notably J.M. Keynes saw in decreasing population growth the opportunity for per capita output to increase rapidly.[34] The real problem, according to him, was the need to ensure that unemployment was not allowed to persist by increasing effective demand through government expenditure and, when required, supplementing existing consumer and investment demand.

Others, particularly socialists, were convinced that the downward trend in population growth was not, in itself, a problem since the key to the future prosperity of Britain was to be found in the redistribution of income to ensure that all enjoyed an income sufficient to enjoy healthy life. This had been the view vehemently advocated by the Independent Labour Party in the 1920s and by Oswald Mosley, when he was a supporter of the Labour Party during the 1920s.[35] Some sections of the Trades Union Congress still felt that the central problem of the inter-war years was unemployment and that, in a way, a slow down in population would not be a bad thing.[36] Others, including Richard and Kathleen Titmuss, suggested the need to regulate future population in such a way as to help the overall development of the economy. Family allowances were, indeed, suggested as a necessary feature of such a policy and were, incidentally, provided for the second child and subsequent children after the Second World War. The Royal Commission on Population also tended to endorse the view that a stationary population was possibly not a bad thing considering the way in which the economy could be regulated. But it also noted that population would continue to rise over the next thirty years and presented the view that the state should plan future population growth by offering family allowances and income tax relief to those contemplating families along with the development of special services for the benefit of children and mothers. Moreover, it supported the introduction of such measures in order to ensure that social inequality was removed and that more children from the deprived families survived their childhood.[37] It concluded:

> Public policy should assume, and seek to encourage, the spread of voluntary parenthood; it should also assume also that women will take an increasing part in the cultural and economic life of the community and should endeavour, by adjustments of social and economic arrangements, to make it easier for women to combine motherhood and the care of the home with outside interests. We submit in subsequent chapters proposals for assistance to families in cash and services. These proposals we regard as doing no more than initiating a programme of family welfare which will have to be kept under continuous review and modified and expanded in the light of experience and deeper knowledge.[38]

In the final analysis, these more sober views were vindicated by events; population continued to increase steadily, after an upward surge in the late 1940s, and some of the views expressed by the Royal Commission on Population were accepted.

Conclusion

Some vital areas of information, such as the extent to which modern and traditional birth-control methods were used, lack any firm, accurate or trustworthy evidence. As a result, it is not easy to arrive at conclusions about the reasons for population trends during the inter-war years. It is difficult to assess whether or not unemployment and economic conditions were vital to the decline in the size of working-class families, or whether the prospect of purchasing new consumer goods conditioned the responses of the working classes. However, certain points can be made. In the first place, it is clear that the working class, along with the middle class, was reducing its fertility – although there were one of two exceptions in some of the most depressed industrial towns. Secondly, this decline in fertility did occur in depressed industrial towns and among industrial groups whose prospects of unemployment were high and whose access to the 'acquisitive way of life' must have been limited by the fact that they were receiving some form of unemployment or health benefit and struggling to survive. In Jarrow, Stockton-on-Tees and other industrial towns it seems unlikely that the prospect of acquiring wealth and property would have exerted much influence upon working-class families struggling for survival. Thirdly, however, it is likely that the 'acquisitive way of life' will have operated amongst the middle class, the working class employed in the new expanding consumer industries, and those migrating from the old industrial areas to the South East and the Midlands. Fourthly, it is obvious that the overall decline in birth rate and population growth which was occurring as part of the demographic transition to small birth and death rates was greatly exaggerated by the poor economic conditions and the unemployment of the inter-war years. It was the speed at which the decline occurred which led to wild suggestions that Britain was on the verge of a race suicide.

In the final analysis, there were many factors operating upon population trends in the inter-war period. Unemployment and economic depression were significant among these, particularly

106

within the working class in the declining industrial centres who had had the knowledge which would permit them to regulate their population increases from the beginning of the industrial revolution, and before. One should not assume that the decisions of working-class families would be substantially affected by new methods of birth control or by new ideas. They had always had the potential to control their fertility and did so when necessary. The economic collapse of the late 1920s and early 1930s provided that necessity, and the results were to be seen in the exaggerated downward movement in population growth.

NOTES

1. R. & K. Titmuss, *Parent's Revolt* (London, Secker and Warburg, 1942), pp. 34–5.
2. G.F.M. McCleary, *The Menace of British Depopulation* (1937); E. Hubback, *The Population of Britain* (1947); N.L. Tranter, *Population and Industrialization* (London, Adam & Charles Black, 1973), pp. 154–170.
3. Deaths exceeded births in 1933.
4. *Royal Commission on Population, Report, 1949*, cmd 7695.
5. J. Stevenson, *British Society 1914–45* (Harmondsworth, Penguin, 1984), pp. 144–5; S. Glynn and J. Oxborrow, *Inter-war Britain: a Social and Economic History* (London, George Allen & Unwin, 1976), ch. 7.
6. Stevenson, op.cit., p. 144.
7. *Royal Commission on Population, Report*, p. 8.
8. Ibid., pp. 9, 15.
9. Ibid., p. 10.
10. Stevenson, op.cit., p. 148, quoting from the Registrar-General's Statistical Review of England and Wales, and Registrar-General, Scotland, Annual Reports.
11. C.L. Mowat, *Britain between the Wars, 1918–1940* (London, Methuen, 1968 edition), table on p. 467.
12. *Royal Commission on Population, Report*, p. 23.
13. B.R. Mitchell and P. Deane, *Abstract of British Historical Statistics* (London and Cambridge, Cambridge University Press, 1962); also quoted in N. Tranter, *Population since the Industrial Revolution; The Case of England and Wales* (London, Croom Helm, 1973), p. 102.
14. R. & K. Titmuss, op.cit., Preface, p. 10.
15. Loc.cit., Report, p. 39.
16. A commonly used sentence.
17. R.A. Soloway, *Birth Control and the Population Question in England, 1877–1930* (USA, University of North Carolina Press, 1982), p. 280.
18. J. Reynolds and K. Laybourn, *Labour Heartland* (Bradford, Bradford University Press, 1987), p. 42.

19. Soloway, op.cit., p. 306.
20. Idem.
21. Idem.
22. Ibid., p. 311.
23. A. McLaren, 'Women, Work and Regulation of Family Size', *History Workshop*, 4, Autumn 1977, p. 72.
24. Ibid., p. 78.
25. P. Knight, 'Women and Abortion in Victorian and Edwardian England', *History Workshop*, 4, Autumn 1977, pp.57–68.
26. Ibid., p. 57.
27. Stevenson, *British Society 1914–45*, p.154.
28. Soloway, op.cit., p. 298.
29. *Royal Commission on Population, Report, Papers*, vol. 1, p. 3, and Tables, 2, 3 & 5.
30. G.C.M. M'Gonigle and J. Kirby, *Poverty and Public Health* (London, Gollancz, 1936), p. 115 records that the birth rate rose from about 35 per 1,000 to 44.25 per 1,000 for a working-class population transferred from a slum area to a new council housing estate.
31. Royal Commission on Population Report, p. 25.
32. Ibid., p. 29.
33. R. & K. Titmuss, op.cit., p. 46.
34. J.M. Keynes, 'Some Economic Consequences of a Declining Population', *Eugenics Review*, April 1937.
35. The Independent Labour Party programme 'Socialism in Our Time', which emerged in the mid- and late 1920s, and Oswald Mosley's *Revolution by Reason* (1925) both developed policies for redistributing wealth and generating new demand.
36. E. Bevin, *My Plan for 2,000,000 Unemployed* (1932).
37. *Royal Commission on Population, Report*, p. 70
38. Ibid., pp. 161–2.

CHAPTER 5

INDUSTRIAL RELATIONS

The First World War saw the rapid rise of trade union membership from 4 million in 1914 to about 6 million in 1918. By 1920, trade union membership reached its inter-war peak of about 8 million. This growth in membership, which had been fairly rapid since about 1906, was the result of a variety of factors, particularly the improved economic conditions, the high demand for labour and the high wages which were paid in war time. Moreover, as the war continued, the government was increasingly dependent on the support of union officials and the status of trade unions rose to a level which had previously appeared inconceivable. The Webbs, the historians of British trade unionism, sensitive to this change, emphasized the point, noting:

> . . . revolutionary transformation of the social and political standing of the
> official representatives of the Trade Union world – a transformation which
> has been immensely accelerated by the Great War.[1]

Such a situation was tolerated by the government in a climate which accepted that the economy had to be controlled. Nevertheless, it was obvious that the impetus which the trades unions had gained would lead to conflict with the government once attempts were made, by government and employers alike, to remove the wartime regulations and return to the competitive situation of the pre-war world. Such conflict became increasingly likely after 1920 when unemployment rose as British trade failed to recover to its pre-war level. Faced with the intense competition of foreign trade competitors, employers resorted to attempts to reduce monetary wages, an action which was given an additional downward twist by the Baldwin government's decisions to return to the gold standard and to reflate the pound in 1925. Indeed, it was this government action which encouraged employers to attempt to reduce the wages of workers by 10 per cent; causing the coal lock-out/strike and General Strike of 1926. A galvanized trade union movement facing the problems of high unemployment and constant wage reductions was bound to find itself in conflict with both employers and government in the inter-war years.

The General Strike is often taken as the symbol of the industrial relations of these years – and is seen as an event which brought to an end the militant trade unionism of almost two decades. Thereafter, it is argued, trade unionism was defeated and the 'Trades Union Congress, which didn't have much support before 1926, had even less support afterwards.'[2] Indeed, the militancy of the 1920s is often compared with the relative quiescence of trade union action during the 1930s. But are these generalizations justified? Did unemployment, economic depression and the General Strike reduce trade unionism to a pitiful weakness? Had the trajectory of Labour's industrial growth been altered by the events of 1926? Did the General Strike marginalize the romantic image of industrial militancy, as Dame Margaret Cole has suggested?[3] Were the defeats of the coal strike/lock-out and the General Strike vital in permitting the Government to return to the political economy of normalcy, which was referred to in Chapter 1? Can the General Strike be seen, in any sense, as the revolutionary strike which the Communists were anticipating? And, was the defeat of the General Strike a watershed in British industrial relations?

The Immediate Post-War Years, 1919–25

Trade union membership continued to grow until 1920 – even though there were reverses for the movement, such as the government's decision to ignore the advice of the Sankey Commission of 1919 and to return the coal mines to the coal owners in April 1921.[4] The wartime machinery of industrial relations still survived – particularly the Whitley Councils which had been formed in order to bring employers and employees together in an attempt to resolve differences without industrial conflict.[5] But in 1920 the economy began to decline, unemployment rose and the government committed itself to following the advice of the Cunliffe Committee to return to the gold standard by 1925. These deflationary policies of various governments added to unemployment at a time when Britain's foreign trade was depressed. Employers therefore resorted to the reduction of costs, most particularly in wages, in order to compete in world markets at a time when it appeared that rising unemployment made their action possible without major conflict.

Employers constantly gnawed at the high level of wages which had been built up during the First World War. They frequently attempted to reduce the basic wage of workers and to reduce the cost of living addition which had been paid throughout the war and in the immediate post-war years. Indeed, it was estimated that the wages of Britain's twelve million workers were reduced by about £5 million per week between 1921 and 1925, although higher estimates have also been made.[6] But this had not improved Britain's competitive position, and all it did was reduce the home demand for products, thus increasing unemployment further. Ben Turner, of the General Union of Textile Workers and soon to be President of the TUC, wrote in 1925:

> It's as much home trade we are suffering from as the lack of foreign trade.
> In fact the reduction in home trade is far bigger than the reduction in
> exports, and this is accounted for by the ten million reduction paid out
> now would give a right big fillip to trade.[7]

Trade unionists increasingly saw underconsumption as the cause of stagnant trade, for, as the manifesto of the woollen textile workers stated on the eve of the 1925 textile lock-out: 'There is no greater fallacy today than to think we could get back to prosperity by reducing wages.'[8] Even before the General Strike there was evidence that trade union leaders were beginning to challenge the notion that wage reductions could solve Britain's economic difficulties and an increasing willingness to threaten industrial action. Up to 1925, however, industrial action had not appeared to work and threatening postures had not generally been successful against employers. Indeed, trade union membership fell by more than

20 per cent, about 1.7 million in 1920 and 1921, in a period when there was more industrial conflict than at any other time in the inter-war years, other than in 1926. The implacable opposition of employers had forced wages down despite the most determined efforts of the trade unions.

This quick decline in trade union power appears to have occurred because of the combination of both internal weakness and external pressure. Apart from the difficulties presented by unemployment and the trade depression, already referred to, some of the leading trade unions found it impossible to submerge their differences in a joint defence against the onslaught of both employers and government. The most famous evidence of this is offered by the events which led to 'Red Friday' in April 1921.

Following the end of the First World War, the leading question in the mining industry was whether or not the state would return the coal mines to their pre-war owners. The Miners' Federation of Great Britain, which had passed resolutions in favour of both workers' control and nationalization, supported state control and in order to avoid industrial conflict the Lloyd George Coalition government set up a royal commission, chaired by Lord Sankey, to investigate the coal industry. Although the Sankey Commission produced four different reports, the majority report – upon the casting vote of the chairman – recommended that the coal industry should continue under national control. However, David Lloyd George decided that a majority of one was not sufficient, even though he had given an undertaking to implement the majority report. The consequence was immediate; the Yorkshire miners struck, unsuccessfully, in July 1919 and some 200,000 miners in South Wales and Monmouth threatened to strike in sympathy. In the final analysis, this sympathetic support did not transpire. Yet the frustration which this 'betrayal' caused among coal miners was to dominate the industry for many years to come. As one historian has noted:

> The bitterness and the troubles of the coal mines for the next seven, or for that matter twenty-seven years, derived in great part from the feeling of both miners and owners that they had been betrayed.[9]

Vernon Hartshorn, then a Derbyshire MP and a South Wales miners' leader, asked in the House of Commons:

Why was the commission set up? Was it a huge game of bluff? Was it ever intended that if the reports favoured nationalization we were to get it? . . .. That is the kind of question the miners of the country will ask, and they will say they have been deceived, betrayed, duped. [10]

Although there were several disputes during the next twenty months, it was not until the coal mines were formally handed back to the coal owners, on 31 March 1921, that serious conflict ensued. On the following day, the coal owners locked out those miners who would not work at lower rates of pay – of up to 49 per cent in the badly affected export area of South Wales – and attempted to suspend national agreements. The government also issued regulations under the 1920 Emergency Powers Act and recalled troops from Ireland and abroad in order to quell the miners and their potential allies. The government feared that the Triple Alliance, forged between the Miners' Federation of Great Britain, the National Union of Railwaymen (NUR) and the National Transport Workers (NTW) at the beginning of the war, whereby each union offered sympathetic strike support under certain circumstances, might be used to widen the dispute. It need not have had such fears.

The expected support of the NUR and the NTW on Friday, 15 April 1921 never occurred, and that day became the infamous 'Black Friday' of Labour history. Although Ernest Bevin's Transport Workers had not come out on strike the real opprobrium of the Labour movement was held for Jimmy Thomas, the railwaymen's leader, whose opposition to sympathetic strike action had been vital to the collapse of the Triple Alliance. He had not helped his cause when he 'trotted blithely down the steps to greet eager reporters with the news "Its all off boys"' and added, to cries of 'Jimmy's selling you' the riposte that "I've tried boys, I've done my very best. But I couldn't find a bloody buyer."' [11]

The immediate outcome of the failure of the Triple Alliance was that the miners were left to fight alone. Eventually, they were forced to accept some significant wage reductions, although the French invasion of the Ruhr, and the consequent interruption of coal output, plus the American coal strike of 1924 helped to reduce and delay the downward trend of coal prices and the rate of decrease in the wages of coal miners. It was to be 1925 before the downward pressure in wages was to again produce the threat of major industrial conflict in the coalfields.

Yet there were other consequences. One was that the wage levels of other industries were forced downwards. In 1921 the employers won back the 5 per cent concession made in 1920 to the woollen workers and successfully reduced the cost of living addition to wages, paid since the First World War, over the next four years.[12] Similar actions were repeated frequently in other industries.

Another consequence was that the TUC was forced to push through its reorganization and to form the General Council, an alternative to its Parliamentary Committee, as its executive body. The real purpose of the General Council was to explore the possibility of establishing effective cooperation between unions. At first, however, it focused upon the need to settle inter-union disputes and it only gradually acquired the right to call for joint industrial action from Congress. By 1925, however, it was strongly pushing forward the idea of forming an Industrial Alliance by which threatened unions could call upon the sympathetic strike support of other TUC unions.[13] Indeed, the left-wing and Communist demands for 'All Power to the General Council,' in 1924 and 1925, helped the General Council to strengthen its demand for an 'Industrial Alliance'.[14] Gordon Phillips has stressed the way in which this objective, and the General Strike, can be seen as an 'expiation of 1921'.[15]

Yet the trade union movement faced many difficulties in the early 1920s. Some unions, most notably the Miners' Federation of Great Britain, were reluctant to invest the General Council with the power to call all unions out on sympathetic strike action and unemployment made it difficult for it to fight against wage reductions. Nevertheless, in 1925 a determined effort was made by the TUC and other unions to reverse the trend. In many ways the stimulus for this came not from the miners but from the wool and worsted textile workers who fought against further wage reductions in 1925.

The summer of 1925 was hardly the most propitious moment for the textile unions to make their stand against further wage reductions. Trade unions were already suffering, and the implementation of the decision to return to the gold standard augured badly for the staple export industries. Yet, in April, the Executive Committee of the National Union of Textile Workers (NUTW) declared its intention of demanding a restoration of the 5 per cent

114

Unemployed demonstrators invade the pitch at half-time during the match between Arsenal and Charlton Athletic at Highbury, 21 January 1939. The police escort two of the demonstrators off the pitch

A party of Welsh unemployed on their march to London to protest against the Means Test. They stopped at Severn Tunnel while first aiders attended to their blistered feet

Slum accommodation in Leeds in 1936 – the back of Stansfield Street, which was about to be cleared

Philip and Ethel Snowdon arriving for a meeting at No. 10 Downing Street, 28 September 1932. It was after this meeting that Snowdon resigned from Ramsay MacDonald's National government

City of Leeds Health Exhibition, 17–26 September 1934. The new design three-bedroom houses were intended to replace slum accommodation. These were built near the Town Hall for the exhibition

Slum housing about to be cleared, 1936

Caroline Street, Leeds *c.* 1935, about to be demolished

The Drummond Street Occupational Centre, Bradford put men to work on allotments

Work training at the mill worked by the Drummond Street Occupational Centre, Bradford

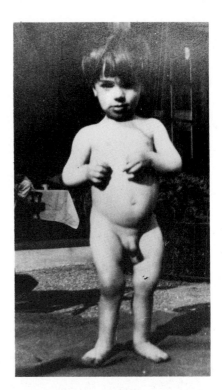

Rickets was still a problem among the children of working-class families; seen here in a 3½-year-old child from Bradford

Quarry Hill Flats, Leeds, showing the day nursery section – an indication of the heightened concern for health in the 1930s

Ramsay MacDonald addressing an audience of 15,000 at North Street Recreation Ground, Leeds, on Saturday 25 May 1929, the eve of the 1929 General Election

Public Health Department, Leeds Municipal Services Exhibition at the
Drill Hall, Fenton Street, Leeds, in 1923

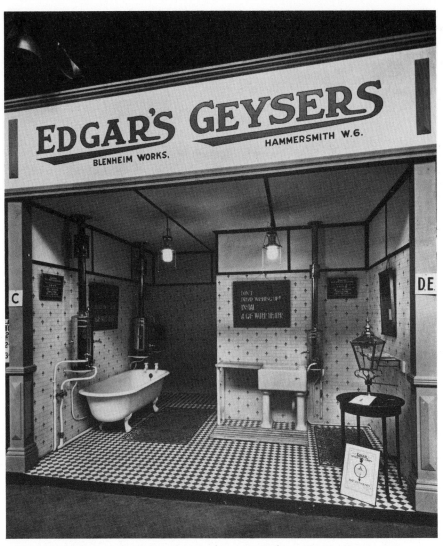

New bathroom facilities advertised at the Public Health Department, Leeds Municipal Services Exhibition, Leeds, 1923

Public Health Department, Leeds Municipal Services Exhibition, 1923

Single back-to-back housing, Leeds *c*. 1936

City of Leeds Health Exhibition, 17–26 September 1934

"E. M. B." POSTERS

E. M. B. 16 for display in November 1937

E. M. B. 34 for display in December 1937

The above poster sets have been specially produced for display on poster frames formerly used by the Empire Marketing Board. The sizes of the posters are: Large posters, 60 ins. wide × 40 ins. deep. Small posters, 25 ins. wide × 40 ins. deep. Price 7/6 per set of five posters and headstrip. They are obtainable by application to

THE CENTRAL COUNCIL FOR HEALTH EDUCATION

1 THORNHAUGH STREET, RUSSELL SQUARE, LONDON, W.C. 1

Empire Marketing Board posters displayed in Leeds, November 1937

An informal conference in the garden of No. 10 Downing Street, between Philip Snowdon, J.H. Thomas and Wedgewood Benn, members of the second Labour government, October 1930

'Healthy children' posters displayed outside Killingbeck Hospital, Leeds, November 1939

Headed by undergraduates carrying banners, the Lancashire contingent of the hunger marchers leave Oxford for High Wycombe, 22 October 1932. Proctors and their bulldogs waited in the centre of the city to take the names of those undergraduates marching

on base wages lost in 1921 and that the cost of living addition should be altered every three months – an action which would benefit the textile workers. This action was endorsed by the National Association of Unions in the Textile Trade (NAUTT) and the matter was put to the employers who responded by suggesting that British industry was less competitive than it had been before the return to the gold standard and the reflation of the pound, and suggested that wages should be reduced by 8 per cent.[16]

The seeds of conflict were sown and, despite offers of mediation from several quarters, the employers issued notices of reduction of wages on 24 July 1925.[17] From that moment the lock-out, or standstill, in the textile trade began. It lasted just over three weeks and the immediate conflict was only resolved by the intervention of the Ministry of Labour and its Minister, Sir Arthur Steel-Maitland, who requested that the employers allow the existing wage rates to continue until a Court of Investigation, which was to be set up, reported upon the woollen and worsted textile trades. When this body, which was composed of an independent chairman and two representatives from both sides, eventually reported it suggested that there should be no change in conditions and wages in the industry.[18]

The significance of this dispute should not be lost. In the first case there were probably between 135,000 and 170,000 woollen and worsted textile workers involved in the dispute, although estimates go up to 240,000, and every union and all sections of the textile workforce were unified in the action which they took.[19] This was a remarkable achievement in an industry which was notorious for its local variation, the disunity of its workforce and the general weakness of its trade union organization. Secondly, the outcome of the dispute was seen as a victory for the workers in their attempt to prevent wages being reduced further. Even before the Court of Investigation confirmed the workers' stand, the trade unions had smelled the scent of victory. On the eve of the agreement to call off the dispute the *Yorkshire Factory Times* commented that the wage retreat had at last 'been stopped'.[20] Presumptious as this was, the feeling was abroad that government policy, as well as the employers' stand, had been defeated:

115

Wages, said Mr Baldwin, have, to be brought down. This is not simply an incautious and unconsidered statement by Mr Baldwin, a slip of the tongue: it is the settled and deliberate policy of the governing class, who have entered upon a course of action which has for its object the deliberate intensification of unemployment as a method of forcing down wages.[21]

The article even invoked the views of John Maynard Keynes as evidence of the foolishness of the government's approach.

Combined with the temporary solution of the coal crisis in 1925, which will be discussed later, the anticipated textile victory buoyed up the whole of the trades union movement. Herbert Tracey reflected that the 'defeatist' mood of the trade unions over the last few years had been transformed. Now it was felt that the General Council of the TUC had struck a blow to maintain minimum wages for all workers by its support of the woollen and worsted textile workers. But the message went further for it was felt that the lesson to be learned was that living standards could be maintained if unity prevailed: 'With the help of the Trade Union Movement, mobilized by the TUC General Council, they were enabled to secure a victory which they could not have won if they were left to fight alone.'[22] In other words they could overcome the debilitating impact of high unemployment and the government's attempts at deflation which had clearly weakened the trade union movement's powers of resistance during the early 1920s.

The moral seemed obvious: the reversal of the onslaught on wages and the defence of a minimum wage, if not the establishment of a living wage, could be secured by an alliance among unions. It was felt that if such unity could be achieved in the poorly organized wool textile trade then it was even more likely that it might be achieved in better organized industries. Indeed, the threatened coal strike of 1925, which occurred at more or less the same time, seemed to confirm this impression. There was, indeed, strong support for collective action with unions within specific industries and between the unions of all industries – something which the TUC encouraged through its new journal Trade Union Unity.

This strategy was particularly evident in the more famous coal dispute of 1925. The events which led to this began on 30 June 1925 when the coal owners decided that they would abolish the national minimum wage, cut wages by about 10 per cent in order to compensate for the government's return to the gold standard with a reflated pound, and to maintain standard profits no matter how low wages fell. The miners refused to accept such changes and the General Council of the TUC committed itself to sympathetic strike action from Friday, 31 July.

The intransigence of both coal owners and the union ensured that conflict was inevitable, and with it the threat of a wider conflict whereby the TUC would at least call for a coal embargo from its constituent unions. Faced with the immediate prospect of a serious coal dispute and fuel crisis the Baldwin government decided to provide a nine-month subsidy to the coal owners, during which time a royal commission, the Samuel Commission, would investigate the coal industry. The fact could not be hidden that the government, despite its earlier refusals, had decided to intervene to avoid serious industrial conflict. Friday 31 July 1925 henceforth became known as 'Red Friday'.

There was much euphoria among trade unionists. The results of both the wool and worsted dispute and the coal dispute convinced some that the tide of wage reductions had been changed and with it, perhaps, the course of unemployment. The *Yorkshire Factory Times*, journal of the wool and worsted textile workers, confidently predicted that the:

> General Council's action in support of the miners and wool textile workers signaled a turn in the tide, the beginning of a definite stand against the policy of wage reductions which economic conditions have enabled the employers to impose in the last four and a half years.[23]

But there were many who were under no illusion that the victory had been won and the tide had turned.

Herbert Smith, President of the Miners' Federation of Great Britain, maintained that the 1925 coal dispute had been 'an affair of outposts. It was a mere skirmish. The main battle has still to be fought and won.'[24] The Communist Party of Great Britain, whose policy at this time was one of 'All Power to the General Council', also posed a question and offered an answer:

> Thirty-four weeks to go – Thirty-four weeks to go to what? To the termination of the mining agreement and the opening of the greatest struggle in the history of the British working class. We must prepare for the struggle.[25]

In 1925, then, it appeared that the position of the trade unions and the pattern of industrial relations were about to change. On the one hand, trade unionists were increasingly confident that the period of post-war wage reductions was about to be halted, even if a battle remained to be fought. As a result there would be more employment and an improvement in the condition of working-class life. On the other hand, there remained the conviction of many employers and Baldwin's Conservative government that wages would have to be reduced in order to maintain profits and to fight international competition. It was the threatened industrial conflict of 1926, the General Strike, which promised to resolve the matter, one way or another.

General Strike, 1926

The General Strike, which lasted for nine days between 3–12 May 1926, was without doubt the most important industrial conflict of British inter-war history. It is the only instance in British industrial history when the vast majority of the organized working class have given their industrial, financial and moral support to one group of workers for any length of time. Indeed, it is the only occasion on which there has been a substantial national strike in support of any industrial group of workers in Britain. Historians have been fascinated with the event and have written extensively on its causes, meticulously recorded the events, and speculated about the conse-quences of its collapse for British industrial relations. On the fiftieth anniversary of the dispute, in 1976, several books appeared on the subject, producing a surfeit of published research to which there has since been no significant addition.[26] As a consequence of this research historians know very well the variety of factors which led to the dispute – many of them already outlined in the earlier sections of this chapter. They are very aware that the problems of the coal industry combined with the clash between government policy and the policies of the TUC ensured that there would have to be some type of conflict in 1926. They are also aware of the regional and local variations in the support for the General Strike. They disagree strongly about its consequences: was it a watershed in British industrial relations, as some Communist writers would have us believe, or did it barely change the course of TUC and trade union policy, as Gordon Phillips has argued?[27]

The main argument presented here is that the General Strike was partly, but significantly, a consequence of the determination of

118

successive governments to reduce wages, thus increasing unemployment in the short term, in the hope of strengthening the pound
and returning to the gold standard – a view which has already been
developed in Chapter 1. Secondly, it must also be appreciated that
there was substantial unity within trade union ranks and that,
despite the suspension of the strike on 12 May, the unions had
signalled their intention not to accept further wage reductions
without some resistance. In this respect it seems unlikely that
successive governments were given the opportunity to return to
normalcy in the manner which they wished. Thirdly, it is doubtful
whether the General Strike could be regarded as the watershed in
British labour history, which it is sometimes claimed to be, or that
it changed in any significant form the pattern of industrial relations.

The context within which the General Strike occurred was one in
which the Baldwin government had returned to the gold standard
and within which employers in exporting countries were faced with
the need to reduce costs, and thus wages, by about 10 per cent. This
had been the cause of the 1925 dispute, and the situation had altered
little between 31 July 1925, 'Red Friday' and 1 May 1926 when the
coal lock-out began. The only change in the intervening period had
been that the government had prepared for the threatened dispute
while the Samuel Commission deliberated about the way in which to
make the industry more efficient and profitable. The government
had divided the country into twelve divisions, circulated Circular
636 in November indicating the responsibilities of local authorities,
passed a Preservation of Public Order Act and received from the
Home Secretary, in February 1926, the statement that 'little
remained to be done before the actual occurrence of an emergency.'[28] Turning to propaganda, the government attempted to open
up the constitutional issues and the Home Secretary, Sir William
Joynson-Hicks put the matter starkly, if exaggeratedly, when he
commented, at a meeting on 2 August 1925 at Northampton that:

> I say to you, coming straight from the Cabinet councils, the thing is not
> finished. The danger is not over. Sooner or later, this questions has to be
> fought out by the people of the land. Is England to be governed by
> Parliament and the Cabinet or by a handful of trade union leaders?[29]

In comparison the trade union movement did little until the
subsidy ended on 30 April 1926, even though it was expected
that the Samuel Commission would be unable to offer a compromise

which might be agreeable to both coal owners and unions. Indeed, when the Samuel Commission reported in March 1926, it was only able to offer the then unacceptable recommendations that the 'amalgamation of small units of production is both desirable and practicable' and that miners should accept further wage reductions as a temporary measure until such reorganization occurred.[30] This was never likely to offer a basis for a wages agreement and the employers issued notices giving the reduced wage rates on 30 April and 1 May 1926, when the subsidy ran out.

In consequence, a special meeting of the TUC on 1 May 1926 undertook to support the coal miners through sympathetic industrial action, giving the General Council primary responsibility for negotiations:

> . . . provided that there was the fullest consultation between the two
> bodies in respect of any developments which might occur, and no
> settlement would be reached without the miners' consent.[31]

And for two days officials from the General Council discussed with the Government the possibility of extending the subsidy. But negotiations were broken off by the government on 3 May once the compositors at the *Daily Mail* refused to set the type for an editorial on 'For King and Country'. The General Strike began, at a minute to midnight, on 3 May 1926.

From the start, there was much confusion about who should come out on strike to support the miners. The General Council of the TUC had decided that only essential, front-line or group one, workers such as railway workers and printers should be called out. In fact, many non-essential, second line or group 2 workers such as those in textiles came out, although the General Council never called upon their services throughout the dispute. The reticence of the General Council was deliberate for it feared the violence which might ensue if all workers came out and was alarmed at the prospect of mass defections leading to the rapid collapse of the dispute if it did not immediately meet its objectives. For, they believed that

> . . . once the strike has reached its highest point . . . then we shall have
> dribblings back to work here and there, and possibly large desertions.[32]

Given the lack of clear and early advice, the General Council's policy was ignored and many second line workers came out in support of the miners. This lack of organization was compounded by the fact that many trades councils set themselves up as councils of action to run the dispute at the local level. They often came into conflict with the local Transport Committees, formed from the local branches of the main transport unions, who correctly maintained that they alone had the right to issue permits for the movement of essential items which would otherwise have been held up in the dispute. This confusion of responsibilities had forced the National Transport Committee, Unity House, London to circulate a telegram on 7 May, with the approval of the General Council, to the following effect:

> We instruct all local transport committees review permits which have been issued. No trades council or Labour Party council of action, strike committee or trade union branch has authority to deal with permits. Please convey to all concerned.[33]

In addition, there was great variation in the areas of support and the surviving local strike records offer a confusing and changing picture of strike activity. Apart from the coal areas, where sympathetic strike action was strongly evident, and the rural areas, where it was not, the rest of the country displayed immense diversity. In London, there were both areas of strong support for the strike, like Battersea, and areas where that support was extremely limited – although far fewer in number.[34] In Yorkshire, the coal areas and Halifax, Huddersfield, Skipton and many other textile towns supported the strike almost 100 per cent, while there was much less support in Bradford, Leeds and Wakefield. In the South East the unlikely towns of King's Lynn and Eastbourne were evidently strongholds of the strike while Aldershot, Maidstone, Dorking, Lowestoft and Yarmouth displayed only lukewarm interest.

The role of the government in publishing the *British Gazette*, its resort to middle-class volunteers and the use of troops obviously reduced the impact of the strike in many regions. The Economic League, formed in the winter of 1919 to 1920 in order to lead a counter-attack by British capitalism against the rise of a mass labour movement, also added greatly to the difficulties of the General Council. It was obsessionally hostile to trade unionism and Arthur McIvor has written:

During the General Strike, the League collaborated with other employers' organizations, such as the FBI, to provide information to the government on coal stocks and shortages, the availability of transport and the organization of strike-breaking operations. Indeed, regional Leagues played an active role in strike-breaking, encouraging the enrolment of volunteer workers, providing lorry drivers and transporting foodstuffs, and publishing news-sheets and leaflets attacking 'the pernicious influence of the reds'. In the coalfields, the district League organized a more sustained propaganda campaign, touring the colliery villages with 'flying squads', vilifying 'Cookism', supporting the Spencer brand of non-political company unionism and propagating the League's new slogan: 'every man is a capitalist'.[35]

There is little doubt that the effectiveness of the strike was greatly impaired by its internal difficulties and external opposition. The 400 or 500 councils of action which were formed were ridden with dispute and inefficiency. It is alleged that these problems made Leeds one of the worst organized towns in Britain.[36] Indeed, Emile Burns' survey of the councils of action, after the dispute, revealed the great extent to which they were badly organized and the degree to which in Middlesborough, for instance, 'each trade acted on its own'.[37] The capitulation of the General Council on the 12 May, and its decision to call off the strike without any guarantees that those involved would not be victimized, might also be seen as evidence of failure. But there was also much evidence of trade union unity and success.

About two million workers had come out in support of the miners, a number which represented almost half the total which the TUC could have called out in support of the miners – and more than it did. There was also a great spirit of unity among the workers and, although the statements were coloured with rhetoric, it was emphasized that at Wolverhampton, 'The whole of the workers stood firm and were prepared to fight to the bitter end' and that at Hull there was 'Alarm – fear – despair – a victorious army disarmed and handed over to its enemies.'[38] In Bradford, it was even suggested that the General Strike might be seen as a victory:

We do not say that the Government has been defeated by the General Strike, for it was not directed against the Government. But we do say that its object [has] been gained, and that after all the stir and excitement, the inconvenience . . . we are back where we wished to be, and with the miners' case under negotiation.[39]

The last comment was obviously wrong, although there remained a rather threadbare conviction that something had been achieved. This view could not easily be maintained as the evidence mounted that, despite their negotiations with Sir Herbert Samuel and the TUC's meeting with the Prime Minister on 12 May, the strike had been called off without any guarantees that those who had been involved would not be victimized by employers and that there would be no immediate resumption of negotiations between the coal miners and the coal owners. Still, there had been unity of sorts.

Little of that spirit of unity could, however, be attributed to the activities of the Communist Party. Though it claimed some influence upon the councils of action in the North East and in London, its impact was minimal. The presence of its members was normally tolerated because they supported the industrial action of the TUC, 1,200 of them being arrested during the dispute, and because some of its leading figures, such as Robin Page Arnot who did sterling work in organizing the councils of action in the North East, were active in the dispute.[40] Their influence was usually patchy and short-lived. In Yorkshire, Shipley was one of the centres of Communist activity but most of its members were arrested early on in the dispute.[41] There was also some violence when the Castleford Communists marched on Leeds, and there were several arrests of communist agitators from Castleford. Typical of these arrests was the case of Isobel Brown. The *Yorkshire Observer*, shortly after the end of the General Strike, reported:

> At Pontefract yesterday Isobel Brown, who said her last permanent address was Moscow, was committed for three months in the second division for having delivered a speech at Castleford on Wednesday likely to cause disaffection. She admitted she had come from London to gain recruits for the Communist Party, but denied any attempt to stir up strife.[42]

None of the efforts of the Communist Party amounted to anything of a significant revolutionary threat about the General Strike and it was Winston Churchill, editing the *British Gazette* for the government, who drummed up more revolutionary potential than really existed. The General Strike, a title not used by the TUC, was simply an attempt by the General Council of the TUC to support the miners against a wage reduction. A few activists might have seen it as more than that, but that was never the view of the General Council.

123

It may well be argued that the government was able to defeat the General Strike by its propaganda campaigns, the arrest of Communist activists, the use of volunteers and by sheer patience, in allowing the General Council's Negotiating Committee to spend several futile days negotiating the Samuel Memorandum in the hope that it would provide a basis for a settlement. But in the final analysis, though the TUC lost some credibility and membership, the government was never able to push forward and capitalize upon any victory it achieved. This was most evident in the fact that the provision banning sympathetic strike action in the 1927 Trade Disputes and Trade Unions Act was never tested in the courts. In many respects the whole General Strike could be seen as an inevitable development which served notice to government, employers and trade unions that each party was not to be taken lightly.

In what respect, then, can the General Strike be seen as a watershed in British industrial relations? It has been suggested by some that the government and employers were left free to reduce wages and to rationalize industry, and trade union membership did decline from 5.5 million in 1925 to about 4.8 million in 1928.[43] Railway workers and bus drivers were victimized by employers and forced to sign documents indicating their intention to leave their unions, and the miners in many districts, though by no means all, found their wages reduced in the wake of the defeat of the miners in November 1926. By the late 1920s and the early 1930s, governments were encouraging employers to rationalize coal along the lines laid down by the Samuel Commission, whereby small units would be incorporated into larger units and be closed, as in shipbuilding, cotton and other industries. It is clear that the views of the unions were ignored. Equally, employers in the wool and worsted industry, having failed to get wage reductions in 1929, forced the textile unions to accept a 9 per cent reduction in wage rates in June 1930, after a ten-week lock-out.[44] There were clear losses for the trade union movement, and a reversal of fortunes for several years, which was amplified by the deepening depression of the late 1920s and early 1930s. Nevertheless, as Gordon Phillips has argued, the pattern of trade union activity and industrial relations was not altered by the General Strike.

It should be remembered that there was no prosecution brought under the 1927 act right up to its repeal by a Labour government in

1946.[45] The decline in trade union membership, and the marked decline in strike activity were already occurring before 1926, as indicated by Table 5.1. Individual trade unions also reflected this continuous decline throughout the 1920s and early 1930s; the coal miners' union declined from 936,653 members in 1921 to 885,789 in 1925 and to 554,015 in 1932 while, for the same dates, respectively, trade union membership in the railway unions fell from 560,875 to 528,764 and 399,184.[46] There also appears to have been no let up in the determination to forge a more effective industrial alliance – even though the General Council stopped short of another general strike. In addition, the pace of wage reduction fell and only one-eighth of the amount was taken off the weekly wage bill between 1930–3 as was taken from the net weekly wage bill for 1921.[47] Also, there was little to suggest that the pattern and the style of industrial relations was greatly altered by the General Strike: the number of workers on strike and the number of days of work lost were already declining well before 1926 and there was a rise of industrial militancy in the late 1920s and early 1930s as unions attempted to resist the further wage cuts being advocated by employers.

Table 5.1 *Trade Union Membership and Rate of Unemployment, 1920–39*[48]
(thousands)

	Membership	Rate of change		Unemployment
1920	8,438	1920–1	−20.55	7.9
1921	6,633			16.9
1922	5,625			14.3
1923	5,429	1922–5	+2.12	11.7
1924	5,544			10.3
1925	5,506			11.3
1926	5,219			12.5
1927	4,919	1925–8	−12.71	9.7
1928	4,806			10.8
1929	4,858			10.4
1930	4,842			16.1
1931	4,614	1929–3	−9.59	21.3
1932	4,444			22.1
1933	4,392			19.9
1934	4,590	1933–9	+43.39	16.7
1939	6,298			10.5

Table 5.2 *Workers Directly and Indirectly Involved in Disputes and the Number of Days Lost, 1920–39*[49]

Year	Workers	Days lost	Year	Workers	Days lost
1920	1,932,000	26,568,000	1930	307,000	4,339,000
1921	1,801,000	85,872,000	1931	490,000	6,983,000
1922	552,000	19,850,000	1932	379,000	6,448,000
1923	405,000	10,672,000	1933	136,000	1,072,000
1924	613,000	8,424,000	1934	134,000	959,000
1925	441,000	7,952,000	1935	271,000	1,955,000
1926	2,750,000		1936	316,000	1,829,000
1927	108,000	1,174,000	1937	597,000	3,413.000
1928	124,000	1,388,000	1938	274,000	1,334,000
1929	533,000	8,287,000	1939	337,000	1,356,000

This is not to deny that there were not some major setbacks. The mining dispute, which had provoked the strike, continued from the end of April until November 1926, when the miners and their families were effectively starved back to work despite the financial support of those unions affiliated to the TUC. There is no denying the suffering of the mining families and the deep hatred which was further nurtured between the miners and the coal owners. The striking miners received no relief though, 'The wives did get a few shillings from the Parish Relief (which all had to be paid back when the strike ended).'[50] The younger men 'started what was called jazz bands' through which to win prizes and raise money for the strike effort.'[51] The local branches of the miners' union set up soup kitchens, with much local help from butchers and shopkeepers. But it was all to no avail. As Kenneth Maher, a miner from Caerphilly, reflected:

> Towards the end of the strike things were awful. No coal, no clothes. We were in rags and a lot of us had no shoes. I remember going with my mother and my brother to a colliery tip about four miles away. The weather was getting very cold. It took us a day to pick two buckets of tiny bits of coal. The tip had been picked clean. Then after eight months the strike collapsed in Nottinghamshire. There was a drift back to work. But in South Wales it wasn't going to be as easy as that.
> The miners went back to work completely crushed — worse off than before. The Powell Duffryn Company came into its own, buying pits up for a few thousand pounds, shutting them down, throwing hundreds out of

work. Thought for the community never entered into it. In the pits they didn't shut down they put their own breed of managers, under-managers and deputies . . . These bosses never mixed with the rest of the community, nor did their wives. They were a law unto themselves.[52]

There is no denying that the miners suffered a humiliating defeat, but was this true of the wider trade union movement?

1927–1939 – Until the 1960s historians generally accepted that the trade unions were on the retreat, relatively toothless and passive, throughout the rest of the inter-war years which followed their defeat in the General Strike. The victimization which occurred, the loss of trade union membership, and the wage reductions all seemed to confirm this impression. The calm industrial relations which occurred in 1927 and 1928 also suggested that the militancy of earlier years had evaporated in the wake of defeat. Dame Margaret Cole, for instance, suggested that the General Strike killed off the 'romantic vision of workers' control'.[53] Clearly, there were some changes and in some industries, most notably coal mining, national wage negotiations disappeared in November 1926 after the collapse of the miners' resistance to the coal lock-out, to be replaced by district agreements. This meant that wages fell sharply in the coal exporting districts of South Wales and the North East but remained the same in the new and expanding south Yorkshire coalfield, where new and deeper mines were producing high quality coal for the home market. Nevertheless, there were many signs that the unions, while still losing members, were still maintaining their resistance against wage reduction.

Neither side of industry was seeking confrontation after the General Strike, and even Baldwin's government was reluctant to pursue the draconian legislation advocated by some Conservative extremists in the autumn of 1926. Indeed, the TUC began to view the prospect of trade unions being involved with the state and the employers in running and regulating the economy. The short-lived Mond–Turner talks advocated this new spirit in industrial relations, which can be viewed as an extension of the concept of the General Council acting as representative of the whole trade union movement in national industrial matters.

These arose out of the feeling that trade unions had to become involved in other spheres of influence if they were to offset any serious injury which might befall them as a result of the General Strike. But, in addition, there arose the possibility of some common agreement with industry over the fact that the economy was being run to the advantage of the City as opposed to industry. The decision to return to the gold standard, and to operate it, often necessitated the rise of interest rates which acted as a burden upon the exporting industries just as the reflation of the pound had made exporting more difficult. By the end of 1926, the General Council was advancing the argument, with some justification, that the General Strike had only been an attempt to warn employers that the problems of industry could not constantly be tackled at the expense of the standard of living of the workers.

Such a view helped trade union leaders to think in terms of coming to some type of arrangement with industrialists who were feeling the pinch of economic policy. George Hicks was well attuned to this possible linkage when, in his presidential address to the 1927 Trade Union Congress, he asserted:

> . . . much fuller use can be made . . . of the machinery for joint consultation and negotiation between employers and employed . . . .. It is more than doubtful whether we have seen the fullest possible development of machinery for joint consultation in particular industries. And practically nothing has been done to establish effective machinery of joint conference between the representative organizations entitled to speak for industry as a whole.[54]

Within a few months, similar statements were being made by the king, Stanley Baldwin, Ramsay MacDonald, Ernest Bevin, and a whole host of trade unionists. Indeed, Ernest Bevin, speaking at a union dinner, maintained that 'if there is a new conception of the objects of industry, then there can be created in this country . . . conditions which will minimize strikes and probably make them non-existent for 25 years.'[55] By January 1928 the preparatory negotiations were going on between the TUC and the Confederation of Employers Organizations and the Federation of British Industries, the two main employers' organisations. The implacable opponents of the past were now, due to a common necessity, moving towards establishing a harmony of interests.

Sir Alfred Mond, of the Federation of British Industries, and Ben Turner, President of the General Council of the TUC, entered into discussions while their respective bodies debated their attitude to the new alliance and the proposals which were being made. The Mond–Turner talks attempted to form a common alliance between the employers and the unions on such matters as unemployment, outlining remedies such a development fund, colonial development, more liberal trade facilities, export credits, augmented pensions for those retiring at sixty-five, the raising of the school-leaving age, and, above all, 'the substitution of modern plant and techniques for existing machinery and methods' – in consultation with the unions and with 'measures . . . for safeguarding workers displaced by rationalization.'[56]

Yet, although the leaders of both sides of industry worked hard to achieve a common agreement on policies to present to the government the talks, and the influence they exerted, began to wither away after a couple of years, and did not survive into the 1930s. The worsening economic situation, and a dramatic increase in industrial conflict between 1929 and 1932, served to sour the possibility of a long-term consensus between employers and trade unionists. Nevertheless, as already suggested, wages did not decrease at the height of the slump of 1929 to 1933 at anything like the level of reductions which occurred in the early 1920s and some type of stability and balance was being established. Trade unions, despite a loss of membership and their apparently weakened position, appear to have performed more effectively after the General Strike than before – which suggests that employers were more reluctant to become embroiled in major industrial conflict and that the unions were, themselves, asserting their rights in more effective and varied ways. The defeat of the TUC in the General Strike did not have the disastrous impact which trade unionists feared. On the contrary, unions appear to have been more effective and even the loss of trade union membership may be a consequence of the inability of the unemployed trade unionists to pay their unions fees rather than due to a loss of sympathy with the unions.

Trade unions, in fact, did rather well during the 1930s. Professor H.A. Clegg has examined the reasons for this in the early 1930s and suggested that employers were not well organized at this time and that there were fewer jobs being lost in the early 1930s than in the early 1920s. In a particularly perceptive passage, he captures the essence of the problem faced by many employers:

Most firms in most industries were not facing disastrous losses, nor even the prospect of disastrous losses. The worst hit firms might decide that they must have a reduction in pay in order to stay in business. Their colleagues, or enough of them, might agree that a reduction in labour costs would improve their prospects too, so that negotiations with the unions could begin. However, when the unions proved reluctant to make concessions, the employers would have to contemplate the possibility of a lockout. Those who were not hard pressed and in no immediate danger of running at a considerable loss might have no strong incentive to vote in favour of a course which threatened them with heavy losses in the immediate future. The conditions of 1930–3 were unfavourable to unity among employers.[57]

Trade unions were in fact in a much stronger position in 1933 than they had been in 1921 or 1922. There had been many amalgamations, the Transport and General Workers and many other large unions had absorbed small unions to form a formidable barrier to employers, there was less interunion rivalry and the authority of the General Council of the TUC was accepted and practically unchallenged. Such Communist opposition that existed, as among the London busmen in the Transport and General Workers, had been marginalized by the post 1926 attempts to remove Communists from trade unions and from trades councils.[58]

By the late 1930s the trade union movement was, in fact, recapturing its lost membership. As indicated in Table 5.1, trade union membership rose by 43.34 per cent between 1933 and 1939, at a time when the economy began to recover and when unemployment was falling. But even more important than that was the fact that trade unions were now exercising new areas of influence and were better organized. In particular, they exerted more power within the Labour Party, were increasingly respected by the National government, and were moving towards the reduction of interunion rivalry.

Trade unions exerted a considerable influence upon the Labour Party, especially after the introduction of the new Labour constitution of 1918. They held a majority of seats on the National Executive Committee. However, they chose not to use their power to interfere too obviously with the policy decisions of the Labour Party and left Ramsay MacDonald to lead his parliamentary colleagues more or less as he wished. There was also a National Joint Council, which brought together representatives of the General Council the National Executive Committee of the Labour Party and the Parliamentary Labour Party, to act as a co-ordinating body for the Labour movement. In fact it rarely met in the 1920s. But the position began to alter after the General Strike, when the trade unions began to take a more dominant role in Labour politics. The National Joint Council, which was renamed the National Council of Labour in 1934, acquired a new constitution, whereby the General Council was allowed as many representatives as the other two organisations. Throughout the 1930s, Ernest Bevin was the dominant figure on this body as he was at Labour Party conferences, shaping Labour's domestic and foreign policy. It was he who, as we shall see, ultimately replaced George Lansbury as the leader of the party with Attlee and who got the Labour Party to move from its general support of peace and pacifism towards the need to prepare to meet the threat of war with European fascism.

All three National governments, which operated under the premiership of J. Ramsay MacDonald (1931–5), Stanley Baldwin (1935–37) and Neville Chamberlain (1937–40), displayed increasing respect for the trade unions in the 1930s. This was reflected in many ways. For instance, Ramsay MacDonald offered knighthoods to both Arthur Pugh and Walter Citrine, in respect of their work for trade unionism. Both accepted what might have been regarded as a rather dubious honour. By the late 1930s, the TUC was being drawn into discussions with the government and textile unions were drawn into the task of reorganizing the cotton industry, through the Acts of 1936 and 1939.[59]

Also, the amalgamation of unions which occurred at a rapid pace throughout the inter-war years greatly improved the organization and effectiveness of the trade union movement as the years progressed. But one of the most significant developments in inter-union relations was the 'Bridlington Agreement' passed at the TUC Congress in 1939, which laid down that no union should attempt to organize workers at any industrial establishment where another union was already represented and negotiated on behalf of the majority of the workers.

Conclusion

Unemployment posed serious problems for the British trade union movement during the early 1920s. Wages fell rapidly and the unions, despite their involvement in many long and protracted

131

disputes were unable to staunch the outward flow of members and funds or to stave off the savage monetary wage cuts which occurred. Ironically, the situation changed remarkably after the General Strike. Far from being the moment when British trade unionism all but collapsed, the General Strike – even though there were other factors at play – sounded a warning to employers that trade unions would resist further wage incursions and that the cost of too muscular an industrial policy could be high. Thereafter, despite the high unemployment years between 1929 and 1932, trade union membership remained remarkably resilient and recovered sharply during the improving trade situation of the late 1930s and trade unions were drawn more centrally into negotiation with national employers negotiations and with the National government. Unemployment, therefore, exerted a powerful, but short-lived, impact upon trade unions and the pattern of industrial relations. While the General Strike might be viewed as a watershed by some historians who feel that the trade union position worsened considerably after 1926, this was clearly not the case; trade unions were less frequently attacked by employers after 1926 than before and the pace of wage reductions slowed considerably. However, there was no change in the strategy and policies adopted by the General Council of the TUC. The purpose behind the formation of the General Council continued to be the need to unite trade unions into an industrial alliance to defend the wages and conditions of workers. The General Strike in no way deflected it from that course and it is difficult to see that event as an historical watershed in the evolution of trade union policies and attitudes. What is remarkable about the inter-war years is the consistency of trade union policies and the forthright manner with which the General Council pursued its intention of forging an effective industrial alliance between its member unions. There were no sudden changes in direction even though employers and government began to modify their attitudes towards trade unions in such a way as to encourage negotiations at the highest level. Far from bringing about the denouement of inter-war trade unionism, the General Strike reasserted, in the fullest form possible, the potential power of trade unionism. It had a cathartic effect upon government and employers and permitted the working classes at least to protect, if not improve, their standard of living.

NOTES

1. B. & S. Webb, *The History of Trade Unionism* (London, 1920 edn.), p. 635.
2. Interview with Mr Scott, a Scottish miner, about the General Strike, conducted by Dr K. Laybourn and Mr J. Popps, May 1979, a copy of which is deposited in Huddersfield Polytechnic Library.
3. *Society for the Study of Labour History, Bulletin*, 34, Spring 1977, pp. 14–15.
4. *Coal Industry Commissioners Report*, cmnd 359, 1919.
5. Named after J.H. Whitley, MP for Halifax and the Speaker of the House of Commons.
6. *Yorkshire Factory Times*, 23 July 1925.
7. Ibid., 28 May 1925, quoting Ben Turner writing in the *Textile Record*, the journal of the National Union of Textile Workers, deposited in the NUTW collection, Archives Department, Huddersfield Central Library.
8. Copies of the printed manifesto are to be found in many of the boxes and bundles of the Amalgamated Union of Dyers' collection at Bradford Archives Department and in the National Union of Textile Workers' collection in Archives Department, Huddersfield Central Library. Also *Yorkshire Factory Times*, 23 July 1925.
9. Quoted C.L. Mowat, *Britain between the Wars* (London, Methuen, 1968 ed.), p. 34.
10. *Hansard*, 18 August 1919.
11. Quoted in P. Renshaw, *The General Strike* (London, Eyre Methuen, 1975), p. 87.
12. J.A. Jowitt and K. Laybourn, 'The Wool Textile Dispute of 1925', *The Journal of Regional and Local Studies*, vol. 2, no. 1, Spring 1982, p. 13.
13. G.A. Phillips, *The General Strike: The Politics of Industrial Conflict* (London, Weidenfeld and Nicolson, 1976), chapter III.
14. Ibid., p. 16.
15. Ibid., p. 13.
16. Amalgamated Union of Dyers, Huddersfield collection, box 2; National Union of Textile Workers Executive Committee Meeting, Memorandum, E.C. 14/249, 4 April 1925; Amalgamated Union of Dyers, Bradford Collection, 126 D77/192, National Wool (and Allied) Textile Industrial Council, Minutes, Memorandum IC 196, 18 May 1925 and Memorandum I C, 197, 198 and 201.
17. Jowitt and Laybourn, op.cit., p. 15.
18. *Yorkshire Factory Times*, 19 November 1925 and the National Association of Unions in the Textile Trades, *Report of the Court of Investigations concerning the wages position in the Wool Textile Trade* (Northern Counties), Bradford, n.d.
19. *Yorkshire Factory Times*, 30 July and 6 August 1925.
20. Ibid., 13 August 1925.
21. Ibid.
22. Ibid., 27 August 1925.
23. Idem.

24. C. Farman, *The General Strike, May 1926* (London, Rupert Hart-Davis, 1972), pp. 28–9.
25. *Workers' Weekly*, 28 August 1925.
26. Most notably, G.A. Phillips, op. cit.; M. Morris, *The General Strike* (London, Journeyman Press, 1976 and 1980), and J. Skelley (ed.), *1926: The General Strike* (London, Lawrence and Wishart, 1976), added to earlier books by Renshaw, op.cit., and Farman, op. cit., and M. Morris, *The British General Strike 1926*, (London, Historical Association), G 82, 1973.
27. Phillips, op.cit., ch. xiii.
28. Cabinet conclusions, 44 (25), 23/50, 316–17, 7 August 1925.
29. Farman, op.cit., p.29.
30. *Report of the Royal Commission on the Coal Industry* (1925), vol. 1, Report, ch. xxii, Summary of Findings and Recommendations, p. 233–4.
31. Report of Special Conference of Trade Union Executives, 29 April–1 May 1926.
32. Lord Citrine, *Men and Work: an Autobiography* (London, 1964), p. 196.
33. Copies of the telegram are to be found in many collections, including the strike records of the Liverpool Council of Action.
34. Morris, *General Strike*, pp.39–43.
35. A. McIvor, 'Essay in Anti-Labour History', *Society for the Study of Labour History, Bulletin*, Vol. 53, part 1, 1988, p. 21.
36. T. Woodhouse, 'The General Strike in Leeds', *Northern History*, vol. xviii, 1982, pp. 252–62.
37. Emile Burns, Councils in Action (1927).
38. Quoted in Farman, op.cit., p. 237.
39. *Bradford Pioneer*, 14 May 1926.
40. *The Socialist Worker*, 6 June 1926.
41. D.A. Wilson, 'Personal Reminiscences from Bradford', in J. Skelley (ed.) *1926: The General Strike*, pp. 352–9; *Yorkshire Observer*, 15 May 1926 reporting the raid on the Shipley Communist Club.
42. *Yorkshire Observer*, 8 May 1926.
43. Look at Table 5.1.
44. *Bradford Pioneer*, 23 May 1930.
45. H. Phelps Brown, *The Origins of Trade Union Power* (Oxford, Oxford University Press, 1986), p. 91.
46. Phillips, op.cit., p.283.
47. H.A. Clegg, *A History of British Trade Unions since 1889*, vol. II, 1911–1933, pp. 526–30.
48. Phillips, op.cit., p.281.
49. Ibid., p. 287.
50. N. Gray, *The Worst of Times: An Oral History of the Great Depression in Britain* (Totowa, New Jersey, 1985), p. 28.
51. Ibid., p. 29.
52. Ibid., pp. 29–30.
53. Look at note 3.
54. Trade Union Congress, Report, 1927, pp. 66–7.
55. Transport and General Workers, Record, January 1927, quoted in Clegg, op.cit., p. 464.

56. Clegg, op.cit., p. 466.
57. Ibid., p. 528.
58. The 'Black Circular' of 1934 attempted to get trades councils to exclude Communist delegates from their meetings.
59. H. Pelling, *A History of British Trade Unionism* (London, Pelican, 1973 ed.), p. 208.

CHAPTER 6

SOCIAL CLASS AND INEQUALITY

George Orwell wrote, at the beginning of the Second World War, that:

> There is no question about the inequality of wealth in England. It is grosser than in any European country and you have only to look down the nearest street to see it. Economically, England is certainly two nations, if not three or four. But at the same time the vast majority of the people find themselves to be a single nation and are conscious of resembling one another more than they resemble foreigners. Patriotism is usually stronger than class-hatred and always stronger than any kind of internationalism. Except for a brief moment in 1920 (the Hands off Russia movement) the British working class have never thought or acted internationally. For two and a half years they watched their comrades in Spain slowly strangled, and never aided them by even a single strike. But when their own country (the country of Lord Nuffield and Montague Norman) was in danger, their attitude was very different.[1]

His main point was that the marked differences in income and wealth persisted between the social classes throughout the inter-war years had provoked little animus and a remarkably timid response from the working class. This indignant representative of the impoverished upper classes sought explanations in terms of patriotism, the indifference of the working class and the upward and downward extension of the middle class which began to smudge the divide between traditional class divisions. But it should be remembered that his was an extremely impassioned and subjective response of a man who had fought in Spain, toured some of the depressed North and committed himself to the increasing intellectual and left-wing policies of the Independent Labour Party.[2] But how justified were Orwell's complaints? Was inequality of income and wealth still gross? How did the high level of unemployment affect the pattern of income and wealth? Did the working class accept their circumstances without demur? Were class barriers collapsing? How did the life of the working class, and other social classes, change?

The Distribution of Wealth and Income

There is little evidence suggesting that unemployment and the poor economic conditions did undermine the overall economic position of the working class during the inter-war years, although monetary wages were reduced constantly until the mid-1930s and wages did decline as a proportion of home-produced income during the early and mid-1930s. After an initial successful assault on wages by employers in the early 1920s, the trade unions revealed remarkable resilience in staving off wage reductions after the General Strike, as has already been suggested. In addition, there were some significant increases in the proportion of income going to the salary earners, suggesting the growth of the service and professional section of society, and a general worsening of the position of those who relied upon profits in the 1920s and early 1930s. There was a similar gradual change in the distribution of wealth, but, as Orwell suggested, the inequalities of wealth remained gross.

Table 6.1 *Percentage of all Wealth Owned by the Top 1 per cent and the Top 10 per cent of Individuals*[3]

		%	
Top 1 per cent	1911–13	69	(Stevenson)
		65.5	(Phillips & Maddock)
	1924–30	60	(Stevenson)
	1936	59.5	(Phillips & Maddock)
	1936–8	55	(Stevenson)
Top 10 per cent	1911–13	90	(Phillips & Maddock)
	1936	88	(Phillips & Maddock)

Table 6.2 *Distribution of Home-Produced Income, 1911–35*[4]

	1911 %	1913 %	1929 %	1931 %	1932 %	1933 %	1934 %	1935 %
Wages	39.5	42.1	41.8	42.8	42.3	42.0	41.5	40.5
Salaries	15.6	25.4	26.6	27.8	28.3	28.0	26.5	25.0
Profits	33.8	25.1	23.1	19.5	18.8	19.8	22.4	25.4
Rents	11.1	7.4	8.5	9.9	10.4	10.2	9.6	9.1

Table 6.3 *Higher Income and Price Level, 1913–37*[5]

Year	No. of persons earning above £5,000	No. with incomes exceeding £100,000	Income of 10,000th person	Cost of living index (1938=100)
1913	13,664	75	6,170	63
1921	28,803	206	10,410	142
1929	29,846	166	9,986	95
1932	22,953	95	8,166	84
1934	19,713	65	7,459	80
1937	26,114	99		

The fact is that the rich retained most of their income and wealth, although there was, quite clearly, some transference of wealth and income from the very rich to the middling rich sections, as indicated in Table 6.3. W.D. Rubinstein has demonstrated, the rich managed to protect and retain most of their wealth and income despite the more democratic nature of society in the twentieth century and the challenge posed by two Labour governments during the inter-war years.[6] The great landowners, such as the Bedfords, Derbys and Sutherlands kept their high position in the realms of the landed rich, despite the decline of inter-war agriculture, and the Roths-childs and the Sterns consolidated their financial position through their work in the City of London. The immediate post-war gloom about the decline of the landed families, as sales of landed property reached a crescendo in the early 1920s proved to be ill-founded, even though the Duke of Rutland and other landed aristocrats, did dispose of substantial parts of their estates.[7] Notwithstanding such erosion, landed wealth showed remarkable resilience and several landed estates were proved at more than £2 million during the inter-war years; the eighth Duke of Northumberland, for instance, leaving more than £2,500,000 in 1930.[8]

Yet, although there remained gross, indeed obscene, inequality in the distribution of wealth, substantial social changes were occurring. Indeed, the changing economic conditions and unemployment did help to alter the balance of social classes and some of the experience of class life. Although much remained unaltered, there is no denying that some significant changes were occurring.

The Classes

Orwell was not alone in observing that England was two, three or four nations; J.B. Priestley had already made much the same observation in his *English Journey*. Priestley's famous observations focused upon the differences between the England of 'cathedrals and minsters', industrial England, and the new post-war England of 'arterial and bypass roads, of filling stations and factories that look like exhibition buildings.'[9] In effect, he suggested that the social and economic divisions were more than ones of mere occupational group. There were clear regional and local distinctions, with their variable impact on economic prosperity, which imposed themselves upon the income, cultural and status divisions which had emerged in the nineteenth century and persisted into the twentieth. Yet, though the concept of class is vague, with social and economic divisions acting only imperfectly to distinguish social groups, the major occupational categories persisted in giving a sufficient basis for social distinction during the inter-war years, even though many differences between social classes were blurred at the margins. Indeed, this lack of distinctiveness owed something to the changes which had occurred during the inter-war years.

In 1934, there were 8,600,000 families, about 73.5 per cent of the total number of families in Britain, living on less than £4 per week.[10] Six million of these families were estimated to earning less than £100 per annum – a very low figure indeed considering that the nation's provision for a family of five in 1935 was 29s 3d (£1 46p) from the Unemployment Assistance Board and 36s (£1 80p) in 1936 – giving an annual income of between £74 and £90 per annum. The majority of these were members of the traditional working class, employed in the staple industries of mining, textiles, shipbuilding, iron and steel and engineering. They represented about half the total number of families of the country and more than 60 per cent of the population, and were those which were most afflicted by the economic ravages of the inter-war years. It was from this section of society that the bulk of the unemployed came. It was they who were scrutinized by Orwell, the Pilgrim Trust and other social investigators. Boyd Orr's malnourished population was drawn almost entirely from this section of the working class and it was their lives which changed little during the inter-war years as Carl Chinn, and other writers have noted. Although, as suggested earlier, their standard of living was higher it had been before 1914 their social position and status remained unchanged.

The children of this section of society were still, as already noted, subject to infant mortality rates at least twice as high as those for the children of the middle classes. In addition, they rarely had the opportunity to escape their environment for they were rarely educated beyond the age of fourteen, the statutory minimum age established by the Fisher Education Act of 1918. The Hadow Report of 1926, which dealt with the education of the adolescent, paved the way for the school-leaving age to be raised to fifteen and contemplated the possibility of secondary education for all, on the basis of the tripartite system accepted by the 1944 Education Act. Yet it should be remembered that the school-leaving age was not actually raised until after the Second World War and that the suggestion that they should receive secondary education was tainted by the official assumption that the children of the working class were innately less intelligent than their middle-class brethren. Indeed post-elementary Hadow schools into which many of them were moved into after 1926 were offering much the same education as the old elementary schools had offered for those children between the ages of eleven and fourten before 1926. Little had changed, and the school conditions and the opportunities for working-class children to do well were always subject to environmental limitation.

Ellen Wilkinson referred to this situation in her history of Jarrow. She particularly noted the squalid condition of many schools. Emphasizing the parsimony of the government and the the economic impact of poverty she wrote:

> There are things which cannot be done even with a 4s 5d education rate when that only produces £22,000, and when, even with the Government grant, there is only £75,000 to spend. The elementary school buildings are out of date and some are insanitary . . . Several of them have not yet got

electric light, which makes modern developments, like school films, impossible. In many the class-rooms are simply partitioned cubicles in what used to be a large hall . . . The sanitary and washing arrangements are primitive . . . The Board of Education will not pay more than 20 per cent. towards the cost of renovating old schools. It is impossible for Jarrow to raise the 80 per cent or the amount needed for new schools; so the children will continue to suffer . ..

In 1936 a survey of Jarrow elementary school children was undertaken by an educational psychologist . . . Her conclusion was that 20.6 of the children were of high intelligence for whom special provision should be made in central or secondary schools. No average for the country is available for comparison, but compared with other areas where similar surveys have been made this figure is regarded as a high one. Unfortunately only 8 per cent of the children can go on to higher [secondary] education.[11]

In many cases, the parents of the brighter children wished them to go to the secondary school in Jarrow, an overcrowded building housing about 400 pupils in which good scholarship results were achieved, but there were serious difficulties facing their children:

To do home lessons on the edge of the table on an overcrowded kitchen is not helpful to concentration on a mathematical problem. The Headmaster in an interview said rather surprisingly that he considered this a greater handicap than any actual malnutrition among secondary pupils.[12]

As a consequence of the difficulties of poverty in which many working-class children were raised, education did not often provide an escape route for them and many, particularly in towns like Jarrow, faced the prospect of juvenile unemployment.

It was this working-class section of society who lived in poor rented, often slum, accommodation, were subject to serious ill-health, and denied the possibility of holidays. Their entertainment, as Ross McKibbin has stressed, came from gambling on horse racing, a feature of working-class financial commitment which never appears in the working-class budgets gathered by social investi-gators. As McKibbin stresses:

Mass betting was the most successful example of working-class self-help in the modern era. It was at every stage of proletarian institutions and bore all the characteristics of the British working class. Although illegal it was almost entirely honest.[13]

141

The aspirations of the working class were narrow; they simply wanted to escape their immediate poverty and to secure some basic improvements in life. As one housewife explained:

> . . . if I won bigger money, I should go in for a new house, which would be built to our own idea, so that we could get a bigger scullery . . . .. Why do they build such small sculleries which make washday a dread.[14]

In short, it was the poorer sections of the working class who were trapped in poverty with little prospect of escape. It was they whose immediate vision was one of attempting to escape from the grind of poverty, and whose children were confined to the lowest levels of education offered in the elementary schools and the secondary, or 'post-Hadow', schools.

Ellen Wilkinson, with the passion of a true crusader who had become an MP for Jarrow, captured the essence of the life of this section of the working class when she wrote:

> Bad housing, overcrowding, underfeeding, low wages, for any work that is going, household incomes cut to the limit by public assistance, or Means Test or whatever is the cutting machine of the time . . . these mean disease and premature death. No goodwill speeches, no glowing perorations about 'the patience of our people under misfortune' alter the plain fact that if people have to live and bear and bring up children in bad houses on too little food, their resistance to disease is lowered and they die before they should. Their babies die too, at an unnecessary and an easily-preventible high rate.[15]

She further examined the appalling rented accommodation in which the working class were forced to live:

> No money spent by the tenants or Council on insecticides seemed able to keep down the swarming beetles in rotting woodwork. The roofs leaked, the walls were damp. Paper hung away in long strips. In some houses the fire grate was loose in the wall and looked liable to fall away at any moment . . . perhaps when full of live coals and with a pan of boiling water.[16]

It is true that some of these poorer working class families were moved into council houses but, as Orwell, M'Gonigle and others have noted, the high rents and rates tended to reduce their living standards and death rates remained high because of lack of income.[17] Poverty surveys were directed at this section of the working class.

Yet, while the traditional working class had little prospect of improving their economic and social opportunities, this was not so for the two and a half million or so families whose income varied between £2 and £4 per week. Indeed, once families were earning over £3 per week in the Midlands and the South East, where the car industry and the new consumer industries were developing, they had the prospect of a much improved standard of living and a significant improvement in their life opportunities. With this went the prospect of renting better housing, of buying the new consumer items, and for those on £4, with small families, the prospect of buying their own semi-detached houses – although it was manual workers who earned more than £4 who were likely to do that. They might even enjoy an annual seaside holiday week. Most certainly these were the sections of the working class who were beginning to benefit from the trend towards paid holidays, which was eventually formalized, after the Amulree Report, and the Holidays with Pay Act of 1938.

Arthur Exell, who worked at Morris Radiators, supplying components for Morris Motors at Cowley in the 1930s, has recorded his experiences as a working man in a new and expanding Morris Motors.[18] There were obviously difficulties at first, when there were no trade unions and 'the factory was run by a mixture of tyranny, favouritism and paternalism'.[19] But pay was good. The sheet metal workers, who cut sheet metal to the design of the drawings of the part of a car, earned 2s 6d (12p) per hour, and did a lot of overtime at one and a quarter time, which means that many of them would have been earning £6 or £7 per week, and be well over the arbitrary divide of £4 suggested as a line for the divide between the working class and the middle class. The polishers, and several other groups could also reach that level of pay. But below these skilled aristocrats of labour were men in the press shop, who would design a press to mass produce a part, and others who would more likely earn 1s 6d per hour, or less, based upon a piece-work arrangement. Even with overtime £3 15s to £4 would be about their maximum weekly pay. Although Exell's reminiscences are coloured by the fact that he was an active Communist and trade unionist, they cannot hide the fact that the pay in the new industries was generally good when compared with the majority of the working classes – and very high in periods of prosperity.

The situation of these workers was very little different from that of the members of the middle classes and, indeed, many of them, in income terms alone, were, from time to time, effectively within that social category. By 1934 there were about 2,500,000 families, or 21.3 per cent of the total, who might be regarded as middle class, based upon the criterion of £4 to £10 per week. At the worst they were little better off than the best paid sections of the working class and at the best they were able to afford a distinctively different education for their children and adopt a lifestyle which aped their financial betters.

Their ranks had been much augmented by the expansion of the salaried sector – managers, clerks, school teachers and civil servants. During the 1920s their proportion of the home-produced income had increased, though it dipped in the 1930s owing to the salary cuts imposed on teachers and civil servants in the wake of the 1931 financial crisis.

It was middle classes who were the major beneficiaries of the economic and social changes which occurred during the inter-war years. In the 1920s their financial position improved and, despite the reductions of income in the 1930s, the cheap money policy which followed the abandonment of the gold standard and the move to protection, permitted them to obtain cheap mortgages to buy the thousands of three-bedroomed semi-detached houses which were being built in the South and the Midlands at between £400 and £450.[20] It was they who bought the new consumer items produced by the new industries and who, as already suggested, were the first to practice family limitation on a significant scale. In education, it was the children of the middle classes who took about three-quarter of the places at grammar schools.

At the peak of economic and social wealth and position were the upper classes, the 617,000, or 5.2 per cent, of families who earned £10 or more per week and often gained their income from profits and rents. At the bottom end of the scale this category could include high salaried officials. At the top it included the wealthiest landowners and industrialists in the land, such as Edward A. Guinness, brewer, who died in 1927 and left £13.5 million and Sir John R. Ellerman, shipowner and financier, who died in 1933 leaving £36.7 million.[21] To this social category, good housing, and a good grammar school or public school education for their children, presented no problem. It was the upper classes who sent 60,000

144

children to public school every year and who did not recognize the need to control family size in the way in which the middle classes did.

During the inter-war years their fortunes had fluctuated a little, dipping in the 1920s, but by the 1930s their incomes were expanding again. In addition, there was some distribution within the income range towards the middling rich, earning between £5,000 to £10,000, rather than the very rich, as indicated in Table 6.3, although this middling category were clearly affected by the economic crisis of the early 1930s when their profits and rents were probably affected greatly by the Wall Street Crash and the ensuing impact upon industry and finance throughout the world economy.

Some of Orwell's complaints were clearly justified. The inequality of wealth and income was still gross, although the rise of unemployment does not appear to have worsened the position of the working classes. There were clearly changes occurring, and the borderlines between social classes, never very clear at the best of times, were probably less precise than they had been before the First World War – though class barriers were by no means collapsing in the real world of health, education and social opportunity. But did the working class accept their continued relatively poor conditions without demur?

Class Conflict

Orwell felt that, by and large, the working class accepted their circumstances without seriously attempting to improve them. In other words, class conflict was limited. Yet other commentators have stressed the degree of class conflict evident in the General Strike of 1926 and the hunger marches of the 1930s. Which picture is correct? Was there a high level or a low level of class conflict during the inter-war years?

The problem with Orwell is that he could only think of class conflict in terms of major insurrectionary conflict. There has been no time in British history when this has ever occurred, although from time to time insurrectionary events, such as the Jacobite risings and Chartism, have appeared to threaten the Establishment. As already stressed, the National Unemployed Workers' Movement and, its mentor, the Communist Party of Great Britain, failed to find the revolutionary spirit which they felt was being dampened and re-channelled by the Labour Party. The fact is that class conflict provided little or no revolutionary potential in Britain and that apathy was far more potent a force among the British working class than action. The political ambitions of the working class had normally been channelled through parliamentary and constitutional routeways. Therefore, while there was support for hunger marches and the General Strike, there was nearly always an emphasis placed upon the constitutional nature of such conflict and, in any case, the working-class interests were always operated through the trade unions to the Labour Party, which emphasized its acceptance of parliamentary politics. Given the parliamentary situation which existed, when Labour governments were minority ones in the House of Commons, and when the National government could not seriously be challenged in the 1930s, it is hardly surprising that working-class protest exerted a marginal impact upon the distribution of wealth and income in Britain. The parliamentary straightjacket which the Labour Party had placed itself in was inimical to violent change.

It should also be recognized that the working class was an extremely diverse social group and that it was fragmented and variegated. One should not expect it to have operated in a unified or uniform manner. And, of course, it rarely did. Yet, there was demur at the problems which inequality caused, even though it was rarely effective.

Conclusion

Orwell's general contention is clearly correct – inequalities of wealth and income persisted and remained marked during the inter-war years. Nevertheless, there were changes and social class divisions may have become more blurred. And, above all the working class acquired for itself a political party, the Labour Party, to improve its position. Though Labour's success was limited to, and by, its parliamentary approach, it used its enhanced relationship with the working classes to develop, particularly in the 1930s, policies to deal with the unemployed, fascism and the Spanish Civil War. This strengthened bond gave new meaning to politics in the age of unemployment.

NOTES

1. G. Orwell, 'England Your England', in *Inside the Whale and Other Essays* (Harmondsworth, Penguin, 1974), p. 73.
2. He joined the Independent Labour Party after returning from the Spanish Civil War.
3. J. Stevenson, *British Society 1914–1945* (Harmondsworth, Penguin, 1984), p. 330; G.A. Phillips and R.T. Maddock, *The Growth of the British Economy* (London, George Allen & Unwin, 1973), p. 96.
4. Mainly drawn from C.L. Mowat, *Britain between the Wars 1918–1940* (London, Methuen, 1968 reprint). p. 492.
5. Ibid., p. 494.
6. W. D. Rubinstein, *Men of Property* (London, Croom Helm, 1981); W.D. Rubinstein, 'Wealth, Elites and Class Structure of Modern Britain', *Past and Present*, 76, August 1971.
7. Stevenson, op.cit., p. 332. The Duke of Belvoir estate (28,000 acres) was sold for £1,500,000.
8. Rubinstein, op.cit., p. 202.
9. J.B. Priestley, *English Journey*, pp. 398–404.
10. Mowat, op.cit., p. 490.
11. E. Wilkinson, *The Town that Was Murdered* (London, Gollancz, 1939). pp. 255–6.
12. Ibid., p. 257.
13. R. McKibbin, 'Working-Class Gambling in Britain 1880–1939', *Past and Present*, 82, February 1979, p. 172.
14. Ibid., p. 162, quoting from J. Hilton, *Why I Go in For the Pools* (London, 1936), p. 26.
15. Wilkinson, op.cit., p. 236.
16. Ibid., p. 246.
17. G.C.M. M'Gonigle and J. Kirby, *Poverty and Public Health* (London, Gollancz, 1936), particularly ch. xv, pp. 264–75.
18. A. Exall, 'Morris Motors in the 1930s: Part I', *History Workshop*, 6, Autumn 1978, pp. 52–78.
19. Ibid., p. 52.
20. The mortgage rate was reduced from 6 per cent in September 1932 to 4.5 per cent in April 1935. The cost of a mortgages, for both 16 and 25 years, fell accordingly. By 1935 a 4.5 per cent mortgage, spread over 25 years, cost 11s 3d (about 56p) per month for every £100 borrowed. Those borrowing £500 for a large semi-detached or small detached house would be faced with monthly payments of £2 14s 9d (£2 74p) per month. This would represent between one-sixth and about one-fifteenth of the gross monthly income of the middle classes. Compared with the comparative cost of home ownership today, the cost of new housing in the 1930s was cheap.
21. Rubinstein, *Men of Property*, p. 44.

SECTION III:
POLITICS IN THE AGE OF UNEMPLOYMENT

CHAPTER 7

PARTIES AND GOVERNMENTS

Unemployment dominated British politics during the inter-war years. Every election, apart from the one in 1918, was fought over the problems of the unemployed – and even the 'coupon' election of 1918 focused upon the debate concerning the need for social reform. The problems which unemployment presented to political parties and governments have already been outlined; the dramatic high-points being the collapse of the second Labour government in August 1931 and the abandonment of the gold standard in September 1931. But what is not often appreciated is that unemployment, and its attendant social problems, helped to reshape the political balance of power of the age and was an important factor in the creation of a new two-party system in which the Labour Party replaced the Liberal Party as the progressive force of British politics in opposition to the almost omnipotent Conservative Party.

Historians have been divided as to the reasons for the political changes of these years. Some have maintained that the Liberal Party was being rapidly undermined before the First World War and that its decline was almost inevitable, others, however, assume that it was the First World War which was responsible for the decline of a vapid Liberal Party – the divisions within Liberal ranks creating the political vacuum into which the Labour Party slipped. Whichever view is accepted, most historians believe that the new political structure of the inter-war years was largely determined by 1918, and the unemployment of the inter-war years is not crucial to either explanation of the structural changes which occurred in British politics. Yet unemployment undoubtedly helped to speed up the Liberal decline and Labour rise since it highlighted the rigidity of the immediate post-war Liberal Party which was clearly unwilling to adapt its policies and ideas on free trade to the new demands of the age. The new advanced economic policies of the Lloyd George Liberals, which emerged in the late 1920s, were developed too late to arrest or reverse the Liberal decline.

The political transformation of Britain was dramatic. The Conservative Party, in various guises, was in government for eighteen out of a possible twenty-one years. During the 1920s and early 1930s, the Labour Party was its serious challenger, to the extent that the Conservative Party was forced to offer social reform in order to meet that challenge. The Liberal Party, no longer a serious political challenger by the late 1920s, meandered through the inter-war years in a state of deep division and shock.

The fundamental political changes of the inter-war years were probably inevitable by 1918, though their pace may have been determined by the level of unemployment and the extent of social and economic reform. Yet many questions remain. The problem of historians is to analyse the reasons and the precise timing of the changes. At what point did the Labour Party take over from the Liberal Party as the second party of government? How seriously did the Conservative Party take the Labour challenge? And, in focussing upon the events of the inter-war years, precisely how important was unemployment in shaping the political changes which occurred?

The Labour Party

Historians have long debated the reasons for the rise of the Labour Party. As indicated above, at one extreme, some believe that its emergence was entirely due to the internecine conflict of the Liberal Party during the First World War, occasioned by David Lloyd George's replacement of Asquith as Prime Minister in 1916.[1] It is argued that the vacuum which this created permitted the Labour Party to emerge. Its development is therefore regarded, by some, as a mere accident of war. At the other extreme, many historians believe that the Labour Party had simply inherited working-class support from the Liberals owing to the fact that trade unions had changed their allegiance when it became obvious that only an independent Labour Party would act in their interests. This second group of historians would therefore argue that the Labour Party was emerging before 1900, and certainly not later than the famous Taff Vale case of 1900 and 1901 – when trade unions appeared to lose the right to strike without facing the threat of financial penalties.[2] Thereafter, they believe that the growth of Labour was practically inexorable given the political circumstances of the times – aided by the increase in the electorate from seven to twenty-one million, following the introduction of the 1918 Franchise Act. The former view tends to ignore the fact that the Labour Party was deeply-rooted in trade-union politics before 1914, while the latter over-looks the great potential which the war had for destroying old values and arrangements.

Although the two main explanations of Labour's growth will remain irreconcilables, the fact remains that the Labour Party did emerge to become the second party in the political system by 1922, and a party of government by 1924. Its rapid post-war development was based upon its close association with trade unionism, already firmly established before 1914, and it seems likely that the First World War simply speeded up the process of political change. It is also fair to suggest that the Labour Party benefited from the rising unemployment of the 1920s for it claimed, successfully in the 1920s, that although it could not solve unemployment, which was a product of a capitalist society, it would at least ensure that the unemployed were guaranteed a level of benefits which would ensure healthy life. This commitment, never really tested in the 1920s, was to help Labour strengthen its credentials as the party of the working class. But how deep-rooted was the Labour Party's political growth? Was its growth inexorable?

Recently, Christopher Howard has challenged the view that Labour's organization was effective in the 1920s: 'The image of a vibrant expanding new party was illusion. Labour was fortunate that its opponents were deceived.'[3] He added that, 'Widespread electoral support bore little resemblance to restricted party membership, however, and disappointments were common.'[4] Unwittingly, Howard appears to accept that Labour's growth was inexorable, within the context of the times, for he argues that it occurred despite the poor level of party organization throughout the country. Presumably the working class were voting for the Labour Party since

153

they saw it as their party and did not need to incentive of a party machine.

Yet, while accepting that the working class was wedded to the Labour Party it should not be ignored that such support was also nurtured by a much improved Labour organization, despite Howard's contrary view. Ross McKibbin and Bernard Barker feel that the Labour Party was making determined efforts to improve both its national and local organization and that, despite some obvious difficulties, it succeeded in doing so. McKibbin, in particular, acknowledges the strengths and weaknesses of the new constituency and party organizations but stresses the overall general improvements which were achieved. To him, however, the overriding developments were the increasing centralization of party organization and the growing predominance of the unions. The party could only go as far as the unions would allow and their influence was apparent at all levels. It was the union organizations in both urban and rural constituencies which guaranteed continuity and finance: 'What emerged was informal, often improvised, but remarkably tough.'[5] In addition, though the party offered its electorate little it was committed to moral ideas and personal liberation to such an extent that it excited passionate enthusiasms. According to McKibbin, the Labour Party became the vehicle of working-class aspirations by the early 1920s. Since the party was dominated by trade unions accepting it meant accepting an intricate network of loyalties rather than accepting socialism. Idealism was in fact rather less necessary, or sustaining, than loyalty within a trade-union dominated Labour Party.

These loyalties were galvanized by initiatives at both the national and local level. The National Executive Committee (NEC) reorganized its activities by appointing four standing subcommittees – organization and elections; policy and programmes; literature, research and publicity; and finance and general purposes. Egerton Wake became the party's national agent and vigorously pursued the policy of giving direction to the rest of the movement, through the organization of regional and local conferences. Indeed, by 1922 each of the party's nine regions had organized at least three regional conferences, many of which were addressed by Wake, Arthur Henderson, the secretary, and a 'star speaker'. Advisory Committees were set up by the NEC on 13 March 1918 in order to help to develop the Party's policies on a wide range of issues and began to publish reports and statements which added to the corpus of Labour policies. The Party also acquired a paper, *The Daily Herald*. Also in the wake of the 1918 Franchise Bill, the Party formed a Women's Section under Dr Marion Phillips and appointed regional organizers to attract to newly-enfranchised women. There were many difficulties, but there is no doubting that Labour's national organization began to improve. Even the most cursory of examinations of the minutes of the National Executive Committee of the Labour Party indicates the feverish activity which was occurring in the immediate post-war years and, in these early days, it was to be expected that mistakes would be made and that new directions would be sought. One Labour Party circular, issued in June 1923, stressed:

> The results of the [1922] General Election have brought forcibly before us the primary importance both of securing the votes of women electors and of getting a large number of women to take part in an electoral campaign. My Executive is of the opinion that it is essential both for winning and retaining Parliamentary seats that special attention should be given to the whole subject . . .[6]

There was certainly no complacency among Labour's national leaders, quite the contrary.

The records of local Labour parties reveal that Labour's feverish organizational activities were not confined to the national party alone. This was abundantly clear in the textile district of the West Riding. Here, the detritus of pre-war Labour politics was quickly absorbed into the more unified Labour Party organization which emerged after 1918. Constituency parties were formed for all the major industrial constituencies. The rather amorphous Huddersfield Labour movement was transformed into the more clearly defined Huddersfield Divisional Labour Party in the spring and summer of 1918.[7] The Colne Valley Divisional Labour Party was formed in June 1917, the Leeds City Labour Party reorganized itself in April and May 1918, and promoted the formation of constituency parties in the six divisions which made up Leeds, while constituency parties were formed for all four of the Bradford seats in April 1919.[8] This reorganization of the local Labour movement was greatly fostered by the appointment of full-time agents, the creation of provincial Labour newspapers and the attempts to create women's sections.[9]

The fact is that the Labour Party had a well-established base for the parliamentary success which it sought during the inter-war years. It was this base which, allowing for the unusual circumstances of the General Election of December 1923, permitted Labour to form its first government early in 1924. Unfortunately, this was an episode which dented the confidence of some of Labour's more extreme socialist supporters due to the fact that Labour was only kept in office, as a minority government, owing to the support of the Liberal Party. During its short period of administration, of less than ten months, it accomplished little of real importance – other than the passing of the Wheatley Housing Act which provided generous housing subsidies to both private and public builders and stimulated the council house building boom of the 1920s. The first Labour government singularly failed to do anything about the level of unemployment, although it made it easier for the unemployed to obtain unemployment relief and extended benefit. However, this failure appears to have made little difference to the fortunes of the Labour Party.

Although Labour was defeated in the General Election of 1924, the election which saw the publication of the 'Zinoviev Letter' with the allegation that it revealed the Communist intention to stir the masses of workers to revolution through using the Labour Party and the Anti-Soviet treaty, its vote increased by more than one million, or about 24 per cent, even though the number of Labour MPs was reduced from 191 to 151.

Between 1924 and 1929, when out of office, the Labour Party clearly strengthened its position. The economic situation and the persistence of unemployment did help but the most obvious factor pushing Labour forward was the General Strike, which occurred between 3–12 May 1926. The Trades Union Congress had called the strike in order to support the coal miners who had been locked out by the coal owners, who were attempting to impose wage reductions upon them. Although the strike was called off, amid bitter controversy, it did benefit the Labour Party. The reluctance of some Labour leaders, most notably Ramsay MacDonald and Philip Snowden, to be too closely associated with the dispute gave the impression that the Labour Party was not fully behind the strikers – although the records of most local Labour parties deny such an impression. In addition, Baldwin's Conservative government took sweeping action against the whole of the Labour movement through the Trade Union Act of 1927, which, among other things, outlawed 'sympathetic' strike action. Nevertheless, there were benefits and compensations for the Labour Party. Trade unionists were incensed with the act and mounted a campaign against it in 1927. Though it was relatively unsuccessful it confirmed and strengthened the trade union connection with the Labour Party in much the same way as the Taff Vale judgement had acted as an annealing force between the trade unions and the Labour Representation Committee in 1901. More trade-union sponsored Labour candidates were put forward in the 1929 General Election as unions recognized the failure of industrial action. Ramsay MacDonald, putting the matter rather bluntly, noted that trade unionists had come to acknowledge that, 'Labour could solve mining and similar difficulties through the ballot box.'[10]

Nevertheless, it was the economic climate, as much as the renewed trade union and working-class support for Labour, which contributed significantly to Labour's victory in the 1929 General Election. Unemployment had continued to remain at more than one million, despite the fact that Britain had returned to the gold standard and free trade in 1925 – actions which, it was suggested, would revive world trade and reduce unemployment. The Labour Party, dominated by the free trade philosophy of Philip Snowden, offered more of the same and was barely distinguishable from the Conservatives in the economic policies they offered – except for the Conservative Party's references to 'safe-guarding of industry', a code-phrase for selective protectionism. What distinguished Labour from the Conservatives was the prospect that an overall parliamentary majority would signify the end of capitalism and the beginning of socialism – even if the commitment to the gold standard, free trade and balanced budgets remained. Indeed, Philip Snowden reflected upon this cautious and measured approach in his manifesto to the Colne Valley electors in 1929:

> We shall not deceive the people by saying the task of National
> Reconstruction is easy, or that it can be accomplished in a twelve month
> [period].
> But we do pledge ourselves to undertake the task with energy and
> determination, confident that in the full-time life of our Parliament we can
> make a great advance in industrial prosperity, in social well-being, and in a
> juster distribution of the fruits of Labour.
> The Labour Party is a Socialist Party. It is opposed to force, revolution
> and confiscation as a means of establishing the New Social Order. It
> believes in progress and in democratic methods.[11]

In the event, Labour had no mandate for socialism. It was returned to office in May 1929 with 287 seats to the Conservatives' 261 and the Liberals' 59. Although the party had secured only 8,360,000 votes compared with the 8,664,000 who voted Conservative, it had won most seats in parliament and it became inevitable that it should form a second minority government, once again relying upon Liberal Party support to keep it in office.

The economic and social problems of the second Labour government have already been outlined in the first chapter. It is sufficient here to merely reiterate two points. The first is that the Wall Street Crash of October and November 1929, and the economic impact which it exerted upon the world markets, increased unemployment to three millions, about a quarter of the workforce, and created the financial problems which Philip Snowden faced in trying to balance the budget in 1931. Secondly, the second Labour government collapsed in August 1931 as a result of the unwillingness of the Cabinet to wholeheartedly approve of Snowden's demand that unemployment benefits should be cut by 10 per cent. During the inter-war years there was no clearer indication of the potency of unemployment in political matters. The fact that a Labour government collapsed as a result of the economic and unemployment situation, caused a precipitate decline in Labour fortunes once Ramsay MacDonald decided to continue as Prime Minister at the head of a National government.

During the rest of the inter-war period, and indeed ever since, Labour politicians and commentators have attempted to explain why Ramsay MacDonald ditched the second Labour government and formed a National Government. This decision has provoked much animus among many who knew him and believed in him, sustaining the view that he had planned to ditch the Labour government. It has long been an axiom of the Labour Party that MacDonald's actions in 1931 marked him as a traitor to the cause. William Lawther remarked that MacDonald was 'bereft of any public decency'. [12] Harold Laski accused him of 'betraying his politics' and 'betraying his origins'. [13] The Labour Party, in order to distance itself from its estranged and inconsistent creator, shrouded his name and reputation with invective. A popular catch at the time ran:

We'll hang Ramsay Mac on a sour apple tree,
We'll hang Snowden and Thomas to keep him company;
For that's the place where traitors ought to be. [14]

There was also the obituary written by J.S. Clarke and sent to MacDonald, which ran:

> Here lies Ramsay Mac
> A friend of all humanity,
> Too many pats upon the back
> Inflated Ramsay's vanity.
> The blarney stone he oft-times kissed,
> But departed in his glory;
> Having been born a socialist
> He died a bloody Tory.[15]

Naturally, Labour supporters have shrouded MacDonald's name in treachery. L. MacNeill Weir, in his book *The Tragedy of Ramsay MacDonald*, was the main critic, suggesting that MacDonald was an opportunist, a liberal rather than a socialist, that he schemed to ditch the Labour government, and betrayed the Labour Party.[16] Although such charges stuck for many years, and still colour the attitudes of Labour supporters towards MacDonald, it is clear, as David Marquand has indicated, that they are largely without foundation.[17] Many may have felt betrayed, but there is little to suggest that MacDonald was any the less of a socialist than others, nor is there hard evidence to suggest that he schemed to bring about the collapse of the Labour government. Marquand's view is quite clear; MacDonald's decision to form a National government was a product of his concern for national interests:

> All his life, MacDonald had fought against a class view of politics and for the primacy of political action as against industrial; for him the logical corollary was that the party must be prepared, when necessary, to subordinate the sectional claims of the unions to its conception of the national interest.[18]

To Marquand, MacDonald's real fault was that he held on to his nineteenth-century principles for too long. His almost religious conviction that the preservation of the gold standard was essential to British economic growth, plus his belief in the primacy of the state over party, ensured that he lacked 'the ability and willingness to jettison cherished assumptions in the face of changing realities.'[19] He was not prepared to take a gamble.

The economic problems caused by unemployment led to the collapse of the second Labour government. The political reper-

159

cussions of the events were devastating for the Labour Party. Its catastrophic election defeat of 1931, when the party was reduced from 289 MPs to a mere 52, was an inseparable consequence of MacDonald's betrayal. But such a decline was illusory – caused largely by the unusual circumstances of the 1931 General Election. Within a year Labour was recapturing some of the political ground which it had lost at the local elections in November 1931. By 1933 it had recovered all the municipal seats it had lost in 1931.[20] Early in 1932 it began its new 'A Million New Members and Power' campaign. Within a year its individual membership had risen by about 100,000. In January 1933 it set up a central By-Election Insurance Fund to help needy constituencies to put forward candidates.

The improved organizational and propaganda activities saw Labour recover many of the parliamentary seats the party had lost in 1931 at the 1935 General Election. In fact, its parliamentary representation rose from 52 in 1931 to 154 – though some had hoped for between 200 and 250 seats. Thereafter, the party made steady progress during the late 1930s as it campaigned for a policy of collective security against the threat of European fascism almost, it seemed, in the face of the complacency of Neville Chamberlain's National government.

There were many reasons for the revival of Labour fortunes. For one thing, the election defeats of 1931 had exaggerated the real losses of the Labour Party. For another, the Labour Party had changed its policy in the mid 1930s from one advocating 'no more war' to one which was prepared to meet the challenge of fascism. But one should not ignore the fact that the Party was also developing its economic policies and identifying closely with the unemployed. They campaigned strongly against the Household Means Test which had been imposed by the National government at the end of 1931, and a Policy Sub-Committee of the party, influenced by Hugh Dalton and Herbert Morrison, attended to the issues of unemployment, banking, housing and transport. These policies were underpinned by the oft-stated general commitment to the introduction of a planned national economy and the desire for the 'socialization of industry'. The whole package of policies was presented in a series of leaflets and pamphlets, such as *For Socialism and Peace* and *Labour's Immediate Programme* (1937).

This commitment and activity was quickly transmitted to the

local level. Very quickly, the local Labour parties identified with the social issues of the day. There was widespread opposition to the Household Means Test, and Labour representatives occupied positions on the Public Assistance committees, in the hope of nudging up relief provisions. Its councillors were responsible for many public works schemes. In addition, they were responsible for many slum-clearance and house-building schemes – the most notable of which occurred in Leeds during the mid- and late 1930s.[21] The slum clearance schemes, and the construction of the Quarry Hill flats were largely stimulated by the short period in which the Leeds City Labour Party held control of the City Council.[22] It is therefore true to say that by the mid-1930s, the Labour Party was truly, as it had never been before, the party of the working class.

Nevertheless, the party could not entirely dissociate itself from the events which led to the formation of the National government, even if the chief villains, as far as it was concerned, were now in political opposition. The fact was put neatly by Barbara Betts, later Barbara Castle, when reporting upon the Labour Party Conference in October 1931: 'It was almost as if it feared to probe too deeply lest it should be disillusioned as to the integrity of Uncle Arthur [Henderson].'[23] But changes of leadership in the 1930s, from Arthur Henderson to George Lansbury and, finally in 1935, to Clement Attlee tended to give Labour a less tainted and more youthful image. This may not have been immediately obvious from the results of the 1935 General Election, for the Party had only just accepted Attlee as its leader on the eve of the election. Yet, during the late 1930s, Labour's clear hostility towards European fascism, and its support of the Republican side in the Spanish Civil War confirmed it to be a party which was prepared to face up to fascism. It marked it out as a patriotic party, in contrast to the general image it had earned during the 1920s.

Recent work has concurred about the basic unimportance of Mosley and the British Union of Fascists.[24] After the Olympia meeting of 1934, which saw the clash between the communists and the fascists, there was little interest in the movement and, as Stuart Rawnsley suggests, it was only a small hard-core of supporters who remained.[25] There were, in fact, few centres of fascist support outside London, Manchester, Birmingham and Leeds. Even in Leeds, occasionally suggested as one of the most powerful and well-organized of fascist centres, there were actually only 100 to 200

161

fascists. Indeed, when Mosley addressed a meeting of 1,500 people at Leeds Town Hall in May 1934 it was estimated that only about 400 fascists were present, 'most of whom had come to Leeds by bus.'[26] The Labour Party rightly dismissed the fascist challenge in Britain. What it could not ignore was the threat of European fascism.

Although some Labour politicians clung to the belief that peace could be maintained, most had come to accept that war was inevitable by 1936, confirmed in their opinion by the outbreak of the Spanish Civil War. Under Attlee's leadership, the Party was drawn, almost inexorably, to a commitment to collective international security and its implication that war was necessary in order to curb aggressor nations. There were groups, such as the Socialist League, which disagreed with the policy line being developed. But the outbreak of the Spanish Civil War resulted in the 1936 Labour Party Conference at Edinburgh support collective security, though it did not approve of rearmament. Also in that year, Ernest Bevin became the Chairman of the General Council of the TUC and Dr Hugh Dalton became Chairman of the National Executive Committee of the Labour Party. The right of the Labour movement were now firmly in control. In 1937 Dalton and Attlee got the Parliamentary Labour Party to support the armed forces estimates and the Labour Party Conference, at Bournemouth, supported rearmament. There was now a new firmness in British Labour Party policy which ultimately permitted them to enter Winston Churchill's Coalition government in May 1940.

For the Labour Party, the inter-war years proved to be successful ones. It was during this period that it became the second major party in British politics, and Britain's leading progressive party. There were clearly many factors for this success. Most obviously, its rising trade-union support ensured that it was to become the party of the working class, a process which was speeded up by the split within the Liberal Party during the First World War. It also seems likely that unemployment and other social problems contributed further to the view that Labour offered the only alternative to the failures of capitalism – no matter how illusory that viewpoint may have been. Combined with other factors, the economic situation in Britain ensured the continued success of the Labour Party, despite the political setbacks of 1931.

The Conservative Party

The Conservative Party was the only other major political party to do well out of the inter-war years. Apart from a short period between May 1929 and October 1931, it was the largest political party throughout the inter-war years. However, this fact is not always recognized since the Conservative Party was often subsumed in office in Coalition and National government arrangements. In fact, there were only two short periods, of ten months in 1924 and of about two years and three months from 1929 and 1931 when it was out of power. It also produced three Prime Ministers, Andrew Bonar Law (1922–3), Stanley Baldwin (1923, 1924–9, and 1935–7) and Neville Chamberlain (1937–40). Throughout its inter-war history, the Conservative Party owed a great deal to Stanley Baldwin who, as Middlemass and Barnes have suggested, was a political giant rather than a political pigmy.[27] As Robert Blake has confirmed, he helped to rebuild the organization of the Conservative Party and to make it more a party of the people by reorganizing the central Office of the party and by encouraging local parties to at least consider the selection of working-class candidates. Indeed, he concludes by suggesting:

> The truth was that the Conservative party under Baldwin had managed to recover a large area of that middle ground in politics which is the key to electoral success and which they lost in 1906, after being in possession for nearly twenty years before that. By the mid-1920s they no longer had the harsh appearance that they had developed in the immediate pre-war years . . . The Conservatives seemed to lack compassion.
>
> Under Baldwin the picture was different. Their social composition did not, it is true, greatly change. The movement of the business men, bankers, industrialists into the party . . . continued . . . .. The Conservatives were still the rich man's party. But there was a new awareness of social problems, a new consciousness of poverty and unemployment.[28]

The fact is that the Conservative Party did become closely involved in the problems of the poor and the unemployed – although their efforts were often seen as less than caring.

Most certainly, Stanley Baldwin's first major political concern as Prime Minister was to tackle unemployment. He had already gained experience of some of the economic problems of the post-war economy in his role as minister at the Board of Trade, from April

1921 to October 1922, and then as Chancellor of the Exchequer from October 1922 until May 1923. When he became Prime Minister he was all too aware of the difficulties which British industry was facing. Before becoming Prime Minister, he had been developing policies designed to 'safeguard' British industry. In effect these were subsidies designed to protect British industry from the competition of even more heavily subsidized goods from abroad. But the commitment of governments was to the gold standard and free trade and, in 1922, Baldwin reflected that, 'a free trade country, such as we are still, finds it very difficult to argue with a country that has a tariff weapon in its hand.'[29] When he became Prime Minister he was determined to rectify the situation and, switching to the traditional Conservative policies of the early nineteenth century, he decided to call a general election and go to the electorate with a policy of protectionism. In November 1923, he stated:

> . . . the crucial problem of our country [was unemployment]. If we can fight it I am willing to fight it. I cannot fight it without weapons. I have for myself come to the conclusion that owing to the conditions which exist in the world today, having regard to the economic environment, having regard to the situation of our country, if we go on pattering along as we are we shall have grave unemployment with us to the end of time, and I have come to the conclusion that the only way of fighting this subject is by protecting the home markets.[30]

The electorate, still besotted with a belief in free trade, rejected Baldwin's campaign for, although the Conservatives were the largest parliamentary party, they were outnumbered by Labour and Liberal MPs who were committed to free trade; the first Labour government was formed as a result. Yet Baldwin never regretted his action. Indeed, in 1935, he reflected of the 1923 General Election:

> Rightly or wrongly I was convinced you could not deal with unemployment without a tariff. After the war opinion was more fluid and open. On political grounds the tariff issue had been dead for years and I felt it was one which would pull the party together, including the Lloyd George malcontents.[31]

There were, indeed, good political grounds for reviving protectionism. In the first place protectionism had been traditional Conservative policy before the emergence of free trade and Joseph Chamberlain had revived some sympathy for the idea in the early

164

twentieth century. The revival of the policy was also calculated to deal with those 'Lloyd George malcontents', such as Austen Chamberlain, who objected to the Conservative Party removing Lloyd George from office in 1922. It was obviously felt that protectionism, a policy which Austen Chamberlain's father had encouraged, might attract Austen and his supporters back to the centre of the Conservative Party. It was also rumoured that Lloyd George might advocate protectionist policies and Baldwin make have called the general election and fought it on protectionist policies in order to undermine any such move by Lloyd George.

Yet the move failed and the Conservative Party dropped the policy for the rest of the 1920s. The Baldwin government which was returned to office in 1924, after the collapse of the first Labour government, was committed to free trade, the gold standard and rationalization. As was indicated in Chapter 1, it was during this period that Britain officially returned to the gold standard and free trade. But the anticipated world trade revival was relatively minor and did not help to reduce unemployment in Britain's staple exporting industries. Unemployment thus remained at well over one million; more than 10 per cent of the workforce.

Nevertheless, this particular Conservative administration did offer social policies which were designed both to indicate its commitment to dealing with social problems and to undermine the challenge of Labour. Indeed, according to Clement MacIntyre, the Conservative Party did change the orientation of its policies between 1922 and 1931:

> There was a realisation that the mantle of radicalism had been seized from the Liberal Party and that the main political division of the twentieth century would not be between the Tories and the Liberals but between Labour and anti-Labour. Accordingly, policies were re-written and strategies revised, firstly, to reflect the changes needed if Labour was to be kept at bay, and, secondly, to accommodate the non-Labour supporters of the old Liberal Party within the modern Conservative Party. The task of the Conservatives was to kill off the Liberals as a credible third alternative and then project the Conservative Party as offering a dynamic alternative to socialism.[32]

Indeed, Conservative spokesmen, and particularly Baldwin, called for economic recovery based upon industrial peace, national unity and class harmony. It was the fear of Labour which led the Conservatives to abandon the Lloyd George Coalition government in

1922 and to anticipate the new social policies of a 'new Conservatism' during the 1920s. It was this concern which was most evident in a timely article in the *Fortnightly Review*, in 1922, which stated that:

> . . . if the return to Conservatism is to be something more than the transient apparition of a spectre from the past, and its voice in national affairs not merely to be a sepulchral warning against the dangers of rash courses, the Conservative leaders must bestir themselves to some purpose . . . [the Conservative Party] must be ready to meet the programme of the Labour Party not simply with a non-possumus but with an alternative which will in some measure satisfy certain of the needs which Labour is concerned to satisfy, and at the same time avoid the perils with which it insists Labour policy is beset.[33]

The message was clear, the Conservative Party would have to broaden its policies in order to attract the newly enfranchised working-class voter and remain in power.

Indeed, the Conservative Party did begin to widen its potential appeal by issuing a plethora of pamphlets in the 1920s: *Aims and Principles* (1924), *What Unionists have done for Workers* (1925), *What the Conservative Government has done for Education* (1928) and *What the Conservative Government has done for Health* (1929). Baldwin suggested that there should be more working-class Conservative candidates,[34] and began to consider and develop social policy within his 1924 to 1929 administration. He spoke of 'a new age, in which people can come together',[35] directed his administration to deal with the reorganization of pensions, housing, the improvements to maternity homes and the reorganization of the poor law. Yet there was always an element of complacency about an administration which enjoyed a substantial parliamentary majority. By the late 1920, following the General Strike and the problem of dealing with the Poor Law authorities, Baldwin decided that the Conservatives would fight the 1929 General Election on its past record rather than a future commitment to major social reform. Baldwin fought what became known as a 'Safety First' campaign.

There have been many attempts to explain Baldwin's 1929 election programme. The traditional one is that both the Conservative Party and government were in decline in the late 1920s and that the party leaders were 'too supine to do anything about this loss of prestige.'[36] Michael Bentley suggests that the actions of the

Conservative leaders were deliberate for the, 'Conservatives made a conscious attempt to eradicate all traces of policy in order to appear stolid and silhouette Lloyd George as a very dangerous thing.'[37] More recently, Philip Williamson has suggested that, in contrast to both the other views put forward, Baldwin's policy was a well-thought out campaign:

> So 'Safety First' was not a substitute for lack of ideas and policies: it was deliberately chosen by Baldwin from a number of possible election platforms. It was not defensive, but a calculated attempt to discredit Lloyd George. It relied heavily on Baldwin's leadership and on the success over the years in persuading the new democracy not to be seduced by socialist abstractions, trade union militancy or Liberal demagogy, but to accept Conservative values as the guarantee of liberty and secure social improvement. And it was expected to be successful.[38]

Most certainly, the Conservatives relied upon a theme song which combined Al Jolson's hit song 'Sonny Boy' with the dependability of Baldwin, the first few lines of which ran as follows:

> When there are grey skies,
> We don't mind the grey skies,
> You'll turn them blue
> Stanley Boy.
> When friends forsake us,
> Let them all forsake us,
> You'll pull us through,
> Stanley Boy.[39]

And Williamson suggests that this line of approach may have been influenced by an important letter sent to Baldwin, by W. Bridgeman, which stated:

> I . . . hope that you will not attempt to outbid L[loyd] G[eorge] or the Socialists in a vote-catching programme . . . it is folly to attempt a competition with irresponsible people, and I believe LG's proposals have given us an opportunity of attacking, instead of defending, ourselves . . ..
> I feel sure we can win if we show no signs of panic, and our only safe course is to depend on our record, and make as few promises as possible.[40]

Such reliance upon Baldwin and the dependability of the Conservatives did not work, and produced within the Conservative Party internal divisions which saw Neville Chamberlain being suggested as a possible alternative to Baldwin and the emergence of the Empire Party, led by Lord Beaverbrook and the press barons, as a challenge to Baldwin's leadership. But Baldwin weathered these political storms with some adriotness and found that the economic policies he favoured emerged, almost naturally, out of the collapse of the second Labour government in August 1931. From then onwards, and throughout the 1930s, the Conservatives operated within the National government and pushed forward the type of protectionist policies which both Baldwin and Chamberlain favoured. The Ottawa Conference of July and August 1932 paved the way for increased trade between the nations which formed the British Empire and thus effectively operated a system of protection. The Import Duties Bill of February 1932 also imposed a general tariff of 10 per cent on almost all imports, and the Import Duties Advisory Committee, which it formed quickly, raised the tariff to 20 per cent on manufactured goods, to between 25 and 30 per cent on luxury goods and to 33 per cent on chemicals and a wide range of other goods. As suggested in Chapter 1, these measures were not, in themselves, particularly successful in reducing unemployment although they possibly helped to promote the housing boom of the mid- and late 1930s.

Throughout the 1930s the Conservative Party was the great beneficiary of the popular support for the National governments which were formed. In the 1931 it raised its parliamentary representation from 261, achieved in 1929, to 472 in 1931 and 387 seats in 1935. From 1935 to the Second World War it was their leaders who assumed the office of Prime Minister. In the final analysis the economic policies pursued in the 1930s, and already outlined in Chapter 1, were those dictated by a massive Conservative parliamentary majority.

The Liberal Party

Ironically, it was the Liberal Party which offered the only serious alternative to the free trade solutions of the 1920s and the protectionist policies of the 1930s – though it was always too weak to make any significant contribution to the economic policies of the country. Indeed, the inter-war years saw the continued decline of the Liberal Party and the persistence of factionalism. As a result the expansionist economic policies favoured by David Lloyd George found little support amongst electors and, thus, in parliament.

Historians have always been fascinated by the decline of political parties. In the twentieth century the most dramatic political collapse has been that of the Liberal Party. For many its decline began before the First World War, as a consequence of its inability to maintain the trade-union and working-class support in the face of the challenge of the Labour Party.[41] For others, mainly committed Liberals, that decline began in 1916 when Lloyd George replaced Asquith as Prime Minister of the wartime Coalition government.[42]

On balance the evidence suggests that the Liberal decline began before the First World War, but there is no denying that the war speeded up this process. It challenged the shibboleths of Liberalism – free trade, the gold standard, retrenchment and peace – all of which were abandoned during the war. But, above all, it divided the Liberal Party for in 1916 David Lloyd George replaced Asquith as Prime Minister of the Coalition government. For the next seven years Asquith's old free-trade section of the party was detached from the Lloyd George supporters. The split was disastrous for Liberalism. In the 1918 General Election Liberal representation in parliament fell from the 272 of December 1910 to 151. In the 1922 General Election, following the decision of the Conservatives to withdraw their support for Lloyd George, Liberal representation was further reduced to 116. The fact is that the Liberal Party declined quickly. The divisions ran deep and Sir John Simon, in the *Liberal Magazine*, of August 1921, said of Lloyd George:

> . . . he incurs Liberal criticism because he sometimes acts like an unprincipled and like an undependable person . . .. Cleverness, ingenuity, adroitness! There has been nothing like it in human history. But, after all, character is more than cleverness. Sticking to a principle is more than adroitly shifting from one position to another. And, in the view of Liberals, Mr Lloyd George has shown himself a faithless trustee of their traditions and beliefs.[43]

The re-union of the Liberals, forced by the action of Stanley Baldwin in calling the 1923 General Election on the issue of protection, seemed to have worked briefly with a revival in the political fortunes of the Liberal Party. But the dramatic decline to 40 MPs in the 1924 General Election was effectively the electoral sign that the Liberal Party was no longer a realistic party of government.

Table 7.1 *The Liberal Vote and Parliamentary Representation, 1910–35*

Elections	MPs elected	Votes	% of total vote
1910 (Dec)	272	2,295,888	43.9
1918			
Coalition Liberal	133	1,455,640	13.5
Independent			
Liberals	28	1,298,808	12.1
1922			
Lloyd George			
Liberals	62	1,673,240	11.6
Asquith Liberals	54	2,516,287	17.5
1923	159	4,311,147	29.6
1924	40	2,928,747	17.6
1929	59	5,308,510	23.4
1931			
Liberal National			
(Simonites)	35	809,302	3.7
Liberal			
(Samuelites)	33	1,403,102	6.5
(Lloyd George)			
Liberal	4	106,106	0.5
1935	21	1,422,116	6.4

This was clearly a moment of major concern for the Liberals. The party was evidently re-united, although deep divisions remained, and ostensibly offering the economic message of free trade which the nation still wished to hear. Yet it was unable to convince the electorate of its political viability. What direction was the party to go in?

The traditional Asquithian-Liberal section of the party, which dominated the constituencies believed in the need to reiterate the established Liberal shibboleths. Exactly this point was made by the Cabinet Committee of the Leeds Liberal Federation in 1921, and adhered to throughout the 1920s. It suggested that it was:

> . . . strongly of the opinion that the time has arrived when hasty
> experiments of a socialistic character, no matter how well intentioned –
> involving heavy public expenditure – should be scrutinised very closely
> . . ... It believes that the Country needs a return of the sane principles of
> 'peace, retrenchment, and reform', which formed the basis of Liberal policy
> a generation ago.[44]

Indeed, few annual reports of Liberal organizations missed the opportunity to reiterate the need for free trade, peace, sound finance and a modicum of reform. From 1917 onwards, many referred to the need for proportional representation and some charged the Labour Party with fomenting class warfare through its parliamentary and municipal campaigns. By 1926 and 1927 local Liberal parties were beginning to note that the Labour Party was responsible for 'dark passages' in the history of Liberalism.[45] Yet they did little to counter the challenge of socialism.

Dr Michael Bentley has suggested, in his book *The Liberal Mind 1914–1929* and in at least one article, that the real problem of the Liberal Party was this lack of flexibility and willingness to think beyond the old shibboleths in a day and age which required new initiatives. Local Liberal Party records bear him out in his assertion of this fixity of purpose and he would appear to be correct in his estimation that:

> Nagging fears and doubts, as well as a shrewd eye for the main chance, had sent some of their number into other parties to leave behind a group of stalwarts to insist that there was a liberal way out of the dilemma, a middle way. 'Look neither to the right nor to the left, but keep straight on', Asquith had told the faithful in his resignation speech of October 1926. But those who obeyed had little enough to focus their blinkered eyes upon by 1929. In a sense they were victims of a paradox; they had chosen their middle way in order to retain their identity; yet it was to be this very middle way which convinced others that they had relinquished it. Everyone believed in liberalism but no one was actually for it – such was the view of one 'lively socialist' after the election of 1929.
>
> Liberals were left to pretend that what they were saying was the fruit not of compromise but of virtue. The advantage of their 'straight road', according to Donald Maclean was that it was hard to get lost by following it. The disadvantage was that 'the liberal bridle-path' could be seen, let alone followed, only by liberals.[46]

The fact is that many Liberals, and especially those in the local constituencies, adopted something of a larger mentality towards change. This meant that most Liberals remained resolutely opposed to the idea that the Liberal Party had to change its policies to fit the new problems facing society. This meant that the views of David Lloyd George carried little political weight within the Liberal Party, and thus within the country.

David Lloyd George had returned to the Liberal fold in 1923 and accepted his position as second in the Party to Asquith until he assumed the role of leader in October 1926. But even before he became leader he was already promoting a new approach to social problems of the day. With the wealth which he had accumulated he began to finance the formulation of a major innovatory social and economic policy based upon four publications – *Coal and Power* (1924), *Land and the Nation* (1924 'Green Book'), *Britain's Industrial Future* (1928 'Yellow Book') and *We Can Conquer Unemployment* (1929 'Little Yellow Book').

These proposed innovatory Keynesian policies were distinct from the economic policies of the Labour and Conservative parties, for they demanded the use of bank credit, the ending of private land ownership, and the use of public works programmes to swallow up over half a million unemployed over a short period of time. These policies even contemplated the nationalization of industry, in rather more detail than had ever been considered by the Labour Party.

Land and the Nation was a rather trenchant report based upon a private investigation into the ownership and use of rural land. It was financed by Lloyd George, without reference to Asquith, and argued that the state should gradually take over the land through committees whose purpose was to ensure that reforms were made to revive the economy of the countryside. In essence it was a development of policies which Lloyd George had advocated at the beginning of his political career. Yet this restatement of his views won him political support from Liberals who looked askance at this quasi-nationalization programme. *Coal and Power* called for an integrated and rationalized scheme for power, a follow up to the Liberal Manifesto of 1923 which suggested that coal and power supplies should be placed under the control of a public board presided over by a minister. This scheme effectively came into existence in Baldwin's second administration with the formation of the Central Electricity Generating Board in 1926.

Yet the last two publications were far more innovative and important. The first of these, *Britain's Industrial Future*, being a report of the Liberal Industrial Inquiry of 1928, was one of the most far-sighted economic documents of the inter-war years. Influenced by J.M. Keynes, one of its fourteen authors, it argued for expansionist economic policies financed by the state through a Board of National Investment and a vast public works programme. It was believed that such measures would stimulate industry and increase employment in the short-term until Britain's economic markets were restored by the revival of world trade and increasing cost-effective output:

> There are two important fields of action in which we can work for the restoration of a vigorous and healthy economic life. On the one hand, we must use all possible means to regain old markets, to, open new ones up, and to encourage international trade on the basis of the division of labour; and on the other, we must endeavour to awaken in British industry a spirit of joint endeavour . . . .. The energetic pursuit of these two policies should in the long run ensure a substantial improvement in the employment situation. At the same time these results are likely to be slow, and if we are right in our conclusion that we are faced at the present time with a certain amount of abnormal employment of a quasi-permanent character, then it is not sufficient to solely rely on the gradual improvement of productive efficiency. Definite and energetic steps must be taken in other directions to restore the balance of our national economic life . . ..
>
> Since the slump of 1921 there has been a prevailing tendency, occasionally interrupted but invariably resumed before there has been time for a real recovery towards parsimony and restriction. This has been the result partly of monetary deflation, but also of a muddle-headed confusion about the meaning of economy – namely. the idea that every form of avoidance of expenditure quite indifferently of whether it consists of really wasteful expenditure or of a capital investment in developing the nation's productive resources, is alike 'economy' . . ... A nation's labour force is by far the most important part of its daily accruing resources, and an inability continued over several years to direct some 10 per cent of it or more to any useful purpose not only involved a disastrous impoverishment of the nation, but is in itself a demonstration that the machinery for directing the available labour into appropriate fields of enterprise has broken down . . ..
>
> We put, therefore, in the forefront of our proposals a vigorous policy of national reconstruction embracing within its scope, inter alia, the rehabilitation of agriculture, still the largest of our national industries; an extensive programme of highway development; afforestation, reclamation, drainage, electrification, slum clearance and town development, and the development of canals, docks, and harbours.[47]

Although this report was ahead of its time, it is also interesting in respect of the fact that it brought together both the traditional and new Liberals. It was the first time, since the 1916 split, that all the major political leaders within the Liberal Party – David Lloyd George, Sir Herbert Samuel and Sir John Simon – had placed their names upon a major economic report. This report was evidently wide enough in scope to appeal to both free-trade and interventionist Liberals. It was this policy, in popular and amended form, which was offered to the electorate in early 1929 as 'We Can

Conquer Unemployment'. The main focus of this shorter document was the employment of 600,000 men, at a cost of £250 million, through a vast building programme of roads and houses.

Although the Liberals improved their position in the 1929 General Election, winning 59 seats compared to the 40 in 1924, their new-found unity and imaginative economic policies had not worked. Thereafter, the party began to splinter and decline. It supported the new Labour government but many Liberals felt that such a course of action was unwise. Most Liberal MPs, except Lloyd George and his family clan, joined the National government and supported it after its general election success in October 1931 from which they improved their position. Yet the Conservative dominance of the new government, and their move towards protectionism, alienated Sir Herbert Samuel and the free traders who left the National government in September 1932. This left the Liberal Party in total disarray – with the Simonites within the National government and the Samuelites and the Lloyd George sections in opposition. The 1935 General Election drove home the fact of their sad decline, for only 21 Liberals won seats in 1935.

As Bentley rightly asserts, the Liberal Party generally reverted to its traditional free trade policies when all the experimentation was over – policies which were always popular in the local Liberal parties. Only David Lloyd George attempted to offer anything different, with his New Deal in 1935.

Lloyd George had launched his programme at a lecture delivered at Bangor on 17 January 1935. In effect he offered a revised and updated version of his 1929 manifesto *We Can Conquer Unemployment*. He also drew inspiration from Roosevelt's New Deal. Yet, apart from a few family friends, there was little support for such views. By this time, Lloyd George was passè. His main supporter was Philip Snowden, a life-long advocate of free trade and Gladstonian economics who had become his close friend, was in a similar category. Writing to Lloyd George, Snowden encouragingly argued:

> The crusade you are beginning for a great and united national effort to revive industry and to rescue the mass of our population from hardship and suffering of unnecessary poverty deserves, and I believe will receive, the support of earnest and sympathetic men and women of all parties and of that large and increasing number of electors who have no party affiliations. This is a time for action . . . the country is waiting for an inspiring lead on a programme of courageous national reconstruction.[48]

174

However, on another occasion, Snowden explained that his free-trade and budgetary views had not changed but that the surplus they had earned now permitted the nation to financially support 'Lloyd George's New Deal'.[49]

Yet history records that the nation was not waiting for a programme of national reconstruction. Two statesmen who were were in the political wilderness by the mid-1930s were hardly likely, or able, to challenge the unthinking protectionist attitude of a National government which enjoyed a substantial parliamentary majority. The British public were cautious and it took the Second World War to inspire a new, and more forward-looking, attitude to the problem of dealing with the economy and unemployment.

Conclusion

There is no doubting that unemployment and the economic depression dominated the politics of the inter-war years. Every major political party was faced with offering solutions to these problems and governments were measured by the effectiveness of their actions. Unemployment was obviously a factor in bringing about both long-term and short-term political changes. Unemployment problems put paid to Labour's political prospects in the early 1930s just as much as it had helped the party to rise to political power in the 1920s. Protectionist policies, designed to deal with unemployment, temporarily ended the rule of the Conservative Party at the end of 1923 just as surely as it helped the Conservative Party to political dominance in the 1930s. Unemployment thus helped to shape the politics of the age, and some political changes were clearly the result of the problems it raised, although long-term social changes were clearly evident in permitting the Labour Party to replace the Liberal Party as the progressive party of British politics. Yet though the issue of unemployment exerted considerable impact upon British politics it does not appear that Britain's political parties came up with much in the way of a meaningful solution to the problem.

The real problem of inter-war British politics was that no major political party, except a small section of a much diminished and effete Liberal Party, was willing to take the political risk of expanding the economy out of the slump by the use of government intervention to stimulate and regulate the economy. The Labour

Party was besotted with the free-trade policies of Philip Snowden, and the Conservative Party wavered between free trade and protectionism. Both parties believed in the need to balance the budget and to operate deflationary measures. Apart from the Lloyd George Liberals, and a few socialists and Oswald Mosley, there were no significant supporters of more expansionary policies. With economic vision so blinkered it was to be expected that the economy would be allowed to drift with the market situation and without significant and positive government direction. But it should be remembered that such hesitation was an endemic feature of British politics during the inter-war years and was even exhibited in the 1930s when fascism, that other major problem of the age, threatened to consume Britain and Europe.

NOTES

1. P.F. Clarke, *Lancashire and the New Liberalism* (Cambridge, Cambridge University Press, 1971); T. Wilson, *The Downfall of the Liberal Party* (London, Collins, 1966); K.D. Brown, *The English Labour Movement* (London, Gill and Macmillan, 1982); K. Burgess, *The Challenge of Labour* (London, Croom Helm, 1980); R. Douglas, 'Labour in Decline 1910–1914', in K. D. Brown. (ed.), *Essays in Anti-Labour History* (London, Macmillan, 1974).
2. G. Dangerfield, *The Strange Death of Liberal England* (London, MacGibbon & Kee, 1966 ed.); H. Pelling, *The Origins of the Labour Party* (London, Macmillan, 1954); R. McKibbin, *The Evolution of the Labour Party 1910–1924* (Oxford, Oxford University Press, 1974); K. Laybourn, *The Rise of Labour* (London, Edward Arnold, 1988).
3. C. Howard, 'Expectation born to death: local Labour Party expansion in the 1920s', in J. Winter, (ed.), *Working Class in Modern British History: Essays in Honour of Henry Pelling* (London, Cambridge University Press, 1983) p. 81.
4. Ibid., p. 78.
5. McKibbin, op.cit., p. 49.
6. Archives of the Labour Party, National Executive Committee, Minutes, June 1923.
7. Huddersfield Divisional Labour Party, Minutes, 23 July 1918.
8. Colne Valley Divisional Labour Party, Minutes, 20 January, 1 May, 9 June 1917; *Leeds Weekly Citizen*, 19 April 1918; Bradford Trades and Labour Council, Minutes, 15 November 1918; Bradford Pioneer, throughout 1918.
9. Laybourn, *The Rise of Labour*, p. 53.
10. Quoted in A. Bullock, *The Life and Times of Ernest Bevin, I* (London, Heinemann, 1960), p. 349.
11. Colne Valley Parliamentary Division, General Election 1929. Election Address of The Right Hon. Philip Snowden, 1 May 1929. Also quoted in K. Laybourn, *Philip Snowden: a biography* (Aldershot, Temple Smith/Gower/

Wildwood, 1988), p. 179.

12. Quoted by D. Marquand, 'A Traitor's Grave', BBC Radio 4 broadcast, 2 March 1977.

13. Harper's, 2 September 1932.

14. M. Foot, 'Ramsay MacDonald', review article of D. Marquand, *Ramsay MacDonald*, Bulletin of the Society for the Study of Labour History, 35, 1977, p. 70.

15. R.C. Challinor, 'Letter from MacDonald to Clarke', *Bulletin of the Society for the Study of Labour History*, 27 (1973), pp. 34–5.

16. L. MacNeill Weir, *The Tragedy of Ramsay MacDonald* (London, Secker and Warburg, 1938).

17. D. Marquand, *Ramsay MacDonald* (London, Jonathan Cape, 1977).

18. Ibid., p. 624.

19. Ibid., p. 795.

20. J. Stevenson and C. Cook, *The Slump* (London, Jonathan Cape, 1977), pp. 116–17.

21. *Leeds Citizen*, 10 April, 11, 17 November, 2 December 1932; 3 March 1933; 26 October 1934; 13 March, 8 May, 18 September 1936; *Bradford Pioneer*, 31 August 1934, 7 June 1935; City of Leeds Labour Party, Minutes, 19 July 1933.

22. J. Reynolds and K. Laybourn, *Labour Heartland* (Bradford, University of Bradford Press, 1987).

23. *Bradford Pioneer*, 9 October 1931.

24. G.C. Webber, *The Ideology of the British Right* (London, Croom Helm, 1987); R. Thurlow, *Fascism in Britain: a history, 1918–1985* (London, Hackwell, 1987).

25. S. Rawnsley, 'The Membership of the British Union of Fascists', in K. Lunn and R. Thurlow, (eds.), *British Fascism* (London, Croom Helm, 1979), pp. 150–165.

26. Labour Party Archives, LP/FAS/34/20.

27. R.K. Middlemass and J. Barnes, *Stanley Baldwin* (London, Weidenfeld and Nicolson, 1969).

28. R. Blake, *The Conservative Party: from Peel to Churchill* (London, Eyre and Spottiswoode, 1970), p. 244.

29. Middlemass and Barnes, op.cit., p. 127.

30. Ibid., p. 229.

31. Ibid., p. 213.

32. C.J. MacIntyre, 'Responses to the Rise of Labour: Conservative Party Policy and Organisation 1922–1931', unpublished PhD, University of Cambridge, 1986, p. 9.

33. Ibid., p. 51, quoting J. Martin, 'The Future of Conservatism', *Fortnightly Review*, cxiii, January 1923. p. 45.

34. MacIntyre, op.cit., p. 52.

35. Ibid., p. 72 quoting S. Baldwin, *Peace and Goodwill in Industry*.

36. P. Williamson, '"Safety First": Baldwin, the Conservative Party, and the 1929 General Election', *Historical Journal*, 25, 2, 1982, p. 386.

37. M. Bentley, *The Liberal Mind 1914–1929* (Cambridge, Cambridge University Press, 1977).

38. Williamson, op.cit., p. 408.

39. Middlemass and Barnes, op.cit., p. 350.

40. Williamson, op.cit., p. 405, quoting from a letter from Bridgeman to Baldwin, 27 March 1929, Baldwin Papers, 175/50–1.

41. Footnote 2.

42. Footnote 1.

43. Loc. cit.

44. Leeds Liberal Federation, Cabinet Committee, Minutes, Report of the Cabinet Sub-Committee regarding the National Liberal Federation submitted 18 July 1921.

45. Yorkshire Liberal Federation, Annual Meeting, 2 July 1927.

46. M. Bentley, 'The Liberal Response to Socialism, 1918–1929', in K.D. Brown, (ed.), *Essays in Anti-Labour History* (London, Macmillan, 1974), p. 72.

47. *Britain's Industrial Future: being the Report of the Liberal Industrial Inquiry of 1928* (London, Benn, 1977), pp. 280–1.

48. Lloyd George Papers, G 18/7/11, 14 January 1935.

49. P. Snowden, *Mr Lloyd George's New Deal* (London, Ivor Nicholson & Watson, 1935).

CHAPTER 8

REACTIONS TO BRITISH AND EUROPEAN FASCISM

Fascism was a product of the deep-rooted social and economic crisis which developed in Europe following the First World War; a period which saw high unemployment, inflation and social instability. Yet, although Britain suffered severe economic depression and rising unemployment, her economic plight was much less marked than that of Germany and Italy. Perhaps for this reason Britain experienced little in the way of a fascist movement in the 1920s; only a few small and insignificant fascist groups, hostile to the Bolsheviks or the Jews, emerged at that time. It was not until the 1930s that a more effective fascist organization, the British Union of Fascists (BUF), was formed under the leadership of Oswald Mosley, at a time when Britain was attempting to deal with the unemployment of between 20 and 23 per cent. When the BUF developed it created something of a stir as the various political parties adjusted to its presence. There was, indeed, quite a furore over its activities, and particularly at the violence associated with its Olympia Meeting of June 1934. Nevertheless, recent work on Mosley and the BUF has concurred about their basic unimportance.[1] It seems likely that both the concern of political parties and of the public at the activities of the BUF was totally out of all proportion to its importance and to the political challenge which it presented; as John Stevenson and Chris Cook wrote 'British fascism was almost a non-starter'.[2] Nevertheless, Mosley's fascist movement merited concern and attention, not least because its emergence seemed to mirror events in Europe. In the end, however, it was European fascism, not British fascism, which exerted most impact upon British politics during the 1930s.

The British Union of Fascists

Sir Oswald Mosley formed the British Union of Fascists in October 1932 as a vehicle for his program which was designed to bring about the economic renaissance of Britain. His 'fascist' ideas had first been shaped by the First World War, which he felt Britain should not have entered. To Mosley, the war had brought an end to traditional party politics and had demonstrated the need for central economic planning. If Britain was to avoid future wars, she had to strengthen her economic and military position and to develop her relations with the Empire in order to deter would-be aggressors. Armed with such views, Mosley entered upon a turbulent political career which saw him move from being the Conservative MP for Harrow in 1918 to, after several political adjustments, becoming Labour MP for Smethwick in 1926.

Mosley's economic philosophy was quickly expressed in *Revolution by Reason* (1925). It advocated a battery of economic and social measures to revive Britain, including the nationalization of the banks and the extension of credit to consumers in order that demand could be increased and that the economy would revive. But planning was deemed essential and Mosley wrote:

> We propose first to expand credit in order to create demand. That new and greater demand must, of course, be met by a new and greater supply of goods, or all the evils of inflation and price rise will result. Here our Socialist planning must enter in. We must see that more goods are forthcoming to meet the new demand.[3]

These ideas were developed further when, as Chancellor of the Duchy of Lancaster in MacDonald's second Labour government, Mosley was involved in the work of the 'Thomas' Committee to deal with unemployment. Dissatisfied with J.H. Thomas' lack of initiative, he put forward his own schemes in the 'Mosley Memorandum', advocating greater expenditure on public works, some forms of tariff protection, the raising of the school-leaving age and the encouragement of early retirement. Mosley resigned in May 1930, when these schemes did not find favour in government circles. But he pursued his policies within the parliamentary Labour Party and the Labour Party issued the 'Mosley Manifesto', develop his policies into a full-scale plan in January 1931, under the title 'A National Policy'.[4] This, more developed, scheme outlined the much criticized recommendation of setting up an inner Cabinet of five which would carry out the needed programme of economic reform.

At first, Mosley's outspoken criticism of the second Labour government attracted support and interest from a variety of MPs, ranging from Nye Bevan to Harold Macmillan. He could not, however, turn this sympathy to good effect and his New Party, formed in March 1931 with the aid of £50,000 from William Morris, the later Lord Nuffield, failed to attract widespread political support and collapsed into political oblivion at the general election of October 1931.

It was only after a trip to Italy in early 1932, to see how fascism operated there, and with the support of Lord Rothermere and the *Daily Mail*, that Mosley renewed his efforts to form a new party designed to instil discipline into the nation, to generate a 'classless brotherhood' and to meet the challenge of communism. Launched on 1 October 1932, the BUF quickly acquired the trappings of European fascism – the 'black shirt' uniform, the commitment to action, the violent conflicts with the Communists and the Jews, and the emphasis placed upon strong leadership. Whatever its economic intent, the fact is that Mosley's fascist movement became associated with the type of violence and anti-Semitism which had become the hallmark of European fascism. The most obvious events of this type were; the conflict between the fascists and the communist at the Olympia meeting in June 1934, the 'Battle of Cable Street' in October 1936 and the fascist election campaigns in the East End of London in 1937.[5] All involved conflict, often violent, between the fascists on the one hand, and the communists and Jews on the other.

The Olympia Meeting of 7 June 1934 was one of the major turning points in the history of the BUF. It was arranged as a grandiose meeting of fascists and their supporters, in anticipation of a triumphant mass meeting at the White City, London, in August. About 1,200 fascists marched to Olympia on the day and the meeting was attended by about 10,000 potential supporters and 2,000 'blackshirts', half of whom were acting as stewards. But, from the start, the event did not go according to plan. There was a rival demonstration by about 2,000 Communists and, according to various estimates, 500 Communists managed to get tickets into the hall. They interrupted events from the start of the proceedings and, exaggeratedly, for Mosley did manage to make his speech, one of the Communist marchers, who did not manage to get into the hall reported:

> So effective was our penetration into Olympia that despite repeated attempts, Mosley was unable to make his speech because of the noise and the fighting between his stewards supporters and the anti-Fascists.[6]

In the end, many of the Communist opponents were ejected from the hall. But it was the manner of that ejection which offended many. Many were kicked and beaten by eight or more stewards before being flung into the street: 'In nearly every case they were bleeding from the head and face and their clothing was badly torn . . ..'[7]

Though Mosley interpreted the actions of the fascists at Olympia as the 'only guarantee of free speech in Britain' that was not how the press, the politicians and the public saw the matter.[8] They saw the fascist stewards as the Nazi storm troopers trampling upon liberty and were quick to dissociate themselves from the image which the BUF had gained. Lord Rothermere and the *Daily Mail* withdrew their support, Conservative MPs who were present vied in their condemnation of the actions of the fascist stewards, the government considered the need to take steps to improve public order, and the public were persuaded to perceive the BUF as an extension of the fascist danger in Europe.[9]

Such visions were amplified by the continuance of fascist violence. The most dramatic evidence of this was the 'Battle of Cable Street' on Sunday 4 October 1936, when a march through the East End of London by the fascists prompted an anti-fascist demonstration, violence, and the injury of seventy people and eighty-eight arrests, eighty-three of whom were anti-fascists. In the wake of this violence the National government pushed forward with the Public Order Act which, among other clauses, prohibited the wearing of uniforms for political purposes in public places or at meetings. Did this signify the end of British fascism? Indeed, why did British fascism fail?

Many reasons have been offered, including the threat of European fascism, the events at Olympia, the introduction of the Public Order Act in 1936, military uniforms, the stability of the political system, the economic recovery of the 1930s and the occurrence of the Second World War.[10] It may have been that its conflicts with the communists exaggerated its importance. A.J.P. Taylor sees its decline more in terms of the failure of leadership:

> Mosley was in fact a highly gifted playboy. From the moment he modelled himself on Mussolini, he resembled nothing so much as an actor touring the provinces in a play which someone else had made a success of in London. Watching newsreels of Mosley on the march through the East End recalls the memory of another Londoner. Oswald Mosley aspired to be the Great Dictator, Sir Charles Chaplin played the role better.[11]

Yet it might also be argued that the major political parties ensured that, despite the attention which Mosley attracted, the fascists were going to be marginalized.

The Labour Party and Fascism

The most perplexing problem facing members of the Labour Party in the early 1930s was how to reconcile their advocacy of peace with the urgent need to deal with the threat of European fascism. This concern was adumbrated in the early 1930s by the rise of Oswald Mosley's British Union of Fascists. Historians have varied in their interpretations of how the Labour Party approached these problems and the effectiveness of its responses.

Michael Newman argues that the Labour Party adopted the view that fascism only emerged where parliamentary democracy was not well established. Since such a system seemed well founded in Britain it chose to ignore British fascism, unlike the Communist Party, which was prepared to fight the BUF on the streets at Olympia and Cable Street. Broadening out his topic, he concludes:

> In this sense, Labour's respect for the constitution and its willingness to collaborate with an increasingly strong State against 'extremism' of the Left as well as the Right did not save Britain from fascism: it merely helped capital at the expense of the working class.[12]

His view is that since there was little chance of a fascist state being formed in Britain the Labour Party ought to have been prepared to tackle fascism in a militant way and to strike a blow against the constitutional approach to politics which simply strengthened capitalism. In rejecting such an approach it was left to the Communists to challenge both British fascism and capitalism in the 1930s.

Yet, such a view argues that the Labour Party should have gone against its declared policies, on the assumption that they could not work, and maintains that it was dilatory in its attitudes towards and actions against British fascism. Neither proposition is necessarily correct. The Labour Party subsequently achieved some measure of socialism under Attlee, despite the hostility of capitalism, and the Labour Party was well informed about the real strength of the fascist challenge. Quite rightly, the Labour Party did not wish to exaggerate the importance of a fringe political group which it had investigated in a detailed national survey, based upon a circular to the secretaries of its constituency organizations in 1934.[13] The Labour Party was well aware of the limited challenge of British fascism and could discriminate between the threat it posed compared with the more serious threat of European fascism.

This survey highlighted the fact that there were few centres of fascist support outside London, Manchester, Birmingham and Leeds – areas where there was a significant Jewish presence or where Mosley exerted some personal appeal. Even in these areas, no political successes were achieved in the local elections despite the determined efforts of fascist groups in the late 1930s.[14]

This thinness of fascist support was particularly apparent in Yorkshire. Bradford was 'not troubled with them' [fascists], 'The Movement does not receive much support' in Dewsbury, and there appear to have been only a couple of modest meetings in Huddersfield.[15] Elsewhere, there may have been more support. It was claimed that there were about 350 members in Sheffield, '50 wear uniform', and in Harrogate the fascists 'appear to confine their attention to younger members of the Tory Party, particularly those interested in sports, rugby and golf players (the boisterous kind of young bloods).'[16] It was feared that the fascists might be 'gaining considerable ground' in the Harrogate area. Nevertheless, any fears about Harrogate and Sheffield becoming centres of fascism proved unfounded. In Leeds, thought to be one of the most powerful and well-organized centres of fascism, it was suggested that there were only 100 to 200 fascists and no regular outdoor meetings, though it was noted:

> The Fascists have very large premises at Devonshire hall. I am informed by one of our Councillors that they are surrounded with Barbed wire. He also says that about 50 or 60 fascists are drilling there regularly.[17]

The fact is that fascist support was limited to the extent that all the fascist groups in a particular region were forced to work together in order to ensure a good attendance at meetings. This was particularly evident in Leeds. When Mosley addressed a meeting of 1,500 people at Leeds Town Hall in May 1934 it was estimated that about 400 fascists were present 'most of whom had come to Leeds by bus.'[18]

Even in the East End of London, a Jewish area which was the stronghold of British fascism, support was limited. Though fascist candidates put forward a strong campaign in the London County Council elections of March 1937, their six candidates for the three two-member divisions of Bethnal Green North East, Shoreditch and Limehouse were defeated and they received less than 20 per cent of the vote.[19]

Stuart Rawnsley's work on the membership of the BUF has also emphasized the limited extent of fascist support, especially after Olympia. In addition he has stressed the crankish nature of many of its supporters and the fact that it drew that support from only a very small section of the working class – even though they may have formed a significant proportion of the BUF's small membership of between 5,000 and 40,000 members throughout the 1930s.[20] Some working-class members, particularly in south Lancashire, were apparently attracted because they were unemployed.

It is clearly dangerous to be too sweeping about the type of support which fascism received, for the evidence is far too diffuse and fragmentary, but it would be fair to accept Wal Hannington's point that the allegiance to the trade unions and the Labour Party prevented the working class and the unemployed being attracted to fascism though he felt that, 'Every locality where the unemployed remain unorganized is a potential breeding-ground for this country, just as it was in Germany.'[21] The trade unions, trades councils and local Labour parties informed their members about the dangers it presented and energized their opposition – albeit in the form of peaceful protest.

The Labour Party was concerned at the threat which fascism posed to its traditional areas of support but the results of its 1934 circular emphasized the limited nature of British fascism. Yet, while it could play down the challenge of British fascism it could not ignore the threat of European fascism. As a result, the Labour Party was forced to alter many of its once-cherished policies during the mid- and late 1930s.

Throughout the inter-war years Labour politicians had been concerned with the preservation of peace. They posed numerous questions. Could European peace be guaranteed by disarmament? How would Germany be prevented from entering another major international conflict? Could French fears of, and hostility towards, Germany be removed? To these questions they offered three policies for peace in Europe: disarmament, collective security through the League of Nations and the restoration of German territories stripped away by the Treaty of Versailles. They accepted that these policies would provide the basis for peaceful co-existence between nations. Yet mutual distrust persisted between France and Germany, Hitler rose to power in Germany, the Italian intervention in Abyssinia revealed the contempt of Italy for the League of Nations, and the Spanish Civil War, the subject of the next chapter, presented the stark challenge of fascism. Some Labour politicians continued to cling to their previous peace strategies but by the late 1930s the majority had come to accept that war was inevitable – a view confirmed by the events in Czechoslovakia, Austria and Poland which preceded the outbreak of the European war. This change of attitude created problems for the large and cumbersome structure of the Labour Party, where the commitment to peace was a deep-rooted and sensitive issue. In a slow, confused, grudging process of adjustment the Labour Party attuned itself to the fight against fascism, and eventually the need to abandon its emphasis upon political independence.

It was Ernest Bevin and the trade-union movement which forced the change of direction. At the Hastings Conference of 1933, the Party had declared its commitment to two potentially contradictory policies. It supported a resolution opposing war by 'organizing working-class action, including the general strike' and yet accepted a resolution committing it to a general reduction of armaments within the security of the League of Nations's commitment to take action against aggressor states. The difficulty was that Labour could have found itself supporting military action against a fascist state at the same time as it threatened a general strike against war.

In fact the Labour Party was deeply divided on how to maintain peace. Arthur Henderson, Ernest Bevin, Dr Hugh Dalton, Clement Attlee, and their supporters, favoured disarmament based upon collective security. The young Hugh Gaitskell, who had become aware of the dangers of fascism on his visit to Austria in the summer of 1933 and was greatly influenced by Dalton, summed up the attitude of this group by arguing that a general strike against all wars was 'an invitation to the fascist aggressors.'[22] A second, rather small, group led by George Lansbury, the party leader advocated pacifism. A third, composed of ex-members of the ILP, favoured an international general strike to prevent conflict and the need for working-class institutions to offer a revolutionary socialist pro-gramme. A fourth, dominated by Sir Stafford Cripps and the Socialist League, a body founded in 1932 by a large minority group of the Independent Labour Party which refused to leave the Labour Party, favoured a 'united front' with the Communists against fascists. Cripps explained that the fascist threat was serious and that Communist hostility towards the Labour Party had ceased. They had 'disavowed any intention, for the present, of acting in opposition to the Labour movement in the country, and certainly their action in many constituencies during the last election gives earnest of their disavowal.'[23]

These factions came into conflict at the 1935 Labour Party Conference. This took place at Brighton in the climate of Italian aggression against Abyssinia and Ernest Bevin, with the support of the trade-union movement, swept away the protests of Lansbury and Cripps' Socialist League to win conference support for collective security through the League of Nations sanctions, including, if necessary, military sanctions against Italian aggression in Abyssinia. Bevin, with the support of the major trade unions, dealt brutally with George Lansbury and his pacifist reservations, effectively forcing him to quit as leader of the Labour Party. Rather dramati-cally, Dalton recorded that Bevin 'hammered [Lansbury] to death.'[24]

The 1935 conference also provoked two major, and related, controversies: the Socialist League mounted a major challenge against the conference policy and constituency parties began to protest that the block-vote of trade unions was limiting their influence within the party. Sir Stafford Cripps linked the two movements by operating in both. Defeated at the 1935 Labour Party Conference, the Socialist League and Cripps attempted to forge an alliance with Tribune (formed to further the 'united front' against fascism), the Communists and the Constituency Labour Party Association through a new, 'united front' campaign.

The international events of 1935 and 1936 tended to confirm the views of both extremes of the Labour Party. Bevin and Dalton felt that Franco's invasion of Spain with his fascist forces justified rearmament, while Cripps and the Socialist League continued to support the 'united front' campaign since the National government was considered to be untrustworthy. As a result the Edinburgh Conference of 1936 passed resolutions leaving the Labour Party supporting collective security but opposing rearmament. Nevertheless, the Spanish Civil War did make a difference for the conference condemned the non-intervention policy adopted by the major powers, for it was being flouted by Italians, Germans and Russians, and recommended that the Spanish republican government should be allowed to buy arms.[25]

After the conference, the Socialist League continued to oppose rearmament, opposed sanctions against Italy threatened as a result of the Italian invasion of Abyssinia, and advocated a policy for the Labour movement of preparing for the 'mass resistance to war', by which was meant a general strike. In January 1937 it patched together a new 'united front' campaign in association with the ILP, the Communists, the Left Book Club and Tribune, around a programme of defence for the Spanish Republic, opposition to rearmament by the National government, support for the struggles of the unemployed and the affiliation of the Communist Party and the ILP to the Labour Party. The campaign was in defiance of the Labour Party ban on joint work with the Communists and the Socialist League was condemned by the Party, its members being forced to choose between disbanding the organization of expulsion. The Socialist League was thus dissolved in May 1937.

The failure of the 'united front' campaign persuaded the left of the anti-fascist movement to reconsider its strategy. The direction of the campaign moved towards a broader 'popular front' to be drawn up between the left in Britain, France and the Soviet Union. When this campaign faltered the idea of the 'popular front' was extended to include an alliance between the Labour Party, the Liberals and some dissident Conservative opponents of the National government, such as Winston Churchill, who were expressing their opposition to appeasement with Hitler and Mussolini.

In this climate, Cripps decided to mount a 'popular front' campaign in 1937 and 1938, in order to encourage Labour to enter a coalition government with anti-fascist and anti-appeasement Conservatives and Liberals if a split could be engineered within the Conservative Party. Indeed, such a split appeared possible in February 1938 when Anthony Eden resigned from the National government because of the attempt by Neville Chamberlain, the Prime Minister, to recruit Italy as an ally against Germany. At that time, as George Orwell reflected, the campaign appeared to be exerting some impact upon British politics for, 'In England the Popular Front is only an idea, but it has already produced the nauseous spectacle of bishops, Communists, cocoa-magnates, publishers, duchesses and Labour MPs marching arm-in-arm to the tune of "Rule Brittania".'[26]

The 'popular front' idea was, however, rejected by the Labour Party, which wished to maintain its political independence, mindful of the general election which was due in 1940. As a result Nye Bevan and Cripps, with several others, were expelled from the party. Their rank and file supporters were also rooted out of the Labour Party in a flurry of activity throughout 1939.[27]

The fact is that after 1936 the tide had turned to the right in British Labour politics. In that year Bevin became Chairman of the General Council of the TUC and Dalton was made Chairman of the National Executive Committee of the Labour Party. In 1937 Dalton and Attlee got the Parliamentary Labour Party to support the armed forces estimates and the Bournemouth Conference supported rearmament. There was now a new firmness in British Labour Party policy.

Although the Labour Party was fragmented in its approach to foreign affairs, and slow to respond to events in Europe, it did strongly oppose Fascism and appeasement even before the 1937 Bournemouth Conference. The right wing within the party had shown more realism about the events in Europe than the left wing. Nevertheless, there remains the issue of the 'popular front' and the 'united front' against fascism – both of which were anathema to a Labour Party hostile to the Communist Party. It also feared that a coalition with the anti-fascist forces might create similar problems to those which the Labour government of 1929–31 faced when relying upon Liberal support to carry out a legislative programme.

The Conservative Party and the Threat of Fascism

What of the Conservative Party, how did it react to the challenge of fascism? The answer would appear to be with less determination than Labour and with fewer changes in policy. By and large, the mainstream of the Conservative Party attempted to ignore British fascism and to appease European fascism.

As already indicated, the Conservative Party was the dominant member of all three National governments which operated from August 1931 until the Second World War. Throughout the 1930s the main body of the party, whether led by Stanley Baldwin or Neville Chamberlain, tended to disown the British Union of Fascists while attempting to appease European fascism. It was the fringe of the Conservative Party, and those prominent politicians who moved to the fringe, who disagreed with one or more of those policies – ranging from the Lord Rothermere, the press baron, to Winston Churchill and, eventually, Anthony Eden.

Some Conservative support for the BUF was evident from its early days and was most obviously stated through Rothermere's *Daily Mail* which, on 8 January 1934, contained an article entitled 'Hurrah for the Blackshirts'. This article inaugurated Rothermere's massive press campaign which helped to thrust the BUF from comparative obscurity into the limelight.[28] Some Conservative MPs began to attend fascist meetings and, as already suggested, there were some young Conservatives who supported fascism that developed in relatively middle-class towns such as Harrogate.

Nevertheless, fascism does not appear to have gained a strong or permanent foothold within most Conservative constituency parties. In areas where fascism had made a significant challenge its presence was likely to be embarrassing. For instance, in Leeds it was the Conservative leader who intervened in a press debate and it was declared that, 'His attitude is anti-fascist and anti-communist.'[29] In addition the fascists threatened 'to oppose Vyvyan Adams, the Tory MP for West Leeds, who has been so active in the House of Commons in asking questions re the Fascists.' Also, the support of many of those conservatives who flirted with fascism came to an abrupt halt after the Olympia meeting. Rothermere withdrew his press suppo. t and Conservative MPs, who revealed some interest in fascism, joined the clamour of condemnation. Indeed, three Conservative MPs – W.J. Anstruther-Gray, J. Scrymgeour-Wedderburn and T.J. O'Connor – had rushed straight from Olympia to Printing House Square to hand in a letter which subsequently appeared in *The Times*. They declared:

> . . . were involuntary witnesses of wholly unnecessary violence inflicted by uniformed Blackshirts on interrupters. Men and women were knocked down and were still assaulted and kicked on the floor. It will be a matter of surprise for us if there were no fatal injuries. These methods of securing freedom of speech may have been effective, but they are happily unusual in England and constituted in our opinion a deplorable outrage of public order.[30]

It was such violence as this, and that perpetrated at Cable Street, which encouraged a Conservative-dominated National government to introduce a Public Order Act at the end of 1936.

If the Conservatives dismissed the British Union of Fascists without too much concern – and most could see no good political reasons for embracing the fascist faith – they could not dismiss the threat of European fascism so easily, and attempted to accommodate it instead. The fact is that the majority of the Conservative Party supported the appeasement line, through the National government, from before the Abyssinian crisis of 1935 to the Second World War.

It is impossible, in a short space, to full convey the complexities of international diplomacy throughout these years. Nevertheless, the fundamental issues can be clearly stated. British governments continued to accept the need for collective security under the Covenant of the League of Nations. Ostensibly, they accepted the need for disarmament and the maintenance of the peace by sanctions, and even military action, organized by the League of Nations against aggressor nations. Therefore, formal protests were made when Hitler announced compulsory military service in 1935 and an increase in military forces, in contravention of the Treaty of Versailles, and when Italy invaded Abyssinia. But in reality such protests were conducted at a low level in order not to interfere with normal, and reasonably good, relations which British foreign secretaries wished to continue and nurture with the offending nations. In the case of the Italians, Sir John Simon, the Foreign Secretary, passed on a friendly warning to Mussolini in February and

March 1935.[31] Later, Anthony Eden, by that time in the Cabinet as Minister of the League of Nations Affairs though still a Junior Minister for Foreign Affairs, went to Rome with the intent of offering Abyssinia territory in Somaliland in return for conceding some of its own territory to Italy. As David Carlton has written, this plan 'represented a willingness to buy off a bully with territory to which he had no legitimate claim.'[32] The plan failed and the Italians invaded Abyssinia in October 1935. In the case of Germany, Simon and Eden travelled to Berlin to have talks with Hitler in March 1935.[33] Evidently, the concern for collective security was not to be allowed to interfere with normal international relations. The process of appeasement had begun in earnest.

Yet the course of appeasement was by no means straight. Baldwin's National government had gone to the electorate in November 1935 against the backcloth of the Italian invasion of Abyssinia, which raised public concern, and a Peace Ballot carried out by the League of Nations Union which indicated that the British public wanted peace and disarmament but was prepared to contemplate military sanctions against aggressor nations. The issue of sanctions against Italy was, therefore, to the fore and the evidence that Sir Samuel Hoare, the Foreign Secretary, had been negotiating with Pierre Laval, his French equivalent, to arrange a plan to settle the Italian–Abyssinian war by giving one-third of Abyssinia to Italy was not well received. Indeed, though the Cabinet had agreed the plan in December Hoare was forced to resign, and replaced by Eden.[34]

Yet the policy of appeasement continued throughout 1936. As David Carlton stresses, Eden was not the most unequivocal foreign secretary. He changed his mind several times about the possibility of oil sanctions against Italy, hoped to be able to win concessions from France, to avoid conflict when German troops unilaterally moved in to remilitarize the Rhineland in March 1936. His mild reaction to the tearing up of the Treaty of Versailles was perhaps explicable by the fact that he saw such events as inevitable and because the Foreign Office was locked into a policy of appeasement. Carlton describes the situation thus:

> Eden was prepared in principle to make concessions not only to Hitler but also to Mussolini if matters could be so arranged as to involve no loss of face. But whereas he had come to the conclusion by the beginning of 1936 that Mussolini was probably not the man to play this game, he remained

192

cautiously optimistic that Hitler might be. He was, therefore, at least until 1938 much more inclined to be hostile to Italy than to Germany. In retrospect this seems to betoken an odd sense of priorities . . . .. Yet in the years before 1938 Eden was obviously closer than his critics to public sentiment. For nothing done by Hitler in the external sphere during Eden's time at the Foreign Office aroused any public reaction remotely comparable to that which engulfed Hoare over Abyssinia.[35]

The detailed record does tend to suggest that Eden was not the consistent anti-appeaser which he claimed to be.

Throughout 1936, Eden pursued a wavering and temporizing course on sanctions against Italy. He was also partly, though not wholly, responsible for the 'non-intervention' policy which Britain and France pursued with regard to the Spanish Civil War, even though it was being blatantly ignored by Germany, Italy and Russia, and though it denied a legitimate Republican government the right of access to the world market for arms with which to defend itself.

There were two motivating factors behind many of these actions of appeasement. In the first place, many of the leading figures in the National government feared the rise of communism in Germany, Italy and Spain rather more than they feared the rise of European fascism. Secondly, they realized too late that European fascism was the real threat to peace and that Britain needed time to accomplish her rearmament. And, as will be suggested in the next chapter, most Conservative politicians were quite happy to see communist and anarchist groups within the Spanish Republican groups beaten by the fascists and their own internal squabbles. Their affinity with the right rather than the left allowed them to overlook the genuine nature of the fascist threat.

Nevertheless, there were a few Conservative politicians who fundamentally disagreed with Conservative policy. The most famous and obvious dissenter was Winston Churchill who, in his years in the political wilderness, was a great critic of both Stanley Baldwin and Neville Chamberlain. His main concern was that the National government had not sufficiently registered the fact that if Spain fell into fascist hands France would then be surrounded by fascist powers – Germany, Italy and Spain. Since Britain was committed to defending France in the case of an invasion, it was obvious to him that Britain would be drawn into a future European war unless fascism was thwarted.

Churchill was soon joined in expressing such a marginal Conservative view by Anthony Eden, one of the leading appeasers of the 1930s. Throughout 1937 and early 1938 relations between Neville Chamberlain, the Prime Minister, and Eden had been strained – largely due to the fact that Chamberlain favoured the policy of enlisting Italian support against Hitler, a policy which was in direct contradiction to that pursued by Eden. Eventually, Eden resigned in February 1938 allegedly as a result of Chamberlain's attempt to make an agreement with the Italians without informing him, although Carlton puts the ball firmly in Eden's court, suggesting that 'Essentially . . . his departure sprang from an unwillingness to treat with Mussolini.'[36] He was fortunate to be seen as an anti-appeaser by the time Chamberlain was negotiating with Hitler and coercing the Czechs into surrender during the Czechoslovakian crisis of September 1938.

Yet David Carlton feels that too much should not be made of the gathering of opposition to Chamberlain's National government policy of appeasement. The fact was that Churchill and Eden were not of like minds and did not associate closely until Churchill became Prime Minister in 1940. Instead, there was a loose group of 20 or 30 Conservative MPs who identified with Eden and a similar group, including Brendan Bracken, Duncan Sandys and Robert Boothby, who identified with Churchill. Their position as outsiders was not transformed until the outbreak of the Second World War when it was Chamberlain's ardent supporters, the 'appeasers' who became the outsiders and the 'guilty men'.

Conclusion

Though Labour joined with the Conservatives in May 1940 to fight the Second World War, under Churchill's leadership, it is clear that despite the almost obsessive concern of the public about the threat of European fascism it was only the Labour Party, slow and cumbersome in its rate of change, which actually squared up to the necessity of facing fascism with military sanctions if necessary. The Conservative Party, which dominated the National government, operated a policy of 'appeasement' to which there was only limited and fragmented opposition from within its ranks.

Perhaps a more determined effort by the Labour Party, and a willingness to operate a 'united front' against the fascists might have forced the National government to change its policy, but that seems unlikely. For one thing, the Labour Party leaders would not contemplate an alliance with the Communist Party, which they rightly feared was merely aiming to use Labour to gain political support and which was involved in almost needless violence against the supremely unimportant British fascists. For another, there was little or no chance that the National government, working with a very large Conservative majority, would be in danger of political defeat even on the matter of 'appeasement'. In addition, it might be noted that British fascism had not substantially changed the attitudes of Britain's major political parties and it could be argued that there was still much equivocation in government as to whether or not Mussolini or Hitler represented the biggest threat. In the realm of secret diplomacy it would appear that public opinion had only a very minor role to play.

What is remarkable is how impervious a government can be to changing public opinion when insulated from the threat of political defeat by a substantial parliamentary majority. It is clear the National government's right-wing attitudes and its hostility to the threat of communism could override public concern within the context of its parliamentary supremacy. This was particularly evident in the case of the Spanish Civil War.

NOTES

1. G.C. Webber, *The Ideology of the British Right* (London, Croom Helm, 1987); R. Thurlow, *Fascism in Britain, 1918–1985* (London, Blackwell, 1987).
2. J. Stevenson and C. Cook, *The Slump* (London, Jonathan Cape, 1977), p. 217.
3. O. Mosley, *Revolution by Reason* (1925), pp. 22–3, quoted in R. Skidelsky, *Oswald Mosley* (London, Macmillan, 1975).
4. Skidelsky, op.cit., p. 248.
5. Stevenson and Cook, op.cit., pp. 208–9 gives details of the results of the London County Council elections in the East End of London.
6. J. Jacobs, *Out of the Ghetto* (London, Simon, 1978), p. 139.
7. Stevenson and Cook, op.cit., p. 235.
8. O. Mosley, *My Life* (1967), p. 301; Skidelsky, op.cit., pp. 365–78.
9. *Daily Mail*, 8 January 1934.
10. Skidelsky, op.cit., from p. 335 and Stevenson and Cook, op.cit., ch. xi.
11. *The Observer*, 7 December 1980.
12. M. Newman, 'Democracy versus Dictatorship', *History Workshop,* Spring 1978, p. 85.

13. Archives of the Labour Party, LP/FAS/34.
14. Stevenson and Cook, op.cit., p. 210.
15. Archives of the Labour Party, LP/FAS/34/233, 235–6.
16. Ibid., LP/FAS/34/22 ii, 24 i.
17. Ibid., LP/FAS/34/20.1.
18. Idem.; also J. Reynolds and K. Laybourn, *Labour Heartland. A History of the Labour Party in West Yorkshire during the inter-war years 1918–1939* (Bradford, Bradford University Press, 1987), pp. 117–22.
19. Footnote 5.
20. S. Rawnsley, 'The Membership of the British Union of Fascists', in K. Lunn and R.S. Thurlow (eds.), *British Fascism* (London, Croom Helm, 1979).
21. W. Hannington, *The Problem of the Distressed Areas* (London, Victor Gollancz, 1937), p. 249.
22. P.M. Williams, *Hugh Gaitskell* (Oxford, Oxford University Press, 1982).
23. *Socialist*, March 1936, quoted in B. Pimlott, *Labour and the Left in the 1930s* (Cambridge, Cambridge University Press, 1977), p. 93.
24. Quoted in Pimlott, op.cit., p. 73.
25. K. Harris, *Attlee* (London, Weidenfeld & Nicolson, 1982), p. 128.
26. Pimlott, op.cit., p. 143.
27. Huddersfield Labour Party, Minutes, 21 February 1939; Halifax Labour Party, Minutes, 25 May 1939; *Leeds Citizen*, 3 February 1939.
28. Skidelsky, op.cit., p. 322.
29. Archives of the Labour Party, LP/FAS/34/20.1.
30. *The Times*, 8 June 1934, quoted in Skidelsky, op.cit.,p. 370.
31. D. Carlton, *Anthony Eden* (London, Allen & Unwin, 1986), p. 62.
32. Ibid., p. 65.
33. Ibid., p. 62.
34. Ibid., pp. 69–70.
35. Ibid., p.76.
36. Ibid., p. 128.

CHAPTER 9

THE IMPACT OF THE SPANISH CIVIL WAR

The Spanish Civil War, which began in July 1936 when General Franco's fascist troops from Morocco landed in southern Spain, exerted a major impact upon the international political scene and, nationally, upon the attitude of the right and left in Britain. K.W. Watkins has written that:

> Probably not since the French Revolution had a foreign event so bitterly divided the British people, and this at a time when national unity was essential for our survival.[1]

This view contrasts sharply with the disillusioned, almost pessimistic, reflections of George Orwell who wrote in *England Your England* that there was no true internationalism amongst the British working class. Apart from the 'Hands off Russia' campaign of 1920 he feels that the British working class had never thought or acted internationally and, 'For two and a half years they watched their comrades in Spain slowly strangled, and never aided even with a single strike.'[2] In a footnote he does point to the aid they gave with money through the various aid-Spain funds but also derides this contribution, emphasising that 'the sum raised . . . would not equal five per cent of the turnover of the football pools during the same period.'[3] Orwell felt that the bulk of British public opinion was behind Chamberlain's foreign policy of 'non-intervention', dissension being voiced by only a few thousand left-wingers, some of

197

whom went on to fight in Spain. In a recent article, C. Fleay and M.L. Sanders have supported Orwell's general stance attacking the Labour Party policy on the Spanish Civil War as being as 'torpid and as ambivalent' as that of the National Government.[4]

The Spanish Civil War has thus been the real focus of recent debate surrounding the British reaction to European fascism. It has raised three major questions. Firstly, what was the impact of the Spanish Civil War upon British public opinion? Secondly, was the Labour Party ambivalent in its attitude towards the Spanish Republican government? Thirdly, why did the National government adopt a policy of non-intervention which, as implied in the previous chapter, aided the fascists at the expense of the legitimate Republican government of Spain?

The Spanish Civil War

The Spanish Civil War began in July 1936 when a Moorish legion invaded southern Spain in support of General Franco's attempt to overthrow the socialist-dominated Spanish Republican government. This action ended an uneasy truce which had existed between the various political parties following the creation of the Spanish Republic in 1931 after King Alfonso's flight from Spain. The situation had begun to deteriorate markedly after the elections of February 1936 returned a coalition of Liberal republicans, social-ists, anarchists, communists and Trotskyists to power, even though the right-wing parties had won a small popular majority. The coalition was uneasy, law and order broke down, there were murderous attacks upon the clergy, churches were looted and destroyed, and there were several major strikes. In this situation, General Franco and part of the army decided to lead a coup d'etat, their action being provoked by the murder of Calvo Satelo, a right-wing politician, on 13 July. The first detachment of the Moors and foreign legionaires crossed from Morocco to the Spanish mainland on 19 July, an action which coincided with military revolts in Seville, Cadiz and Barcelona.

To most Western observers the Spanish Civil War was simply a conflict between the supporters of the Republican government and Franco's fascist rebels, supported by Germany and Italy. It was in fact more complex and multi-layered encompassing Basque and Catalan independence movements, a landlord–peasant struggle and a civil war between communist and anarchist groups in Catalonia. George Orwell wrote of the civil war within a civil war, for he was present when this conflict erupted in Barcelona.[5] There was also religious conflict. Quite often Catholic groups gave support to Franco against the Socialist Republican government, on the grounds that the latter was responsible for the burning of churches and the murdering of Catholics. But one should not ignore the fact that there were many Catholics who found themselves opposing Franco because of their support for the independence movements.

These subtleties of the war did not entirely evade the British public. Pro-Republican Catholics did express their opinions in newspapers such as the *Leeds Citizen*.[6] There was deep concern by Catholics at the bombing of Guernica by German planes in support of Franco's cause.[7] Nevertheless, it was the basic European conflict between fascism and socialism which was reflected most in the concern of the British public. As Watkins wrote:

> The Spanish Civil War was a mirror into which men gazed and had cast back at them not a picture of reality but the image of hope and fears of their generation. For many it became the supreme moral issue of their time.[8]

There is no doubt that part of the Catholic community in Britain reacted strongly to the destruction and damage of Catholic churches. Indeed, Eoin O'Duffy, who led an Irish contingent to Spain to help Franco, maintained that they had gone to fight the battle of Christianity against Communism, a view which was confirmed for them by the Irish Dominican father, Revd Paul O' Sullivan when he said:

> You are fighting in God's holy name, for God's glory, in God's defence, to save our holy Faith, to save Christianity. to save the world from the fiendish atrocities which have been perpetrated in Russia, in Mexico and now in Spain.[9]

Equally, there is no doubt that trade unionists were fervently hostile to the actions of Franco. Accounts of atrocities on both sides clearly helped to partly divide British public opinion along social, religious and economic lines. Some obviously saw the events in Spain as fascism limbering up for an even greater conflict; Spain was seen as an experimental laboratory for the arms, equipment and strategy of the fascist powers.

Many of those who went and fought for the Republicans were not always clear about why they were there, except that they felt a revulsion against fascism and a general feeling that they had to do something in the face of the frustrations of the 1930s. Jason Gurney, who joined the International Brigade, wrote of such feelings:

> The despair we felt at our inability to control our own destinies was not concerned solely with the rise of Fascism throughout Europe and the danger of it in or own country; the Depression had proved that the ruling class could not control the system it had itself produced.[10]

Many others who went to Spain would have concurred.[11] Before the National Government banned Britons going to Spain at the beginning of 1937 there were already more than 600 men in the British Battalion of the International Brigade, organized by the Communist Party of Great Britain, while others, such as George Orwell, identified with the Independent Labour Party activists who fought with POUM, a Catalan anarcho-syndicalist group. Yet others fought and identified with a plethora of socialist and anarchist groups who fought on the Aragon front, in the defence of Madrid, and at the battle of Jarama in February 1937. But they were gradually forced to withdraw from Spain. Orwell returned in 1937, disillusioned after the conflict between the communists and anarchists in Barcelona.[12] The British section of the International Brigade withdrew from Spain with the full organization on 15 November 1938. Thereafter, the fascists rapidly captured the major cities and the war came to an end on 1 April 1939.

British Public Opinion and the Spanish Civil War

The impact of the Spanish Civil War on British public opinion must be seen within the wider context of the international events of the 1930s. The rising tide of European fascism began to concern the British public, as well as some politicians, from the mid-1930s onwards. The Abyssinian crisis, referred to in the previous chapter, was the first really serious issue which moved British public opinion against fascism. It clearly influenced the League of Nations Union 'Peace Ballot', held in June 1935 and involving about eleven and a half million people, the majority of whom voted in favour of disarmament and the need for collective military action against aggressor nations should economic sanctions fail. It also dominated the general election of November 1935 and influenced government foreign policy throughout 1936. And it was against this backcloth of public concern that the Spanish Civil War began on the 19 July 1936.

The Spanish Civil War exerted a profound impact upon British public opinion, despite Orwell's contrary view. Although few British citizens fought in Spain, and there was little in the way of public protest and demonstration, there is ample evidence of public concern – particularly for the Spanish Republican government. The need to halt fascism began to be seen almost as a life and death matter. This affected not only the dedicated left and the organized working class but the whole of British society.

The size and range of the relief activities undertaken shows the strength of public support for the Spanish Republican government. At the national level there was a National Joint Council for Spanish Relief, chaired by the Duchess of Atholl, a Conservative MP, though dominated by Liberal and Labour. This committee acted as the co-ordinator for the activities of many other organizations, including the Spanish Medical Aid Committee, the Spain Foodship Youth Committee, the League of Nations Committee, the Peace Pledge Union, and various local councils of action and *ad hoc* bodies. Most towns had Aid Spain Committees, which collected tins of milk, bars of soap, money for medical aid as well as holding meetings to explain the cause of Republican Spain. While many of these bodies were underpinned by Labour and working-class support it should be recognized that they attracted support from across the social and political spectrum. As a result twenty-nine food ships – the organizing of which proved to be a good way of strengthening support, were sent to Republican Spain during the three years of the civil war. Collections for medical supplies were also undertaken and the first British Medical Unit of doctors and nurses, organized by the Spanish Medical Aid Committee, left for Spain as early as August 1936. Several towns raised money to send their own ambulances to Spain bearing the town name. The Spanish Medical Aid Committee reviewing the situation at the end of the first year had sent out forty-seven ambulances, eighty trained personnel, had constructed two base hospitals and several field hospitals and had set up a convalescent home – the Ralph Fox Memorial Home in memory of a well-known author and critic who had died in action in Spain during 1936. About ten months later, in a report to an

International Congress at Paris it was stated that the Spanish Medical Aid Committee had helped to set up nineteen hospitals throughout Republican Spain, some front-line hospitals and seventy-two ambulances. [13]

There were in fact many organizations supplying help to the Republican government. They raised money in a variety of ways, from auctioning sketches of Picasso's *Guernica* to showing, up and down the country, the films *The Defence of Madrid and Spanish Earth*. [14] British miners raised £80,000 for Spain, the Labour Party Spain Committee collected £49,000. Some towns, such as Bradford, provided facilities for Spanish refugees. Indeed, Bradford set up a home for Basque children up Manningham Lane, though it was largely financed by the Trades Council.

Several writers have rightly reflected the widespread nature of the political support for the Republican government and accepted C.L. Mowat's comment that the various *ad hoc* bodies which emerged 'were, in effect, "popular fronts" drawing in members of all parties.'[15] Support for the Republican government was widespread throughout all the social classes and across the political spectrum. This contrasts sharply with the limited support for the Spanish fascists. In fact when the *Daily Mail* launched an appeal for an anti-red ambulance it did not raise sufficient money to send even one to the Spanish fascists. [16]

Nevertheless, it was the British Labour movement which was the backbone of support for the Spanish Republican government. Yet this fact does not seem to have impressed Orwell and some other, more recent, writers.

The British Labour Movement and the Spanish Civil War.

The crux of the criticism directed at the Labour Party, in particular, is that while it provided food and medical help it did little to try to persuade the British government to end its policy of non-intervention towards Spain. This view has been expressed most effectively in an article by Fleay and Sanders. In their work on the Labour Spain Committee they conclude:

> The party's identification with the cause of the Spanish Republic was never translated into practical aid for winning the war. Whether possible or not, it was never contemplated. The Labour party leadership failed consistently to put principle into practice, while the rank-and-file opposition to party

politics, as expressed by the Labour Spain Committee, confused imperatives and failed to effect a radical change of policy.[17]

Watkins comes to a similar conclusion, although he argues that the Labour Party's hostility to working with the Communist Party was the reason for its failure to force the National government to abandon its non-intervention policy.[18]

These criticisms are, in many respects, justified although it would seem a bit far-fetched for historians to believe that the Labour Party, even in alliance with the Communist Party, could have forced a National government with an overwhelming parliamentary majority, to have capitulated to external pressure. In addition to which, the Labour Party was facing the anguish of having to adjust its attitude towards peace and disarmament, commitments which had been established in the wake of the First World War, when faced with the threat of European fascism and the Spanish Civil War. The process of change was never likely to be easy.

The real problem was that although Ernest Bevin and the trade union movement had swept away pacifist opposition, and won conference support for collective security for the League of Nations at the Labour Party's Brighton Conference of 1935, it was by no means fully committed to rearmament. Indeed, throughout 1936 there was much confusion in Labour Party ranks. This is beautifully illustrated by the actions of the Bradford Trades Council, whose secretary was also the secretary of the Bradford Labour Party. In 1937 it's Year Book reported:

> Having in mind the proposals of the Government for a very considerable increase in the armaments of the country, and also the piling up of armaments in other European countries with a consequent danger of war, the Council in March passed a resolution calling the TUC to discuss measures which might be taken to oppose such an armament programme and to prepare plans for action to prevent the outbreak of war.[19]

In the same source a later piece was written on Spain, which noted:

> We have witnessed a further attempt on the part of the Fascist element in Spain to supersede the democratically elected Government of the People of Spain by force of arms. The magnificent fight which the Spanish workers have waged against the Fascist . . . has been the wonder of the world . . .. the Council organized a Mass Meeting in Bradford to place the true facts before the public, and also opened a Spanish Workers' Relief Fund in conjunction with the TUC Solidarity Fund . . ..

We wholeheartedly condemn the Government's policy of Non-intervention which has permitted the Fascist countries of Italy and Germany to pour into Spain vast amounts of arms, ammunition, men, whilst it has denied the Spanish Democratic Government the legal right to purchase necessary supplies to defend the State. By its attitude the 'National Government' has done much to advance the cause of Fascism . . ..[20]

The Labour Party's confusion was a result of the rapid change of events. At first the party supported the policy of non-intervention, advocated by the French and British governments in August 1936, and gave this policy its cautious support at its conference in October 1936. The trade unions dominated the conference and endorsed the policies of their leaders. By that time, however, the constituency parties were complaining of trade-union domination at conference, and formed the Provisional Committee of Constituency Labour parties to challenge this feature of Labour conferences. The rejection policy of non-intervention by many of the constituency Labour parties tended to become tied in with their challenge to the trade-union domination of the Labour Party, and probably lost its impact and relevance in the wider debate about party democracy. As a result the Labour Spain Committee had to be formed in March 1937 to fight the battle for the rejection of non-intervention within the Labour Party.[21] It had three main purposes. Its first objective was that of urging the National Executive of the party to call a conference of the whole Labour movement in order to reassess their policy. Secondly, it wished to mount a national campaign to force the National government to allow the Spanish Government to buy arms. Thirdly, it wished to co-ordinate all anti-fascist groups supportive of the Republican government into one single movement.

The effectiveness of the Labour Spain Committee was impaired both by the fact that it was was associated with the movement in the constituency Labour parties and also because it was effectively advocating a a popular front against fascism, which the Labour Party continued to reject throughout the 1930s; after the political disasters of 1931 it wanted no treating with its political enemies whether of the left or the right. The Labour Party leadership also felt that the British people were not, as yet, ready for war: 'In Great Britain the position was that no Government would be able to secure public support for any action which the people believed would lead to war.'[22]

204

Nevertheless, whilst a joint campaign with the Communist Party and other political organizations was entirely out of the question, the Labour leadership felt compelled to adjust its policy with regard to Spain. Shortly after the Edinburgh Conference, the National Council of Labour, which brought the executives of the TUC and the Labour Party together, agreed that the Spanish government should have its commercial rights restored.[23] By June 1937 the National Council of Labour, effectively speaking for the Labour Party, decided to reverse its Edinburgh policy and to oppose non-intervention. This policy was confirmed at the Labour Party's Bournemouth Conference in October 1937. In addition, the conference was forced to accept the need to organize a campaign to compel the National government to drop its policy of non-intervention, an action which led to the formation of the Spain Campaign Committee.

Fleay and Sanders feel that this committee achieved remarkably little, placing no significant pressure on the National government to drop its policy of non-intervention. Its main work appears to have been the organizing of humanitarian aid to Spain, such as the 'milk for Spain' appeals. Indeed, as part of this campaign Yorkshire Labour town constituencies had sent over 150,000 pints of milk to Spain and more than 10 tons of pasteurised milk by February 1938.[24] In addition, the Secretary of the City of Leeds Labour Party, A. L. Williams, in assessing the contribution made by his organization between March 1937 and March 1938 noted:

> . . . the Labour Party in Leeds had done quite a lot of work in support of the Spanish Government. Last year, nearly £300 had been collected for the Spanish Fund, and within the space of a month, including Xmas holidays, no less than three large indoor meetings had been held, of which one was the Town Hall meeting at which one of the largest collections ever received at a Labour meeting in Leeds was taken up. Also the division had been responsible for organizing 5 cinema meetings and a number of smaller meetings during the campaign weeks. All these meetings concerned themselves with the Spanish question.[25]

Given the Labour Party's lack of political action on the Spanish issue it is hardly surprising that the Labour Spain Committee renewed its efforts to call for a national conference, which it organized in October 1938. On this occasion, it once more called for the formation of a popular front against fascism, which did not endear it to the leadership of the Labour Party.

The Labour Party's response to the Spanish Civil War was clearly more humanitarian than political. It was confused, slow to change – a factor amplified by the fact that there was no party conference between October 1937 and May 1939 – and deliberately hostile to the idea of working with other anti-fascist groups. Its opposition to the Communist Party, in particular, prevented it from even attempting to mount a mass political campaign in favour of the Republican government. Yet is also harboured doubts about whether there was widespread political support for the Republicans. Labour leaders doubted whether they had convinced the population of the need to support Republican Spain:

> If our propaganda has failed, it has failed because we have been unable to arouse the British people in such a way as to make them feel that the cause of Republican Spain was their cause in such a measure that they would take every risk, even the risk of war to make the Republican cause in Spain prevail.[26]

In fact a series of public opinion polls, conducted between February 1938 and January 1939 revealed that between 57 and 78 per cent of those who expressed an opinion favoured sympathy for the Republican government, and even a willingness to take action against Franco's fascists.[27] Only between 7 and 9 per cent expressed sympathy for Franco. The Labour Party quite clearly underestimated the extent to which the British public was horrified by the rise of fascism in Spain.

The National Government and the Spanish Civil War

Given the extent to which the British public supported Republican Spain, why was it that the National government kept to its policy of non-intervention? Was it because of its natural sympathy for the right and its hostility of the left? Was it because its parliamentary majority prevented any real possibility of its position being threatened? Was it because of the commitment of both Stanley Baldwin and Neville Chamberlain to the process of appeasement? Alternatively, was it due to the fact that the Labour did not mount an effective campaign against its position?

There is no doubt that the majority of the Conservative MPs in the National government were quite pleased with the developments in Spain. Their main concern in 1936 was the threat of socialism and communism in Europe and in Spain. The burning of churches by the Spanish Communists and Russia's increasing support for the socialist-dominated Republican government: some of these were quite clearly pro-Hitler and pro-Mussolini. A significant proportion supported the appeasement policies being put forward by Chamberlain. As suggested in the previous chapter, only a few agreed with Churchill and with Eden, after his departure from the National government, that fascism posed a major threat to Britain. Although the Labour Party failed to mount a sufficiently large campaign against the non-intervention policy, there seems little doubt that the government would have continued along its agreed course. Perhaps, as with the Abyssinian episode, public opinion might have been sufficient to temporarily deflect the leaders of the National government from their chosen course, but it seems unlikely that Chamberlain's government would have been so easily, or temporarily, blown off the course of appeasement. The fact that the Labour Party did not lead public opinion as strongly as it might have done meant that the National government had an easier ride than it might otherwise have expected.

Conclusion

The Spanish Civil War clearly conditioned British public opinion to the impending threat of conflict with European fascism. It was, as already suggested, the mirror into which people looked to have their fears reflected. Without doubt the sympathies of the British people were with the Spanish Republican government – and they demonstrated their support with a humanitarian response. But the National government was locked on course for appeasement and, with the parliamentary majority which it enjoyed, there seems little doubt that even a powerful political campaign by the Labour Party, in league with other anti-fascist groups, could have changed its policies. For the left, the Spanish Civil War proved to be something of a crisis. For the right, the real crisis came when appeasement proved to be a bankrupt policy as Britain drifted towards war in September 1939.

NOTES

1. K.W. Watkins, *Britain Divided; The Effect of the Spanish Civil War on British Political Opinion* (London, Nelson, 1963).
2. G. Orwell, 'England Your England', *Inside the Whale and Other Essays*.

3. Ibid.
4. C. Fleay and M.L. Sanders, 'The Labour Spain Committee: Labour Party Policy and the Spanish Civil War', *Historical Journal*, 28, i, 1985, p. 197.
5. G. Orwell, *Homage to Catalonia* (Harmondsworth, Penguin Books, 1974), pp. 116–72.
6. *Leeds Citizen*, 30 April, 7 May and 14 May 1937.
7. Ibid., 7 May 1937.
8. Watkins, op.cit., p. 13.
9. Ibid., p. 86.
10. J. Gurney, *Crusade in Spain* (London, Faber and Faber, 1974), p. 26.
11. M. Sperber, *And I Remember Spain: A Spanish Civil War Anthology* (1974).
12. Orwell, op.cit., p. 217.
13. Watkins, op.cit., passim and C.L. Mowat, *Britain between the Wars, 1918–1940* (London, Methuen, 1958, 1968 ed.), pp. 577–82.
14. Central Division of Leeds Labour Party, Minutes, 9 February 1937; *Leeds Citizen*, 16 April 1937; Bradford Trades Council, Minutes, 11 February, 18 March and 15 April 1937; Huddersfield Labour Party, Minutes, 31 May 1938.
15. Mowat, op.cit., p. 579.
16. Watkins, op.cit., ch. 5.
17. Fleay and Sanders, op.cit., p. 197.
18. Watkins, op.cit., ch. 5 and particularly pp. 194–5.
19. Bradford Trades Council, Year Book,1937 (Bradford, 1937), report for 1936, pp. 7,9.
20. Ibid., p. 11.
21. Fleay and Sanders, op.cit., p. 188.
22. Report of Labour Socialist International/IFTU Meeting, 4 December 1936, Spanish Civil War, LPA, SCW/5/3. Quoted in Fleay and Sanders, op. cit., p. 190.
23. Fleay and Sanders, op.cit., p. 190.
24. *Leeds Citizen*, 11 February 1938.
25. City of Leeds Labour Party, Minutes, 16 March 1938.
26. Fleay and Sanders, op.cit., p. 195.
27. Idem.

CONCLUSION

Robert Graves and Alan Hodge do not do justice to the protracted nature of the problems of the inter-war years by lightheartedly suggesting that these years were a 'long weekend'. Many of the other epithets used to describe the inter-war years are more apposite. The fact is that from the view of the working classes, whose members were likely to be on poverty or to be living a precarious existence within its vicinity, a breadline existence was a common and familiar experience in a period which might well be regarded as the 'wasted years'. But the problem of the inter-war years has always been one of perspective and emphasis. Did the improvements for those who were in constant employment – those members of the working class in the new expanding industries and the rapidly growing salaried middle class – outweigh the dire social conditions which were experienced by the traditional working class in the declining staple industries?

This contrast was beautifully illustrated in a mid-1980s BBC television series 'The Dragon Has Two Tongues', which dealt with the history of Wales. When it came to the inter-war years the co-presenters offered their alternative visions of Wales – the one reflecting upon the happy and joyous years of the 1930s, driving along Llandudno sea front in a Lagonda, the other standing amid the ruinous remains of Cardiff docks and complaining about the poor social and economic conditions which was the lot of most Welsh folk. Such stark contrasts, essentially based upon class perspectives, are not easily reconcilable.

This book has necessarily been one-eyed – more concerned with the social and economic conditions of the working classes than of the middle classes. Yet it should not be forgotten that it was the working-class problems of unemployment and ill-health which posed the major difficulties for British governments during the inter-war years, and only in the mid- and late 1930s did this have to take second place to the rising threat of European fascism.

Inevitably, the debates about the inter-war years have concerned these issues – seeking to measure the degree of change and improvement in the lives of the working classes. They pose many questions. Did poverty decline? Were the majority of people healthier and better off than before the First World War? To what extent did society adjust to its economic problems? How much action was taken by governments to alleviate unemployment and poverty? In the final analysis the argument of this book has been less optimistic than those put forward by John Stevenson, Chris Cook and D. H. Aldcroft. It has argued five main points. In the first place has stressed that governments simply failed to properly tackle the problem of unemployment because of their commitment to balanced budgets, regardless of whether they operated in a free trade or a protectionist context. Though widely discussed by the 1930s, the expansionist and contractionist policies of J. M. Keynes' multiplier did not have a great influence upon the National governments. Secondly, it is maintained that the majority of the working classes lived in poverty or near to poverty, with consequent ill-health – although the middle classes and the better off members of the working class ensured that about half the total British population were probably better off. One can debate forever the extent of poverty in these years but it should be remembered that few detailed poverty surveys actually dealt with the worst areas of unemployment where poverty was clearly a more acute problem than it had been before the First World War. Thirdly, it is argued that the depression of these years was not offset by the economic progress made in the Midlands and the south-eastern consumer industries – although the working classes in these regions were certainly prospering. Fourthly, it asserts that the association between the working classes and the Labour Party was strongly enhanced by the economic conditions of these years. Partly in consequence the Liberal Party plummeted into political oblivion and Labour became the political alternative to the Conservative Party in Britain's two-party political system. Labour was already clearly already identified with the working class by the end of the First World War but the economic conditions of depression and unemployment strengthened that link as never before, and possibly since. Fifthly, it appears that, despite the social deprivation which persisted a large proportion of the British population, and particularly those in the impoverished working class, were aware of international events and hostile to the threat of European fascism. Amid acute deprivation, the majority of the working class identified with those oppressed by fascism although, as with their own circumstances, they were able to do little about the matter.

The perplexing question for many observers is why was continued poverty accepted almost in silence? To put it more bluntly, and exaggeratedly, why wasn't there a revolution? Certainly, Wal Hannington and National Unemployed Workers' Movement found it difficult to organize the unemployed despite the high level of unemployment throughout the inter-war years. But, perhaps, one should not be surprised at the limited response of the unemployed and the poor. In the first place, many of the unemployed expected to find work. When this did not occur, because of the high level of unemployment in some towns, unemployment became almost institutionalized and absorbed within the framework of the community. And in any case, as Carl Chinn has made clear, it was the wives and women of the poor who bore the brunt of poverty and the street matriarchs who helped to ensure that survival was possible for the working classes. The struggle for existence consumed most of the efforts of the working-class poor and appears to have contributed to the feeling of apathy and futility commented upon by many social observers. Secondly, unemployment was essentially a regional problem which affected only a minority of people directly. It did not impinge upon the mind of the general public except in periods of acute distress.

Nevertheless, there is no doubting that unemployment, and its consequences, shaped the politics, the economics and the social life of the inter-war years. The collapse of the second Labour government, ill-health and many of the social difficulties of these years were almost directly, though often partly rather than entirely, attributable to unemployment. It was this experience which, in the context of the Second World War, permitted the Beveridge Report the luxury of being able to demand full employment for the post-Second World War generation. It was the memory of unemployment and the failure of successive inter-war governments to deal with it which, linked with the new wartime radicalism, provided the climate of opinion out of which the post-war Labour government's welfare state was able to emerge.

BIBLIOGRAPHY

Primary Sources

Manuscripts

Amalgamated Union of Dyers' collection, West Yorkshire Archives Department, Bradford.
Archives of the Labour Party, National Executive Committee, Minutes.
Bradford Archives, 22 D77/3/2/8.
Colne Valley Divisional Labour Party, Minutes (Huddersfield Polytechnic Library).
Huddersfield Divisional Labour Party, Minutes (Huddersfield Polytechnic Library and Huddersfield Central Library).
Leeds Liberal Federation, Minutes (West Yorkshire Archives, Sheepscar Library, Leeds.)
Lloyd George Papers.
National Union of Textile Workers' collection, Archives Department, Huddersfield Central Library.
Public Record Office, Cab. 23, Cabinet Conclusions and Cabinet Papers/Memos.
Public Record Office, Cab. 24., various reports on unemployment.

Books and Reports

E. Bevin, *My Plan for 2,000,000 Unemployed* (1932).
A.L. Bowley and Burnett-Hurst, *Livelihood and Poverty* (1915).
A.L. Bowley and M. Hogg, *Has Poverty Diminished?* (London, P.S. King, 1925).
A.L. Bowley (ed.), *Studies in the National Income 1924–1938* (1944).
J.& B. Braddock, *The Braddocks* (London, MacDonald, 1963).
Britain's Industrial Future, being a Report of the Liberal Industrial Inquiry of 1928 (London, Ernest Benn, 1928, 1977).
Bradford Medical Officer of Health, *Reports, 1876–1940.*
Bradford Trades Council, *Year Book*, 1937.
H. Fenner Brockway, *Hungry England* (London, Gollancz, 1936).
Emile Burns, *Councils in Action* (1927).

J. Campbell, M. Spring Rice, *Working-Class Wives* (1939, also London, Virago, 1981).

Carnegie Trust, *Disinherited Youth* (Edinburgh, Carnegie UK Trust, 1943).

Census of England and Wales, 1921 and 1931.

Lord Citrine, *Men and Work: An Autobiography* (London, 1964).

Coal Industry Commissioners Report, cmnd 359, 1919.

M. Cohen, *I Was One of the Unemployed* (London, Gollancz, 1945 and E.P., Wakefield, 1978).

First Interim Report, Cunliffe Committee on Currency and Foreign Exchange after the War.

General Register Office, Census of England and Wales. 1951, Housing Report.

J. Gray, *The Worst of Times: An Oral History of the Great Depression in Britain* (London, Barnes and Noble, 1985).

J. Gurney, *Crusade in Spain* (London, Faber and Faber, 1974).

Hansard

W. Hannington, *Unemployed Struggles* (1936).

W. Hannington, *The Problem of the Distressed Areas* (London, Gollancz, 1937).

W. Hannington, *Ten Lean Years* (London, Gollancz, 1940).

W. Hannington, *Never on our Knees* (1967).

E. Hubbock, *The Population of Britain* (1947).

A. Hutt, *The Condition of the Working Class in England* (London, 1933).

J. Jacobs, *Out of the Ghetto* (London, Simon, 1978).

H. Jennings, *Brynmawr*.

D. Caradog Jones, *The Social Survey of Merseyside* (London, Liverpool University Press and Hodder Stoughton, 1934).

T. Jones, *Whitehall Diary*, vol. II 1926–1930, (ed.) R.K. Middlemass (London, Oxford University Press, 1969).

O. Mosley, *Revolution by Reason* (1925).

O. Mosley, *My Life* (1967).

H. Llewellyn Smith (ed.) *The New Survey of London Life and Labour* (London, P.S. King. 1974).

G.F.M. McCleary, *The Menace of British Depopulation* (1937).

G.C.M. M'Gonigle and J. Kirby, *Poverty and Public Health* (London, Gollancz, 1936).

P.L. McKinley, article, *Journal of Hygiene*, 1929.

Ministry of Health, *Annual Reports*, including the 1931 report.

Ministry of Health, *An Investigation into Maternal Mortality (1937)* cmnd 5422.

Ministry of Health, Maternal Morbidity in Wales (1937) cmnd 5422.

J.L. Munro, *Maternal Mortality and Morbidity* (1933).

J. Boyd Orr, *Food, Health and Income* (London, Macmillan, 1936).

George Orwell, *The Road to Wigan Pier* (London, Gollancz, 1937 and Harmondsworth, Penguin, 1962).

Pilgrim Trust, *Men Without Work* (Cambridge, Cambridge University Press, 1938).

J.B. Priestley, *English Journey* (London, Heinemann, 1934, 1968, 1976).

Registrar General, *Statistical Review of England and Wales*.

Report on the Overcrowding Survey in England and Wales, 1936.

Report of the Royal Commission on the Coal Industry, 1925.

213

Report of the Royal Commission on National Health Insurance 1926, Majority Report.
Report on Social Insurance and Allied Services (Beveridge Report) 1942.
Report on Wages, Hours and Work in the Wool Textile Industry in Yorkshire, 1936.
E. Roberts, *A Woman's place. An Oral History of Working-Class Women 1890–1914* (Oxford and New York, Oxford University Press, 1984).
B.S. Rowntree, *Poverty: A Study of Town Life* (London, Longman, 1901).
B.S. Rowntree, *Progress and Poverty: A Second Social Survey of York* (London, Longman, 1941).
B.S. Rowntree, *Poverty, Health and Income* (London, Longman, Green & Co, 1941).
Royal Commission on Population, Report, 1949.
P. Snowden, *Mr Lloyd George's New Deal* (London, Ivor Nicholson & Watson, 1935).
R.K. Titmuss, *Parent's Revolt* (London, Secker and Warburg, 1942).
R.K. Titmuss, *Birth, Poverty, and Wealth* (London. Hamish Hamilton, 1943).
H. Tout, *The Standard of Living in Bristol* (Bristol, Bristol University Press, 1934).
Trade Union Congress, Report, 1927.
E. Trory, *Between the Wars: Recollections of a Communist Organizer.*
E. Wilkinson, *The Town that was Murdered: The Life-Story of Jarrow* (London, Gollancz, 1939).
Yorkshire Liberal Federation Annual Meetings.

Articles

'Glamorgan Police Files', *Society for the Study of Labour History*, Bulletin 38, Spring 1979.
J.M. Keynes, 'Some Economic Consequences of a Declining Population', *Eugenics Review*, April 1937.
G. Orwell, 'England Your England', *Inside the Whale and Other Essays* (Harmondsworth, Penguin, 1974 ed).

Newspapers

Bradford Pioneer
Daily Mail
Leeds Weekly Citizen
Observer
Out of Work
Socialist Worker
The Times
Workers' Weekly
Yorkshire Factory Times
Yorkshire Observer

Secondary Sources

Books

D.H. Aldcroft, *The Inter-War Years 1919–1939* (Batsford, 1970).

B.W.E. Alford, *Depression and Recovery? British Economic Growth 1918–1939* (London, Macmillan, 1972).

M. Bentley, *The Liberal Mind 1914–1929* (Cambridge, Cambridge University Press, 1977).

H. Berkeley, *The Myth that will not die: The formation of the National Government 1931* (London, Croom Helm, 1978).

R. Blake, *The Conservative Party: from Peel to Churchill* (London, Eyre and Spottiswoode, 1970).

N. Branson and M. Heinemann, *Britain in the Nineteen Thirties* (London, 1973).

N. Branson, *George Lansbury and the Councillors's Revolt: Poplarism 1919–1925* (London, Lawrence and Wishart, 1979).

K.D. Brown, *The English Labour Movement* (London, Gill and Macmillan, 1982).

A. Bullock, *The Life and Times of Ernest Bevin I* (London, Heinemann, 1960).

K. Burgess, *The Challenge of Labour* (London, Croom Helm, 1980).

J. Campbell, *Nye Bevan and the Mirage of British Socialism* (London, Weidenfeld and Nicolson, 1987).

D. Carlton, *Anthony Eden* (London, Allen & Unwin, 1986).

C. Chinn, *They Worked All Their Lives: Women of the Urban Poor in England, 1880–1939* (Manchester and New York, Manchester University Press, 1988).

P.F. Clarke, *Lancashire and the New Liberalism* (Cambridge, Cambridge University Press, 1971).

H.A. Clegg, *A History of British Trade Unions since 1889*, Vol. II, 1911–1933 (Oxford, Oxford University Press, 1985).

S. Constantine, *Unemployment in Britain between the Wars* (London, Longman, 1980).

C. Cross (ed.), *Life and Times of Lloyd George: The diary of A.J. Sylvester 1931–1945* (London, 1975).

G. Dangerfield, *The Strange Death of Liberal England* (London, MacGibbon & Kee, 1966 edition).

B. Eichengreen, *The Gold Standard in Theory and History* (London, Methuen, 1985).

C. Farman, *The General Strike, May 1926* (London, Rupert Hart-Davis, 1972).

S. Glynn and J. Oxborrow, *Interwar Britain: a Social and Economic History* (London, George Allen and Unwin, 1976).

K. Harris, *Attlee* (London, Weidenfeld & Nicolson, 1982).

K. Laybourn, *Philip Snowden: a biography* (Aldershot, Temple Smith/Gower/Wildwood, 1988).

K. Laybourn, *The Rise of Labour* (London, Edward Arnold, 1988).

D. Marquand, *Ramsay MacDonald* (London, Jonathan Cape, 1977).

R. McKibbin, *The Evolution of the Labour Party 1910–1924* (Oxford, Oxford University Press, 1974).

R.K. Middlemass and J. Barnes, *Stanley Baldwin* (London, Weidenfeld and Nicolson, 1969).

B.R. Mitchell and P. Deane, *Abstract of British Historical Statistics* (London and Cambridge, Cambridge University Press, 1962).

M. Morris, *The British General Strike* (London, Historical Association, 1973).

M. Morris, *The General Strike* (London, Journeyman Press, 1976 and 1980).

C.L. Mowat, *Britain between the Wars 1918–1940* (London, Methuen, 1968 ed).

H. Pelling, *The Origins of the Labour Party* (London, Macmillan, 1954).

H. Pelling, *A History of British Trade Unionism* (London, Pelican, 1973 ed).

H. Phelps Brown, *The Origins of Trade Union Power* (Oxford, Oxford University Press, 1986).

G.A. Phillips, *The General Strike: The Politics of Industrial Conflict* (London, Weidenfeld and Nicolson, 1976).

G.A. Phillips and T.T. Maddock, *The Growth of the British Economy* (London, George Allen & Unwin, 1973).

B. Pimlott, *Labour and the Left in the 1930s* (Cambridge, Cambridge University Press, 1977).

S. Pollard (ed.), *The Gold Standard and Employment Policies between the Wars* (London, Methuen, 1970).

J. Reynolds and K. Laybourn, *Labour Heartland: a history of the Labour Party in West Yorkshire during the inter-war years 1918–1939* (Bradford, Bradford University Press, 1987).

W. D. Rubinstein, *Men of Property* (London, Croom Helm, 1981).

J. Skelley (ed.), *1926: The General Strike* (London, Lawrence and Wishart, 1976).

R. Skidelsky, *Politicians and the Slump 1929–1931* (London, Macmillan, 1967).

R. Skidelsky, *Oswald Mosley* (London, Macmillan, 1975).

R.A. Soloway, *Birth Control and the Population Question in England, 1877–1930* (USA, University of North Carolina Press, 1982).

M. Sperber, *And I Remember Spain: A Spanish Civil War Anthology* (1974).

J. Stevenson, *Social Conditions in Britain between the Wars* (Harmondsworth, Penguin, 1977).

J. Stevenson and Chris Cook, *The Slump* (London, Jonathan Cape, 1977).

J. Stevenson, *British Society 1914–1945* (Harmondsworth, Penguin, 1984).

R. Thurlow, *Fascism in Britain: a history 1918–1985* (London, Hackwell, 1987).

N.L. Tranter, *Population and Industrialization* (London, Adam & Charles Black, 1973).

N.L. Tranter, *Population since the Industrial Revolution: The Case of England and Wales* (London, Croom Helm, 1973).

B.D. Vernon, *Ellen Wilkinson* (London, Croom Helm, 1982).

K.W. Watkins, *Britain Divided: The Effect of the Spanish Civil War on British Political Opinion* (London, Nelson, 1963).

B. & S. Webb, *The History of Trade Unionism* (London, 1920 edn).

G. Webber, *The Ideology of the British Right* (London, Croom Helm, 1987).

L. MacNeill Weir, *The Tragedy of Ramsay MacDonald* (London, Secker and Warburg, 1938).

J. White, *The Worst Street in North London: Campbell Bunk, Islington, Between the Wars* (London, 1986).

P.M. Williams, *Hugh Gaitskell* (Oxford, Oxford University press, 1982).

T. Wilson, *The Downfall of the Liberal Party* (London, Collins, 1966).

M. Wynn, *Family Policy* (1970).

Articles

M. Bentley, 'The Liberal Response to Socialism, 1918–1929' in K.D. Brown (ed.), *Essays in Anti-Labour History* (London, Macmillan, 1974).

R.C. Challinor, 'Letter from MacDonald to Clarke', *Society for the Study of Labour History*, Bulletin 27, 1973.

R. Douglas, 'Labour in Decline 1910–1914', in K.D. Brown, *Essays in Anti-Labour History* (London, Macmillan, 1974).

A. Exall, 'Morris Motors in the 1930s: Part I', *History Workshop*, 6, Autumn 1978.

C. Fleay and M.L. Sanders, 'The Labour Spain Committee: Labour Party Policy and the Spanish Civil War', *Historical Journal*, 28, 1, 1985.

W.R. Garside and T.J. Hatton, 'Keynesian Policy and British Unemployment in the 1930s', *Economic History Review*, xxxviii, 1, February 1985.

S. Glynn and A. Booth, 'Building Counterfactual Pyramids', *Economic History Review*, xxxviii, 1, February 1985.

E.P. Hennock, 'The measurement of poverty: from the metropolis to the nation, 1880–1920', *Economic History Review*, xl, May 1987.

C. Howard, 'Expectation born to death: local Labour Party expansion in the 1920s', in J. Winter (ed.), *Working Class in Modern British History: Essays in Honour of Henry Pelling* (London, Cambridge University Press, 1983).

M.E.F. Jones, 'The Regional Impact of an Overvalued Pound in the 1920s', *Economic History Review*, xxxvii, 4. November 1984.

J.A. Jowitt and K. Laybourn, 'The Wool Textile Dispute of 1925', *The Journal of Regional and Local Studies*, vol. 2, no. 1, spring 1982.

K.J. Hancock, 'The reduction of unemployment as a problem of public policy, 1920–1929', *Economic History Review*, xv, December 1962.

R. Hayburn, 'The National Unemployed Workers' Movement 1921–1936: A Re-Appraisal', *International Review of Social History*, vol. xxxviii, part 3, 1983.

P. Knight, 'Women and Abortion in Victorian and Edwardian England', *History Workshop*, 4, Autumn, 1977.

B.C. Malament, 'Philip Snowden and the Cabinet Deliberations of August 1931', *Society for the Study of Labour History*, autumn 1980, p. 32.

A. McIvor, 'Essays in Anti-Labour History', *Society for the Study of Labour History*, Bulletin, vol. 53, part 1, 1988.

R. McKibbin, 'Working-Class Gambling in Britain 1880–1939', *Past and Present*, 82, February 1979.

A. McLaren, 'Women, Work and Regulation of Family Size', *History Workshop*, 4, Autumn 1977.

R. Middleton, 'The Constant Employment Budget Balances and British Budgetary Policy, 1929–1939', *Economic History Review*, xxxiv, 2 May 1981, p. 278.

M. Mitchell, 'The Effects of Unemployment on the Social Conditions of Women and Children in the 1930s', *History Workshop Journal*, 19, Spring 1985.

M. Newman, 'Democracy versus Dictatorship', *History Workshop*, Spring 1978.

R. Pope, '"Dole Schools": The north-east Lancashire Experience, 1930–1939', *Journal of Educational Administration and History*, vol. ix, no. 2. July 1977.

S. Rawnsley, 'The Membership of the British Union of Fascists', in K. Lunn and R. Thurlow (eds.), *British Fascism* (London, Croom Helm, 1979).

J. Redmond, 'The Sterling Overvaluation in 1925: A Multilateral Approach', *Economic History Review*, xxxvii, 4, November 1984.

W.D. Rubinstein, 'Wealth, Elites and Class Structure in Modern Britain', *Past and Present*, 76, August 1971.

C. Webster, 'Healthy of Hungry Thirties?', *History Workshop Journal*, 13, Spring, 1982.

J. White, 'Campbell Bunk: A Lumpen Community in London between the Wars',

History Workshop, 8, autumn 1979.

N. Whiteside, 'Counting the cost: sickness and disability among working people in an era of industrial recession, 1920–1939', *Economic History Review*, xl, no. 2, May 1987,

P. Williamson, '"Safety First": Baldwin, the Conservative Party, and the 1929 General Election', *Historical Journal*, 25, 2, 1982.

T. Woodhouse, 'The General Strike in Leeds', *Northern History*, vol. xviii, 1982.

Unpublished Research

H.J.P. Harmer, 'The National Unemployed Workers' Movement in Britain 1921–1939: Failure and Success', unpublished PhD, London School of Economics and Political Science, 1987.

R.H.C. Hayburn, 'The Responses to Unemployment in the 1930s, with particular reference to South East Lancashire', unpublished PhD, University of Hull, 1970.

N.J. Leiper, 'Health and Unemployment in Glamorgan 1923–1938', unpublished M. Sc., University College of Wales, Aberystwyth, 1986.

C.J. MacIntyre, 'Responses to the Rise of Labour: The Conservative Party Policy and Organisation 1922–1931', unpublished PhD, University of Cambridge, 1986.

S. Shaw, 'The Attitudes of the Trade Union Congress towards Unemployment in the inter-war period', unpublished PhD, University of Kent, 1979.

INDEX